HEROD'S DISPENSATIONS

Harry Clifton was born in Dublin in 1952, and has travelled widely in Africa and Asia, as well as more recently in Europe. He won the Patrick Kavanagh award in 1981 and has been the recipient of fellowships in Germany, France, the United States and Australia.

He has published eight collections of poems, including *The Desert Route: Selected Poems 1973-88* and *Night Train through the Brenner*, all from Gallery Press, with *The Desert Route* co-published by Bloodaxe Books in Britain. *On the Spine of Italy*, his prose study of an Abruzzese mountain community, was published by Macmillan in 1999. A collection of his short fiction, *Berkeley's Telephone*, appeared from Lilliput Press in 2000. His previous collection of poems, *Secular Eden: Paris Notebooks 1994-2004*, was published by Wake Forest University Press in 2007 and won the *Irish Times* Poetry Now Award. His latest titles are *The Winter Sleep of Captain Lemass* (2012), shortlisted for the *Irish Times* Poetry Now Award, *The Holding Centre: Selected Poems 1974-2004* (2014), *Portobello Sonnets* (2017) and *Herod's Dispensations* (2019), all published by Bloodaxe Books in Britain and Ireland and by Wake Forest University Press in the USA.

He has taught in Bremen and Bordeaux universities, as well as Trinity College and University College Dublin. He returned to Ireland in 2004. He was Ireland Professor of Poetry in 2010-13.

HARRY CLIFTON

Herod's Dispensations

BLOODAXE BOOKS

ISBN: 978 1 78037 451 2

First published 2019
in Britain and Ireland by
Bloodaxe Books Ltd,
Eastburn,
South Park,
Hexham,
Northumberland NE46 1BS,
and in North America
by Wake Forest University Press.

www.bloodaxebooks.com

For further information about Bloodaxe titles
please visit our website and join our mailing list
or write to the above address for a catalogue

Supported using public funding by

**ARTS COUNCIL
ENGLAND**

Cover design: Neil Astley & Pamela Robertson-Pearce.

Printed in Great Britain by Bell & Bain Limited, Glasgow, Scotland, on
acid-free paper sourced from mills with FSC chain of custody certification.

ACKNOWLEDGEMENTS

Acknowledgements are due to *The Stinging Fly, Poetry East, The Irish Times, The Stony Thursday Book, The Poetry Review, The Manhattan Review, The Times Literary Supplement, Temenos, Poetry Ireland Review, Poetry Salzburg, Icarus, The High Window, Reading the Future* (Arlen House), *The Dublin Review of Book*s, Qualm website and Stoney Road Editions where some of these poems first appeared.

CONTENTS

Item(s) checked out to
D4000000349414

Herod's dispensations / Harry Clifton.

<u>Date Due:</u> **9 Nov 2020**

<u>To renew your items</u>

Online at librariesireland.iii.com Ph: (01) 4941900

Mon-Thu 9:45am to 8pm, Fri-Sat 9:45am to 4:30pm

Paperless overdues coming soon!

From December 1st we will no longer post overdue
notices. Please sign up to receive email notices via
your online library account.

To the Next Generation

These days, like the leech-gatherer
In Wordsworth, I keep the wolf from the door
Of indigence, and take the weather
On the lonely moor.

The gibbet creaks in the wind. The body is gone.
Here comes a soldier, home from the war.
Napoleon, he tells me, is no more,
The work of healing is done

And the million sutures closed, below on the plain
Where the bloods are drawn.
I ask myself private questions now, in the dawn,

About women and poems, the impossibilities
Of old age, dipping for pondlife in the rain
As a child looks up to me.

Redesdale Estate, 1956

for Catriona Crowe

First, this old clock. As I dismantle it,
A child of indeterminate age
On the garage floor, the cogs and flywheels
Buzz, the hour-hands race and stop,
Go back on themselves,
And I peer, like a little god,
In the workings of time. Steady,
The ticking starts, suburban days
Falling into place
Like memory. Glass front doors
And front room windows
Are black depths, to be looked into
Afterwards, when the time is right.
But for now, each pebbledashed house
Is a Freudian box of tricks,
Pre-conscious, locked in itself,
Respectable, safe, like Nineteen Fifty-six.

Pounds and ounces, pennyweights and grams –
A grocer's measuring instruments
Sift reality, slicing ham
And butter, trowelling sugar in brown paper bags
For all of us blow-ins, on whom the hag
Has roosted, the hag of Ireland,
Stateless... Lord Redesdale,
Whoever you were, you gave us the myth of a State,
You left us your name
To conjure with, on your sold estate,
And fled to England, clutching the deeds.
De Valera set us down here, and bade us breed.

A new generation. A clean slate
For history to write on. Non-attachment
Our middle name. Sleepless, we hear
The cattle-drive, to the milking-sheds
Of Stillorgan, in the early hours,
Like the lost morning of a mythic race
Our fathers snore through. De Valera,
Give us our pasteurised milk, and cleanse our blood
Of impurities. Banish the gypsy horses,
Their mounds of fertile dung,
From our gardens. Tinsmiths' fires
Will burn themselves out, the caravan train move on –
Give us leave to live here...
                              O the pain
That first winter of consciousness –
Snowballs, tainted with copper sulphate,
Crash against my ears. The Zen command
To awaken! Child, it is too late
To run in tears to Mother.
She points to the orphans, filing through the estate
From nowhere to nowhere, shadowed by Sisters
Terrible in their winged headgear
Out through the age of innocence, into the years
Undreamt by De Valera, Connolly, Pearse.

Endgame

> The old fog calls
>
> SAMUEL BECKETT

I never belonged in my father's house –
His unread Bible on the shelf
My silent coming of age.
In the kitchen, pregnant pauses,
Whispering. Behind pages
Of the *Irish Times*, the man himself

Hiding from Ireland in Ireland.
People used to call,
I remember, in the old days –
Musical instruments, coats in the hall,
Sectarian difference, shouting. Trays
Of edibles, hand to hand,

As once in Joyce's *Dubliners*.
I ask myself now, would I want it all back.
Anything but, in the name of Krapp.
A hundred houses, back to back
Against nothingness. Foghorn-blur
In Dublin Bay, as a ship

From Liverpool or Holyhead
Reversed through time into history.
The shouting has stopped, the whispering
In the kitchen has died away.
I lift to my eye instead
The spyglass in the Beckett play

And see, through the matte grey
Of a Sunday afternoon
Without God, Dún Laoghaire
In focus, millions on a pier –
Those who can never do themselves in,
Those who can never pray.

The Accursed Questions

1

The girl behind the bar is in love with you, do you know that?
Look at what happened to Kierkegaard, Dostoyevsky –
Sad lives, early deaths, the world no better a place.

It is cold in the kitchen, but you feel nothing,
Reading... The Russians, too, never felt their own weather
In all those fictions. It came from within them.

People out walking, on the East Pier,
Swarm in their thousands, ghosts of the Nevsky Prospekt.
Where do they come from? Where on earth do they vanish to?

2

Grey-haired now, the girl behind the bar
Has given up on children... And for forty years
No one has disturbed it, the white cold silence of the kitchen.

The bollards are still grass-grown, on that other pier
Across the water, where time stops
And a decommissioned lightship rusts at anchor.

Half the world has gone to its death. But you,
You are still eighteen, the ice on the Neva
Still unbroken, life unreal outside the hermitage wall.

After Mao

Her beauty was cold to the touch
Like marble. She was not there
In flesh or spirit. Two or three words
In a foreign tongue, and the rest
Silence. On she worked,
Ignoring her own nakedness,
Her slavery skin-deep and her dream
Off limits. And the streets
Outside, the city cold around her,
Night growing out of nowhere.

Money and strange hours, a room.
There was a train once, through China –
Father to Mother, out of which grew
Like a taproot, singlemindedness,
Detachment, lights in passing,
Distances...
                    That country
Is everywhere, its separations
Early, its children turned to stone.

Across the River

I crossed them again, the Liffey
And the Lethe, and there it all was,
The seventies, north of the river,
Nothing changed. The smells of food,
The same lit pubs, with a failed generation
Drinking inside them, in a blue fug
Clinging to the loose-stitch and the breast-swell
Of a girl's pullover, who would go on
To age, make children,
Break with the crises, the excitements
Of Saturday night, for the grey of Sunday afternoon.

There were no more Sundays now
But I smelt the docks, on the farther side of Lethe,
The ghosts of the transit sheds
For cattle and emigrants, shipped to Liverpool –
Abbatoir of souls...

Local colour, raised to the power of infinity
Once, long ago. Back then,
Staring much, I saw too little.
Now, a gull might cut right through me
For all I knew, and everything be remembered
Out of nowhere, the city reassemble itself
From the ruins of the seventies,
I its soul-survivor,

And the bad poetry, the only real poetry,
Still being sold, from an upstairs loft
On Middle Abbey Street, by a dropout
From the future, loose-stitched, heavy-breasted,
Careless of second comers. Mnemosyne,
Daughter of memory.

Ruins

My generation, dropping like flies –
At least in Stalingrad
There were ruins, a battleground.
Here, the buildings rise,
The minds collapse. As John of God
Slides by, a halfway house

For the saint, the suicide
And the family sacrifice,
I stay in lane, in the living tide
Of windscreens and car-bonnets,
Deaf to the silent cries,
The incoming round with my name on it.

The offensive has begun.
A woman walked into the sea
Just yesterday. A man was hung,
Self-hung, from the hook of desertion
There behind suburban curtains,
Disbelieving in victory.

Anne and David, Geraldine –
Enough that I drive by
Once in a while, at the violet hour
Of medication, Gethsemane hour
For the hero, the heroine.
Let me leave you where you lie

Undecorated, even by God,
The children of a neutral state
Who went down fighting, hand to hand,
With your own shadows, self-destroyed,
Caught in the suction of the void
That let the city stand.

Daytime Sleeper

A Shanghai night-poet
Keeping Chinese hours
Looks across the lights of Dublin
At the sleeping powers

On western time. A little wine
But mostly tea, exfoliating
Leaf by strange green leaf
In earth-dark, where the soul alone

Drinks to itself in the windowpane.
After Mao, the masses, slaughter,
Brotherless, the lonely daughter
Of the Policy of One

Is staring out, through bloodshot eyes,
At emptiness a Trappist monk
Might waken to, and never blink
In time or history. O for advice

From that strange soul-sister
Out of Asia, someone new,
A veteran of Anabasis,
A follower of Chuang Zhu,

A Gnostic at the hour of sex
Who sees through all the books...
She must be sleeping by now,
Her hair cut straight across her brow,

Her dregs brewed out, her left brain's
Dreaming mind a hemisphere
Ahead of me, already night
In Shanghai as I write.

The Egg-wife

Mainly remembered for the wind that blew
Beneath her door, as the negotiations,
Not difficult, continued… Sheepdogs too,
Barking, whimpering for admission

From the big cold, the distances outside,
The hinterlands. How it would be in winter
We could imagine – Aga stove at centre,
Two small children taken in her stride…

Egg-whites, spreading evenly on a pan,
Their yolks unbroken (ours the brokenness).
Telegraph poles, an infinite succession

Over the skyline. Somewhere about, her man,
And flesh as grass in the wind, that summer day –
Hardly selling, giving her eggs away.

Therese and the Jug

Marriage is the monastery of our time

LEONARD COHEN

She liked the jug, because it was cracked.
If it had a flaw
It was perfect. Under God's law
It was made whole by what it lacked –

Or so you tell me, matter of fact,
As you water a whiskey
Last thing at night, or sweeten Darjeeling tea
With the milk and honey of tact.

How many decades now
Since we entered the enclosed order
Of ourselves, to raid and replenish the larder
Of imperishables? The marriage vow

Grown ordinary, seems to keep house
And break bread with us, through and through,
At communal vespers for two
Like a hidden spirit. Patient Therese,

Our patron saint of the infinitely small,
Examines the wedding plunder, stainless steel,
Anything bedsheets might reveal
The morning after…Total recall,

If it ever came, would be shattering as a mirror
We stand before daily,
Man and wife, success and failure –
Childless love, imperfect as a marriage

Or that fissured jug, its flaw that integrates
A world around it, so you say,
A world left behind, for the Little Way
Of ovulins and fetherlites.

Before Christ

She left me a tax letter, on the table.
Deal with that, she said. Unopened,
Unread, it lay there, hours on end.

Something Roman, I said to myself,
Sent from another realm, to bleed us dry,
The people of the spirit, her and I.

A name, a telephone number. Yellow paper,
Dry, official. I would never get through
To anyone real, with my unresolved question.

Nor would it go away. Like Caesar
Or the State, a moving shadow
As the pen moves, the shadow of a hand,

A man and his shadow, co-writing,
Simultanaeous, in invisible ink,
Two histories, of Israel and of Rome.

How many massacres, I wondered,
Deserts and messiahs, Herods, Pilates,
Tax collectors with inviolate souls

Had it taken, for this privileged trance
I lay back into, abdicating everything,
To exist? *No answer necessary*

I might have told her, at eleven,
As she left, through the extra-temporal door.
Now, as I finish this, it is almost four.

A Flight into Egypt

Sixteen years we lived among alien people,
Cities without bridges to be burned,
Uncertain roofs – protecting ourselves, a couple
Gone into hiding, who would one day return
When the balance of power changed, and the attitudes.
Meanwhile, strangers were kind. The terrible places,
Unexpectedly, were generous with food,
Indifferent for the most part, sometimes even gracious.
And to this day, our books on the shelf,
Our suitcases unpacked, I ask myself
If ever it might happen again –
Protection of innocence, Herod's dispensations,
Transit lounges, midnight railway stations –
No, not even whether, only when.

Pity and Terror

Whoever they are, they hate it. They're afraid –
    The man of foreign extraction
In the second row, and the woman beside him
Out of Ardmore studio, following the action,
Clutching his elbow. '...Die, you shagging bitch,
Or take off back to Crewe across the water –
Do you hear me?' Listening, the daughter
Backs towards the audience, stopping barely an inch

Beyond their double glaze of pity and terror,
    The pair of them.
Again the voice of a mother, through the terrible mirror
Held to the nation. 'What did you ever care
For Irish freedom?...Your father, the I.R.A....'
A trembling hand pours tea, from a real pot,
In mythic space. A distant radio plays.
They're dreaming of the interval, like as not,

That mystery couple... Sure enough, it arrives,
    The space of enlightenment
Everyone here has swung for, in a previous life –
The liberal buzz and murmur, Synge's rioters
Gone quiet for an age, between the acts,
In changing motley, waiting. Her and him
The interval bell as certainly drags back
To earlier darkness, as the lights again grow dim

On old age propped on pillows, tea turned gin,
 A table set for one.
Will anything change? Will anyone burst in
From a better world 'Oh Christ, I thought you were gone...'
To work white magic? Lonely on a wall
The lights of a passing car. And time crawls,
The daughter listens again. 'That radio,
Turn it off... It was all such a long, long time ago...'

And no, they do not like it. They're afraid,
 Wishing themselves in bed,
Far into each other, a million miles away
On the other side of Abbey Street, Burgh Quay,
Bursting through traffic and rainfall,
Grimed cafés and savage pubs, and the laws
Of iron necessity, to a curtain-call
Beyond Ireland, a freedom without applause.

Art, Children and Death

I love only art, children and death

ALEXANDER BLOK

A literary man blows in from Cork
On literary business. Glad of a chat
In the lonely hour between the end of work
And the railway station. This and that –
Divorces, second families, his book
And the pasting it took in last week's *Irish Times*,
And still, one goes on writing... Coffee, talk,
The long perspective. Some day, when it comes,
There will be no one, in the latening roar
Of an age that passes. Only Heuston Station –
Transients, plastic tables, paper plates,
The crumbs of controversy, reputation –
Only the provinces, out past Inchicore,
The children's children, and the train that waits.

Disfavour

I, Heinrich Heine,
No longer or not yet
In favour, decline
In this lazaret

Of Paris, attended
By a peasant childwife,
Her infantile mind
Still believing in love.

Outside, no greenery,
Only a street.
Serves you right,
The Volk would say,

For heaping ironies
On our Black Forest trails,
Our darkness, in *Harzreise*,
Germany: A Winter's Tale.

Alone among German poets,
The critics harangue
Me, you never wrote
A decent drinking-song.

And those I defamed
Disown me, withhold
My inheritance.
Changing my name

From Harry to Heinrich,
I try assimilation,
No good, in the current mood –
Cosmopolitan! Stinkjude!

Disintegration
Of the lower spine –
Six mattresses
Support you, Heine,

More than the rise of nations.
You were never one of us,
They tell me. Your country
For you, is syphilis,

The tertiary stage.
Deaf to the call
Of a new, heroic age,
I turn my face to the wall,

Prefer disease
And living women
To the kiss of death,
The anthologies.

London, 1992

The Stage-door
Neary's, Chatham Street

They slipped out the back, through the stage-door,
Cut in here. Old bottles, lining the shelves,
Tobacco-smoke, the noise... For half an hour
They could be their real selves

As I remember them, with the greasepaint off.
Always the actor must fail
In the last performance, coat-trailing,
Legless, having his cough

Loosened, his pockets shaken down...
I watched, invisible for years
Up here in the gods, as the laughter-drowned,
The tragic, the cast in order of appearance

Burnt themselves out, like the legendary gas lamps
Along the counter – growing into my role
Of opera phantom, prompter through a hole
At Method, Stanislavsky or High Camp,

Only needing words and whiskey-breath,
An art-girl or a leap of faith,
An interval, a space between the acts
To contemplate the truth, if not the facts.

The Achill Years

If the Greeks experienced despair, it was always
through beauty and its oppressive quality

ALBERT CAMUS

1

Graham, Paul and Robert, lost at sea
Between dreams of art and a weekly farmer's market,
Pedalling into the wind for all these years,
And Louis too, and Mannie, warped like trees
Outside each others' windows, in the mind-darkening
Onset of Atlantic drizzle, pocking the Ice Age lakes –
You're only the latest... Take yourselves to bed
Or leave forever. Either way, bring food
For an island interlude, where the spirit breaks
Like whiskey on the rocks, in the Hotel Amethyst,
Waiting for clearance, and the high blue days
Of space into vertigo, vertigo into space –
Everyone else half-drunk on Irish mist,
Stumbling home, through a world of appearances.

2

The disconnect with the landscape,
The vacuum, you would say,
From man to nature, far Dooega
Through to Dookinella,
Brings out the drinker in each of you.

You are sucked out, like an egg,
Through your own eyes
Into azures, greys,
Which, if you understood them
Properly, would be horrors of a kind.

32

And yet, you stay on the island,
Painting. Years pass
Unchanging, the mountains in the distance,
The sea at hand, the canvasses
Accumulating,

Priceless, worthless.
Others, trying too hard to see,
Get drunk on air, and shoot themselves
From loneliness, despair –
The huge inscrutability,

The island, with its question.
Words are too social,
Too intimate. All eye, no mind,
Where the anti-poet thrives,
Is what survives.

Horace

Sick of that bloody poet, everywhere
Smart casual, urbane and circumspect,
Choosing his words with a little too much care
To be real any more, command respect
Or say a single thing worth listening to,
It came to me the only road to go
(Not martyrdom) was sheer, deliberate death
Made to seem like accident – too slow
To be suicide, too chaotic for myth
To be shaped of it afterwards. Satires? Odes?
No, silence. And the Roman gods
Discredited, through whose eyes,
At too many wine receptions, weighing the odds,
I watched the art of perfect compromise.

The Bible as Literature

In a locked, upper room,
For the authorities were about,
The disciples waited. And Christ came –
On his hands, his feet,

The stigmata. Transpierced
His side, where blood and water,
(Suffering innocence)
Issued, just for the record.

On the agenda, one item –
The impossible. Was it the wall
He had come through, or the window,
Breathing, passing along

The knowledge beyond death,
The leap of faith
Involved, from here on out,
In getting up in the morning,

Going about the business of the world?
There were stones to be etched,
New lectors to amaze. A day
Might supervene, or ageless centuries,

Before He, who had floated out
The window, floated back in again
With the ending to the Book.
Meanwhile, *vox populi*

And the literary games –
False messiahs, brought in chains
From Antioch all the way to Rome,
Dying to make their names.

At Racquets

Let's play hardball. Hamlet and Horatio
Back from Wittenberg, Laertes in from Paris –

Fencing, sex, and fallings-out at tennis,
At the sagging net of an outer court,

The heart of a long-lost summer... Politics,
Power, return us to Denmark. Watch us leap and smash

In chalk-marked space, a court within a court,
A play within a play, as fathers, mothers,

Drift onstage, for the fifth act
And the pile of corpses – venoming foils

For the sons already wounded, too far gone
For school debate, who dropped out

Long ago, with points to score
In love and war, on either side of the question.

The Pit

One by one, you are led to the pit
And in you stare, at all those gone before you,
Naked, splayed on top of each other,
Caught in their last wild grimace. Who would spare you?
No one, nothing. Somewhere Holy Writ,
This day, in Heaven, thou shalt see thy Father –
Doubled up, they laugh at your distress,
The executioners... Knowledge without bitterness,

Is that what you were promised? Piles of clothes,
Belongings. Loved remembered images,
Still or moving. Time accelerated,
Hair gone grey. To remember, to suppose,
Irrelevant now. Your cities still undamaged,
Streets of a different epoch. Loved and hated
Men and women, scorch-marks on a wall,
Shadows, from an age before the Fall.

Millions of flies have settled everywhere
Once, long ago. Our urns, our ashes, laughable
To you now, and our neighbourhoods
Deathless. You would say how lucky we are,
Unimaginable, in our future, beyond the rubble
Of cities, the battles of bad and good,
The categories – our mortgage on existence
Year by year, our time without history,

Everything rebuilt, a simulacrum
Of the real, a street of haunted people
Drawn together by intangible fear,
Meeting like lovers, under the steeples
Of a deconsecrated church – our Kingdom Come
Each other, our heavens blue and clear,
Our past eradicated, in the pit,
Our deaths that never come, our ruins lit.

Wreckfish

As a wreckfish cruised
I imagined it, fathoms underwater,
At large in the real blue

Of the human catastrophe,
Not this tanked aquarium light,
These people, oxygenated.

Bones of armadas
White as a ribcage
Glided through, and picked-off insights

Tiny as snails... A go-between
In half-lit worlds, insurance,
Undertaking. A loner

Among shoals, in the clockwork surf
Exploding on fake reefs,
With nowhere to dive to,

Nothing to resurrect –
A twenty-pounder
Among minnows, circling blindly

In its mirled dimension,
Bubble-hiss, too long in the tooth
For our million years,

Our trivia. Hull-haunter,
Soul-monger, slowing me down
To the sluggish beat

Of its cold-blooded heart,
Inhabiting me, as I moved between
Disaster, salvage, art.

The Dry-souled Man

Yvor Winters 1900–1968

1

Where you end up, in the boiler basement room
Of Stanford faculty, Professor X
Who never lived, who thinks he knows Crane's poems,
Can't get to you. The staff of '66

Are shacking up with students, getting stoned
In hope of tenure. Listen, planes up there –
American self-belief, and its counter-tone,
Soul music. California grows long hair,

Undresses, wanders nude in its own parks
Through jasmine weather, Emersonian highs,
Haight Ashbury, Berkeley... far overhead, the B-52s
For Vietnam. 'I'm sorry Winters, your work

Is a disgrace to this department...' Kennedy said
In that chairman's office, long ago.
Kennedy, and how many millions, are dead.
Droning in close formation, even now

His demons thrive, in the moist-damp atmospheres
Of south-east Asia, the 'blood-smell of prey'
As Saint Augustine says. The demons of emotion –
Waves of amplified sound, Pacific oceans...

2

Now, so near retirement, past all that,
A desert lies behind you. Santa Fe –
Your sick young self, in quarantine on the plateau
Of New Mexico, under a rainless sky,

All day long to write and drink, in shacks
Of blue adobe, towns without streetcar lines,
Sleep with dark *mestizas*, the daughters of copper mines,
Recover your rhythm, get your breathing back.

Someone or something is there, outside the door.
Is it Professor X? Or is it Crane
Back from the underworld, like Orpheus?
'Winters, for all your talk of the dry-souled man

You need a drubbing...' Silence, it's too late
To change conviction now. Pacific mist
From Pasadena to the Golden Gate
Rolls in like tear-gas, and the campuses are lost

To the long-hair ideologues. Remote, archaic,
The dangerous years of poetry, bad sex
And playing with fire. Today, the pride of the stoic
In his own endurance – secular crux,

Dry measure, as the bombers drone overhead
And the beat goes on. Outside that basement room –
Your *Forms of Discovery* stacked on shelves, unread –
The unmistakeable sweep of an iron broom.

Trance

1

Somebody said 'There's a job going
In Africa...' And the next thing

I was on that plane. Which year?
I don't remember. *You are here*

Said the map, and that was enough.
I taught some classes, fell in love

And watched a government collapse.
Savannahs, storms, cross country trips,

Alone not lonely in a Volks,
Through a wilderness of withering stalks...

The wide blue sky, the laterite belt –
Everything seen and nothing felt.

2

Somebody said 'There are children dying
In Asia...' And the next thing

I was on that plane. Don Muang –
Americanised. Simon and Garfunkel sang

Through tannoy, at the shakedown points.
The camps, the women rolling joints

Are all I remember. Blazing food
For jaded palates. And the giving of blood

Up-country, in a lying-down faint,
And coming-to, a secular saint

With lives in my hands, long working hours
And a dreamy feeling of power.

3

Everything heatstruck, in a trance –
Adrenaline, auto-immune defence,

Fantastic overcompensation
Roaming the earth, and saving nations,

Touching down in my own backyard
With a jolt and a mocking word,

A blow from a Zen instructor's wand,
And slowly, slowly coming round

Through days and years, in patient rooms,
To the self as home from home,

To nearness, touch, the strength to feel,
To the limited, to the real.

Auden in Shanghai

Okay, you wrote one sonnet. In between,
Poetry in abeyance. Afternoon flings
In the bath-house – Chiang, the local scene.
For who would want to read about such things

In Nineteen Thirty-eight, with the opium wars
Turned ideological, and the Japanese
Hovering? Off to the Front then, in closed cars,
Where no one sees, through the smoke of generalities,

Your one dead Chinese soldier... Decades on,
The ghost of Chiang, with therapeutic oil,
A person not a category, someone real

With a home to go to, and real needs,
Massages you. Don't ask him what he reads
If he ever did, or which side ever won.

Anabasis

Saint-John Perse, Peking 1917

Forbidden to the city, looking out
Beyond Mongolia, lies the hinterland
Of imagination. Watchtower and redoubt,
The lost Qing dynasties, are grass in the wind.
Gone the binary world of time and place,
The Occident, the Orient, interchangeable –
Pieces in a chessgame... On he plays
With Liang Kichao, with Liu. Already the Stranger

Forms inside him, like a pure idea –
He who writes the book of yellow dust,
Who contemplates the ends of civilisations,
The beginnings... Of all hours, these the happiest
While the stable-boy from the Legation
Grooms his desert stallion, tamed before the Fall,
And tree frogs, a mosquito off the wall
Perch at his plate, a woman pours green tea

And the epic goes on forming. *Anabase –*
The movement of peoples, after Xenophon,
To and from the ocean...
                              Here inland
The north-west wind. She lights the Russian stove
In the winter garden, where a lizard plays
At killing insects, and the War goes on.
Liang Kichao has moved. A counter-move
From Liu Tsiang-tsen. Outside, blown sands

Of plague, oblivion, warlords at the gate.
Tomorrow to set up a quarantine.
Tomorrow Li and his hundred concubines
To be sheltered here, in this state within a state,
The diplomatic zone... Minutiae,
Duties. Let the real thing grow
Inside, where no man sees it. Lei Hi-Gnai
His chessmates call him. Thunder beneath the Snow.

And some day, come the summer, he will go
Behind the veil of time and history
Where the gods lie around, in smashed theogonies
Of stone, to sleep in the ruins of Tao-Yu
And wake to the human caravan setting out
All over again, forever going west –
The wild geese flying, absence of whereabouts,
Mountain cold, an epic space as vast

As Inner Mongolia, setting itself free.
By the roads of all the earth, the Stranger to his ways...
The child of an island race, in the Gulf Stream,
Who sees it all already in a dream
(Gone the binary world of time and place).
The horse on the desert route, who scents the sea
And dies inland. The son without a mother
Grown into a man eternally other

Sleeping under the stars, in high Xinchan
Tonight, Beijing in the distance, incoming flights,
Thalassal surge of traffic, avenues of lights...
Here comes the boy, from the other side of time,
With eggs, a pullet, legends of Verdun,
The boy from the stables, beating a little stone drum
Below by the river, for the ferry across
From Tiananmen Square to Xenophon's wilderness.

from **Red Earth Sequence**

1 *The Mouth of the Yangtze*

All that flying time at body heat –
And now at last descent… The spirit-worlds
Of Sichuan, Tibet, have drained away
To shipping lanes and Japanese defeat,
Drowned Studebakers, yesterday's bar-girls,
Gold teeth gone, who walked the Shanghai streets
In Nineteen Forty-five and saw the flash
Five hundred miles away – Hiroshima
Or the end of the world… If time, eternity
Ever meet, tomorrow or today,
My criminal essence and my need to pray
Will break apart on impact, in the South China Sea,
Or make it through, on a wing and a prayer
To a deathless landing. No one will meet me there.

2 *The Life on Zhentong Street*
(for Huiyi Bao)

Smell it, the osmanthus. Heavy, sweet,
The essence of China, as the poet said.
For days I hang out here, on Zhentong Street,
Making a world, recovering, lightheaded

After time-zones. Children, break my heart
For childlessness. Street-women, sprawl at ease
On your public sofa. Life has beaten art,
The innocence and the sleaze.

The vulcaniser's spark, the cobbler's awl
Monopolise the empire, great in small.
Laughter claps a hand to its own mouth

In pure embarrassment at the power of mood.
Past the point of beauty, short of death,
Never does plain water taste so good.

3 *Autumn in Chengdu*

At the slightest rain, a flowering of umbrellas
Fourteen storeys down. The human sea,
The 'ocean of suffering', or so they tell me –
Deaths, rebirths... How many days now, all alone
At the heart of reality, in the white noise
Of a jammed radio, the fuzz on the internet,
Do I cut myself off, the better to atone
For ever living? It is not time yet
For the leaves that never fall, on the trees of Chengdu –
But the cripples and the hydrocephalic boys
At the Buddhist gates, the lama's cry
On the loudspeaker, powerfully coming through
The smog of appetite, are reaching me
Even now, and teaching me to die.

4 *At the White Night Café*

A poet of the Meo tribe, smoking weed,
Ignores me, ostentatiously. Ms Zhai
With a hand-held camera, looks herself in the eye.
'It is time, now, for our honoured guest to read.'

Professor Chan sits down. I see John Wong
Stealing, surreptitiously, anything he is able,
From the uncleared plates on the revolving table.
Xu translates. A travesty, all wrong –

But who will care? The smoke and mirrors, drinks,
The zither-pluckings ancient as Du Fu,
The spot-lit stage, projectionist on cue,

Inspired misunderstandings, age to age,
Are crowding in on me, as the stone page
Turns, I clear my throat, and darkness blinks.

5 *Red Earth*

Huge as China, tiny as a door
To a higher incarnation... No one there
To meet me, no one to say goodbye.
Such is the infinite courteousness, I could die
On the wrong side of language. Where I go
There is only silence. Everywhere, crowded floors
Of airports, Himalayan air
In the distance, or the nearness of gingko trees –
Mongolian space, the nomad's empty stare
In total externality. Two currencies,
Origin, destination, burn a hole
In my pocket, whatever each is worth.
Meanwhile, the body in transit. And the soul
Eternally foreign, vaster than red earth.

Zhoukoudian

> Praise to you harsh matter, which one day will be dissolved
> with us and carry us into the heart of Reality

>TEILHARD DE CHARDIN

1929

We were digging deep in time, towards nightfall,
A light snow falling, and the journey back
To Peking ahead of us, when the spade struck
Something in the matrix. 'Davidson Black,'
Said Pei, 'will want to see it all...'
So we axle-cranked that travertine of rock

By rail-line forty long kilometres
To the Cenozoic Lab. Where Black, that night,
Would cancel his engagements, I remember –
All that klieg-lit world of socialites,
Fowl and oyster feastings through December,
Winter palaces and glib ice-skaters –

Chipping away, with dental instruments,
At the myth of creation, the dogma of the Pope,
While Teilhard, who would hang by his own rope
Of Catholic heresy, watched the protuberant
Forebrain coming clear, as the human ape
Of Zhoukoudian, the one in a billion chance,

The stealer of fire, the ghost in the machine,
Sinanthropus, or Peking Man,
The heresy for which nothing can atone
But death of temple, church, the image of Christ
In smithereens, the bible turned to dust –
Unearthed itself in each of us alone.

2016

Was I there? Am I here tonight,
A soul-abandoned body hearkening back
From Dongshimen district, to the ghost of Black,
The old hostesses? Pei the Japanese shot,
And Teilhard died, a pastor without flock
In a New York room – anathema, frozen out,

The founder, so they say, of his own religion,
Gnosis… In the zone of institutes,
Embassies, and the flags of nation-states,
The massage-parlours glow, and the winter kitchens
Billow cooking-smoke from the street below.
The skull unsocketed, that never nictates,

Sees everything, at all hours. Through the wall
A woman wild as wind off Asian steppes
Empties her bladder in the toilet-bowl
Of the unholy. No Creation, no Fall –
A man in the background swearing, that is all.
I stand on the bathroom scales and weigh my soul

By its only law – true matter. Co-religionist,
Gnostic, heretic, Teilhard, I,
As the spirit in my shot-glass drinks itself dry
In dehydration, drink to his lonely ghost
Out there in the Beijing night – and the rise of Man,
The death of God, and dark Zhoukoudian.

Come and See Us Sometime

People grow old, their quarrels cease
Dividing them, as the common fate
Kicks in. The man with the prize,
Ten books on the shelf,
The man you used to hate,
Turns out, against all odds, to be yourself.

The enemy you shrank from, a friend in disguise,
Turns to the wall and dies.
Too late, now, for the word to be said.
Let our dusts mingle
And be nothing. Let our headstones
Lean, at a charitable angle,

Into each other's space,
Conspiratorial, wise
Beyond the binary knowledge of the living
As a child comes, all eyes
For the future, through the maze
Of unforgiving.

To the Philippians

And he humbled himself, obedient unto death

SAINT PAUL

Open-eyed, she stares into the void,
Occasionally blinking, seeing nothing. Interrogative
You might say, but no longer of people,
Not at this hour, when the wards, the corridors
Are empty, and the Filipinas chat
In the nurses' station, and the stacked bags
Of human rubbish, bleeding on the floor,
Await removal. Slow, the movements of symphonies
Belly and pulsate, like jellyfish,
Through the weightless ozone. You would like to speak,
You have nothing to say. The sockets of her eyes,
And behind them, nothing. Was that a smile, a sigh?
And suddenly her loud enormous yawn
Unfettered by convention, declaring boredom
Absolute, collapses into silence
As the time-line straightens, systole, diastole,
Dead to the world again, unripples and flows on.
That was not a question in her eyes.
Acceptance is absolute. Matter reigns.
Write your name in the book of visitors,
A citizen of Philippi, in a declining age,
With the void staring back at you
And the road to Damascus nowhere travelled on.

57

Toronto Suite

It was unimaginable,
The freezing dark out there
Beyond room temperature
On the nineteenth floor –

My cubit of perspective,
Solitude. Far below,
The ongoing work of the ferries
In death-chill, darkness...

I was ripe for collection,
I and my dog-eared volumes,
Watching, as Lake Ontario,
Lost but for lights

That were islands of the blessed
On its waters, stopped
Like a clock without hands,
And only the hours went on,

The millions below in the lobby,
And the single heartbeat
On the ansafone, glow-dilating
In its votive space.

Ballinafull, 3 July 2014

Dermot Healy 1947–2014

It was like an eye opening,
An eye, or a space
Between nature and itself –
And through it poured the days,

The years, the mountain-shapes...
There was a smell of hay,
And swallows, elbowing their way
Between nothing and nothing,

Keeping the elements open wide
And summer at the full.
In the high corner of a field,
On this side of the wall,

A human crowd, a passing bell.
This being Ireland, sea in the distance,
Wind and skies, the changeable –
In short, existence

On the latch, or the hook,
Like a sashed country window,
An eyelid, or an inch of light
Propped open by a book.

Death's Door

Christ, the weight of that coffin. And the plot
So bottomless from above, is overflowing
With generations. There it is, the root
Of every dark emotion – down there, growing.
Please, can I die now? Tired, I straighten up,
The whole of life behind me, all my dead
From Antofagasta to Luton, Cargin to Bray Head,
Adding to themselves, as nothingness
Weighing a ton, and biting like a strap
Against my shoulder, shucks itself off. The river
Has become a strait, and the race of men
Is changing into gods who live forever.
Standing back, I make a Sign of the Cross,
And death's door shuts against me once again.

Goodbye to China

Stripping for death not love,
I lose myself in the Chinese crowd.
We have no shame,
There is nothing to prove,
And none of us needs a name.

Everything has been said before
In this or another language.
Steam surrounds us, we are ghosts
Resurrected from self-image,
Clothes on a bath-house floor.

An earth-gnome, batlike ears
And giant phallus, gives me the eye.
Where are the women now, I cry,
My Xiaoqin, my Wenming Dai?
Where are all those years?

We are setting out, a host of souls,
The fiction of gender
Behind us, the pathos of roles –
Of time and distance, Xian, Chengdu,
Of passports and controls,

The pathos of history, Sichuan strikes,
Of railwaymen in 1911,
Stevedores in Shanghai,
Of Mao Tse-tung and Chou En-lai
And dreams of an earthly heaven.

Setting out, we are setting out
Past Xinchan range
And Lingquan temple, time and change,
Forbidden City, Tiananmen,
After the end, before the beginning

Brings us round again –
An accidental brush of lips
At Beijing airport, one winged seed
I keep inside the leaves of a book
For just this hour of total need

And zero expectation
All I can cling to, conjure with,
All I have with which to grow
Tomorrow, through another death,
Another incarnation.

Praise for *Wayward*

A *New York Times Book Review* Editors' Choice

'An urgent, deeply moving, wholly original novel by one of the
most wildly talented writers in America. This is Spiotta's best
book yet, rich with all the joyful immersion-in-culture that
characterised her earlier work, and of which she is a master, but
with, it seems to me, more heart, hope and urgency. There's
not a smarter, more engaging, more celebratory writer working
today than Dana Spiotta, and here she shows us to ourselves with
stunning, sometimes lacerating, honesty, but also with a feeling
of genuine hope for us, i.e., with kindness. I finished the book last
night and woke this morning both fonder of, and more terrified
for, America' George Saunders

'A dazzling lightning bolt of a novel which illuminates the
sometimes exhilarating, sometimes heart-breaking moments
of connection and disconnection in our lives. What begins as
a vertiginous leap into hilarious rabbit holes ends as a brilliant
meditation on mortality and time. How does she do it? Only
Dana Spiotta knows. I'm just happy to see her work her magic'
Jenny Offill

'What a thrilling experience to take a wayward journey along with
Dana Spiotta's heroine, in the social landscape of America when
America is probing its future, in a woman's complex internal
landscape as she forges forward. *Wayward* is a fiercely funny and
deliciously subversive novel' Yiyun Li

'Furious and addictive ... Sam [is] an ideal guide, rash, funny,
searching, entirely unpredictable, appalled at her own entitlement
and ineffectuality – drawn with a kind of sceptical fondness ...
So much contemporary fiction swims about in its own theories;
what a pleasure to encounter not just ideas about the thing, but
the thing itself – descriptions that irradiate the pleasure centres
of the brain, a protagonist so densely, exuberantly imagined, she
feels like a visitation' Parul Sehgal, *New York Times*

'Dana Spiotta is one of the most alert, ambitious, nuanced and, yes, smartest of our contemporary novelists ... Spiotta's novels, always rich with ideas and atmosphere, often focus on the arts ... Here, architecture connects to *Wayward*'s larger meditations about impermanence and decay – human, structural and even national' Maureen Corrigan, *Fresh Air*

'In literature and film, something happens when women hit forty, or nowadays perhaps forty-five: the earth opens up and swallows them, until they're spat out again decades later as grandmothers or wise old aunts in peripheral roles. The menopausal (or in this case, perimenopausal) protagonist is rare, which is just one thrilling aspect of Dana Spiotta's new novel, *Wayward* ... There's much comedy in the asking, but the novel makes clear that the answers aren't straightforward ... Spiotta's novels are unfailingly dense with life – the textures, digressions and details thereof – and *Wayward* is no exception. Spiotta offers grand themes and beautiful peripheral incidents ... she writes with sly humour and utter seriousness; a rare articulation of midlife now' Claire Messud, *Harper's Magazine*

'Masterful ... a mordant, coruscating indictment of these times, liberal politics, affluenza, self-improvement and social identity ... *Wayward* explores the ironies and frailties of modern life, the human tendency to constantly gaze inward to become better, to move further ... [Spiotta] swings for the fences' *Washington Post*

'Exhilarating ... *Wayward* reads like a burning fever dream. A virtuosic, singular and very funny portrait of a woman seeking sanity and purpose in a world gone mad' Joanna Rakoff, *New York Times Book Review*

'*Wayward* is a strikingly human and affecting story ... gloriously cool, deftly assembled, brimming with mood ... a hymn to iconoclasm, a piercing novel about what we lose and gain by when we step out of life's deepest worn grooves' *Vogue*

'A comic, vital new novel' Alexandra Schwartz, *New Yorker*

'Riddled with insights into aging, womanhood and discontent, *Wayward* is as elegant as it is raw, and almost as funny as it is sad' *Philadelphia Inquirer*

'*Wayward* is about rescuing your life from the mess you've made of it so far, while your body goes haywire ... Simmering under Spiotta's deceptively breezy, fluid description of everyday life in 2017 Syracuse are large and perplexing questions about the eternal interplay of idealism and pragmatism, of the longing for a better world and the reality of human frailty ... Sam dissects many flavours of contemporary delusion and distraction with consummate precision' Laura Miller, *Slate*

'A wonderfully mischievous and witty story ... A knockout' *Publishers Weekly*

'*Wayward* takes on marriage and motherhood – and shatters our safe, tidy concepts of each. Razor-sharp ... *Wayward* stands tall in its representation of these harried times' *San Francisco Chronicle*

'Defiantly, poignantly a novel of middle age ... One of the many strengths of *Wayward* is its unflinching portrayal of anger both personal and collective' *Los Angeles Times*

'Spiotta writes beautifully about parenthood, aging and other calamities that come with being alive in an unforgettable meditation on the indignities of life in the modern age' *Town & Country*

'Spiotta mines [her] material with laser precision and wit' *People*

'An engrossing, interior mother-daughter story that expands into a sharp social commentary' *Kirkus*

'Breathtaking ... a strikingly intelligent book, sometimes funny, sometimes painful ... a book that masterfully explores the pressures of being a woman in a hostile society. The characters are stubbornly defiant, and Spiotta does a wonderful job depicting [Sam and her daughter Ally] in their twin rebellions. A brilliant novel with love – never a simple subject – at its core' Michael Schaub, *Minneapolis Star Tribune*

Wayward

DANA SPIOTTA

virago

VIRAGO

First published in the United States in 2021 by Alfred A. Knopf
First published in Great Britain in 2021 by Virago Press

1 3 5 7 9 10 8 6 4 2

A CIP catalogue record for this book
is available from the British Library.

Hardback ISBN 978-0-349-01641-2
Trade paperback ISBN 978-0-349-01642-9

Printed and bound in Great Britain by Clays Ltd, Elcograf S.p.A.

Papers used by Virago are from well-managed forests
and other responsible sources.

Virago Press
An imprint of
Little, Brown Book Group
Carmelite House
50 Victoria Embankment
London EC4Y 0DZ

An Hachette UK Company
www.hachette.co.uk

www.virago.co.uk

For Agnes and Emy

A kind of wild forest blood runs in your veins.

MARY RUEFLE, "PAUSE"

2017

ONE

Sam

—————

I

One way to understand what had happened to her (what she had made happen, what she had insisted upon): it began with the house. It was the particular house, but it also was where the house was and where she discovered she wanted to be. It was a run-down, abandoned Arts and Crafts cottage in a neglected, once-vibrant neighborhood in the city of Syracuse.

The house sat high on a tiny lot on Highland Street, which ran atop a hill that bordered a long expanse of grass and trees. It looked like a small, sloping park, but it was actually a cemetery, the old graves scattered across the rise. Unless you were squeamish about graves—Sam wasn't—the sloping green hill was quite pretty. Highland itself offered a wide view of downtown. You could see the steeples of churches, and you could see how the small city was in a valley surrounded by hills. You could even see the kidney shape of Onondaga Lake, although it was often partly obscured by low-hanging clouds. If you turned your head to the left, or if you looked out the side windows of the house, you could see Syracuse University up on another hill. You would locate it by the quilted low white bubble of the Carrier Dome (named for the nearly absent Carrier corporation—all that remained were a handful of jobs, the dome, and Carrier Circle, a treacherous traffic roundabout that Sam hated). Soon after you spotted the dome you would notice the various spired and turreted campus buildings.

The decision to leave her husband—the act of leaving, really—began the moment she made an offer on the house. It was a Sunday; Sam woke up at five a.m., unable to continue sleeping. She attributed this unnecessarily early waking to the approach of menopause. Her period still came each month, but odd things had started changing in her body, even her brain. One of which was suddenly becoming awake at five a.m. on a Sunday, her mind shaking off sleep with unnegotiable clarity, as if she had already drunk a cup of coffee. And just as with coffee, she felt alert, an adrenal burst, but she could also feel the fatigue underneath it all, the weariness. That morning the wood floor was cold against her bare feet, but she couldn't find her slippers. It was still dark. She tried not to wake her husband. She used her phone to illuminate the way to the bathroom. She peed, flushed, washed. She brushed her teeth without looking in the mirror. She pushed up the blinds to peek outside. The sky was gradually lightening with the dawn, and half a foot of snow had fallen overnight. It was one of those Syracuse March snow dumps. Everyone complained because it "should be spring," but why say that when it never was spring in March in Syracuse. Besides, snow in March was often spectacular because of the spring light. The sunrise that was creeping up now cast a pink-and-gold glimmer, and a little crust of ice on top of the snow glittered from the sky and from the streetlamps. The trees, the roofs of the houses, even the salt-crusted cars looked beautiful. And like most spectacularly beautiful effects, it was almost too much, too dramatic, nearly lurid. Sam loved the drama of a March snow. March meant the sky would be bright, blindingly bright, not the cloudy darkness of January or the dingy gray monotony of February, the worst month. As the day progressed, sharp shadows would be cast across the snow crust, your eyes would squint from the brightness, and, with no wind, you might unzip your coat. Syracuse in these moments could be a Colorado ski slope. March was different because the light brought the promise of spring, and the snow made everything lovely, freshly covered and pristine.

But here was the important part: Sam figured that she was the only person on earth who thought March snowstorms were wonderful, and this made her feel a bit proud of herself. Always she liked to imagine herself as subtly different from everyone else, enjoying the tension and mystique of being ordinary on the surface but with a radical, original interior life. For example, back when Sam used to shop the sales at the Talbots in DeWitt with the other suburban ladies of her class and age, she separated herself. Sure, Sam had discovered that the classic A-line or sheath dresses made of solid-colored ponte knits were so forgiving, so flattering ("flattering," that tragic word) to a grotesque midlife misshapenness—a blurriness, a squareness, really. But despite being there and shopping because of an "insider" email-blast notification of a super sale, Sam believed that she was different from the other women. Inside she was mocking the calibrated manipulations, mocking herself, noting the corporate branding and lifestyle implications of the preppy styles and colors. The classic plaids, the buttons on the sleeves, the ballerina flats evoking a tastefully understated sensibility. It even occurred to her that the other women could be having the same interior thoughts and that the idea of conformity—at least in modern America—was never consciously sought after. No one older than a teenager thought, *I want this because everyone else has it.* No, Sam knew that you were sold the idea that you could be independent-minded even as you bought what everyone else bought. You were allowed to keep a vain and precious sense of agency. This was the very secret to consumerism working in a savvy, self-conscious culture. Her sense of resistance was as manufactured as her need to buy flattering clothing. Nevertheless (!), Sam also believed that her having such self-critical, self-reflexive thoughts as she shopped set her apart from the other women. Surely. So she still believed herself to be (however stealthily) an eccentric person, not suited to conventions of thought or sensibility.

Lately this desire to be contrary to convention had taken on a new urgency well beyond clothes or matters of taste. An unruly, even perverse inclination animated her. It had been looking for a place to land, for something to fasten on. So now (not before), this odd inner state pushed her toward a highly destabilizing wildness (a recklessness) that she couldn't suppress any longer.

She pulled on the same clothes she had worn the day before: stretched-out jeans and a black cowl-neck sweater. She no longer wanted to open her closet full of clothes. Why did she need so many, so much? In the last few months, things that used to captivate her no longer did.

She crept downstairs and made herself a coffee.

It was Sam's habit to check out the real estate listings online. She had the bored-housewife pastime of attending open houses. She knew many of the other people there also had no intention to buy but had come to snoop into other people's lives or to calculate land values or to imagine a fantasy life brought on by the frame of fresh architecture. This last impulse made sense to her. She had even wanted, at one point, to study architecture (and history, and women's studies, and literature), but she had talked herself out of it and, in what she characterized to her friends as a retro move, she had gotten married and then pregnant instead. She settled for becoming an architectural amateur. And a "stay-at-home mom" (a term she found degrading, as if she were a prisoner under house arrest).

Unusual old structures (Syracuse had many) excited her: they were a visible-but-secret code, the past rendered in materials that could be seen and touched. For example, the abandoned People's AME Zion Church on East Fayette Street. Its tiny perfect form sat on a sturdy, intact limestone foundation. Paint-peeled crumbling white brick rose into a modest bell tower next to a large Gothic-pointed stained-glass window. But the building was lost in the concrete dead zone around I-81, grown over with box maple saplings and covered with graffiti, the windows long boarded up. It belonged to the oldest Black congregation in Syracuse, built a hundred years ago to replace a structure at another site that dated to the 1840s, when it had been a part of the Underground Railroad. Sam had seen old photos of this church when it was a thriving center of the Fifteenth Ward, before the neighborhood was destroyed in the name of urban renewal. Yet it sat stranded and forgotten. Syracuse had so much history that it could neglect wide swaths of it. When Sam saw a building that no one else seemed to see anymore, she would stop her car, get out, walk around the perimeter, and even lay her hand on a brick as a form of communion and respect. Fascinating old buildings and houses, empty or still in use, called to her from all over the city. She sometimes drove out of her way just to glimpse one of her favorites.

But open houses gave her the rare chance to go inside, which was a much more intimate experience. As soon as she crossed the threshold into a house's space, she could feel it shape who she was—or would be—in some deep way. Whenever she had a chance to walk inside one, she did, which always worked as an act of imagination, an act she loved. What would it feel like to live here, wake up here, argue with your husband here?

This open house intrigued her because it was cross-listed on an Instagram account for architecture nerds:

Unique Arts and Crafts bungalow designed by Ward Wellington Ward in 1913. For sale for $38,000! Intrepid buyers only—needs complete rehab. Most original details intact. 110 Highland St., Syracuse, 11am–2pm Sunday. See link in bio for more #cheapoldhouses#saveoldstuff#bungalow#restoration #casementwindowsforthewin

She was the only fantasy lurker attending the open house at 110 Highland Street that Sunday morning.

The house was falling apart. The house was beautiful.

It had leaded glass windows, built-in shelves, and hidden storage benches. Two of the benches were framed by wood-beamed closures ("the inglenook") and sat at either end of (oh, what she longed for!) an elaborate tile-lined fireplace ("Mercer Moravian tiles"). Sam imagined sitting in the nook, gazing at the fire, reading a book. The tiles were dirty with layers of dust but still intact. She could pick out a narrative in the relief images. ("Saint George and the Dragon," the agent said.) The clay finish was a rustic, uneven glaze, the colors pink, green, and white. She touched her fingertips to the tiles and felt an undeniable connection. Someone on some podcast had talked about "grounding." It was when you walked outside with bare feet and let the earth connect with your body. It was supposed to right you, your circadian rhythms or something. Help you get over jet lag. Or maybe it was to mitigate the endocrine disruption of chronic toxic exposure. Or to counter EMF, the low-level but constant electromagnetic waves from Wi-Fi and cellular towers. Or maybe all of that, grounding promoted as a systemic cure-all. Sam scoffed at the idea, even despised it as New Age crap, yet as her fingers touched the tiles, she felt *grounded*. There was no other word for it, as if a corrective current flowed from the house through the dusty tile and into her hand and, truly, her whole body.

The tiles were set against patterned deep red brick topped by a mantel made of dark oak, also dirty but intact. Maybe it was Gustav Stickley or it was William Morris who wrote about the Arts and Crafts ideal, how the fireplace should be a work of everyday art. It looked handmade and warm, and its beauty was in its utility and simplicity: she was cold, she needed a fire. The hearth drew her in, invited her to sit. She now understood the fireplace as a form of secular worship. She imagined it would make her feel close to something elemental. ("Obviously, the chimney will have to be looked at.") To keep her sanity over the long Syracuse winter, Sam needed this beautiful, old, heat-squandering open fire. At her house in the suburbs, they had a glass-fronted gas fireplace that gave off some regulated, efficient BTUs of heat and a low, exhausting fan hum. The gas flame had a cold blue at its center.

"This house is on the historic register as the Garrett House. It even has a Wikipedia page. Designed by the architect Ward Wellington Ward."

"Yes, I read that in the notice," Sam said. "I'm familiar with him." She had seen some of his house plans at the Onondaga Historical Association. Meticulous, in colored pencil and ink. The three W's of his name, the repetition of the "Ward"s at each end, the short-long-short look of it, all drawn in that distinctive Arts and Crafts lettering. Everything was a work of art, even his name.

"Oh good. So you know his houses are very special. Garrett had it built in 1913. After he and his wife died, it fell into neglectful hands, but none of the original details are ruined. Clearly it needs some TLC: a heating system, electrical updates, new roof, mold abatement. Possibly a chimney rebuild. Better drainage in the basement. Shore up the foundations. But it's still a wonderful house, no?"

"Yes," Sam said.

Later she drove to the big suburban Wegmans and bought some wild halibut, diced sweet potato, and triple-washed organic baby spinach for dinner. She also got Ally's favorite fruit, mango, and her husband's favorite cereal, No-Grain Vanilla Granola, and several liter bottles of that German mineral water she liked. She took the groceries to their house. No one was home yet. And then, instead of cooking, she got in her car and drove back into the city. It was nearly six, and the sun was starting to go down. The sky was backlit, iridescent, spring bright, and as she drove she watched the clouds close to the horizon glow pink and orange. She drove back to the city because she had to see the house in this dusk light, this ridiculous, almost garish light. She crested the hill. She pulled into the house's tiny driveway. The roofline was steep, and the shitty asphalt tiles were coming undone. But. The front windows and the side windows faced the sunset. The city in all directions gleamed, and it looked as if an ocean lay beyond the clouds, some giant lake or shore. Ward Wellington Ward, this architect, he must have known. He thought of the sky and the trees as he designed his house; he knew how much you need those early-spring sunsets in Syracuse, even if they glisten off a foot of snow.

She retrieved the business card from her coat pocket and called the real estate agent. "I want it," the words coming up from some reptilian (perhaps paleomammalian, limbic, sublimbic) area of her brain, some part of her she never knew existed. "I want to make an offer, I mean. Can we do that today?" It felt easy. She signed the papers and wrote a check for the deposit. Inner life had spilled out and become outer life. She wrote an X in the box to waive the inspection. As is.

What drew her to the house was its nature: the house was a paradox, both rustic and elegant. It was contrived to be functional, but emotionally functional. After all, who needs a built-in bench by the fire? The huge hearth was clearly inefficient. Beauty was its own value, as was the experience of living. It felt hand-constructed, personal. Yet it reeked of artifice, "Arts and Crafts" meant to evoke home and nostalgia through cozy appropriations of English cottages and, oddly enough, some idea of a country church. Also, the state of the house. Dirty, falling apart, empty for too long.

It was wrecked. It was hers.

She got in her car, and she looked back once more at the house, maybe to imprint its image in her heart, the way you might look at a departing loved one. Sam noticed a white bit of paper tucked into the front door's frame. She got out of the car and walked over to see what it was. She plucked a corner with two fingers, and as she pulled it, she felt a heavier paper stock than she was expecting. Almost like an index card, but smaller and more rectangular, palm-sized. She turned it over. It had letterpress printing, blue on creamy white:

BEWARE: NTE IS COMING

Sam shrugged. What was NTE? Was it an ad? A religious message? Or a sort of warning? But the production values of the message gave it weight and substance, so she tucked the little card into her jean pocket.

She drove back to her home in the suburb, and only then did she realize, as she drove, that she was leaving her husband. Matt. That she would go live in the broken-down house in the city, the unloved, forgotten house with the view of the unloved, forgotten city. Why? Because she alone could see the beauty. It was meant for her. She couldn't—shouldn't—resist. And saying yes to this version of her life would mean saying no to another version of her life.

As she drove, she held her phone in her left hand, pressed it awake, tapped her password, and tried not to glance at the device as she found her way to the Favorites screen and pressed "Ma." She touched the speaker icon, and then she looked at the road, once again admonishing herself for driving and messing with her phone. It was a steady beat, that admonishment, and yet it changed nothing.

"Hello?" her mother said, as if she didn't know it was Sam, as if she didn't see Sam's name on the phone, as if Sam didn't call every day.

"Hey, Ma."

"Hi, sweetheart."

"How are you? Are you feeling—"

"I'm fine," she said, like a warning. Sam's mother, Lily, was sick but Sam wasn't supposed to ask her about it; "please don't dwell" on it, she had told Sam.

"Good." Sam pushed it off, undwelled. She would dwell elsewhere.

"But are you okay? You sound strange."

"Yeah, I do," Sam said. She laughed.

"What happened?"

She told her mother about the house in detail, the words rushing out with infatuated breathlessness.

"You really made an offer? Did you sign a contract?"

"Yes," she said.

"Does Matt know?"

"Not yet."

"Sam, you have to discuss this with him. You might have to cancel it. I think you have three days, right?"

"I don't want to cancel it." She felt herself getting tearful.

"You can't buy a house and not tell Matt—"

"You don't understand. It's not just a house."

"—even if it is cheap. It's cheap for a house, but not cheap like an impulse buy of some shoes or something. Come on, Sam. Are you trying to provoke something?"

"No! Don't be ridiculous. I will tell him, I'm going to tell him."

"I'm ridiculous? You're not thinking. This is silly, irrational."

"I know it is. That's the point. I know it."

"Call me after you talk to him. Talk to him. Do you want me to call him?"

"No! I'll talk to him myself."

Sam didn't tell her husband that night, or the night after. She ignored her mother's voicemail. She instead sent her an email saying everything was fine and she would update her soon. She had planned on calling her closest friend, Emily, but Emily had gotten on her nerves lately. Plus Sam's mother's reaction made her hesitate. Not about her decision, but about discussing it. She didn't need to crowdsource her fucking life, did she?

When Sam woke in the early morning of the third day, she felt her usual weariness about her sudden awakening, and then she remembered the house and felt a strange giddiness, an excitement. That evening, when her daughter, Ally, was at an away soccer game, Sam finally confessed to Matt what she had done. Not the way she had rehearsed it while driving in her car, with calm logic and gentle segues. But like a lunatic, impulsive and incoherent. It was interior monologue made audible. It included an elaborate description of 110 Highland Street. Then:

"I have to leave this house," she said. "I'm sorry." As if she were leaving the house instead of him. She had once fallen in love with their large cedar-and-glass, open-plan, contemporary suburban home. High ceilings and new white-pine flooring. Concrete patio with a fire pit. Surrounded by dense woods that made it feel private, no other houses to contaminate the view. *They* had fallen in love with it. But now she felt the hollowness in the doors, the casual way it was built, which was apparent in the details. Living in it left her cold. (Actually freezing in the early mornings. Baseboard heating in these huge spaces, conceived by some cheap contractor. They did have radiant heat under the floor tiles in the master bath, and she found herself huddling there, taking bath after bath, not willing to leave, all winter long.)

"What are you talking about?" Matt said, barely looking at her. He was reading something on his phone; he didn't have time for this. That made it easier on Sam, much. Out it fell.

"I can't stand it here, in this house." Sam's voice trembled; the intensity of her emotion surprised her. She touched the door of the small bath off the kitchen. "Who puts a bathroom off a kitchen, you know? And this door—" She pounded on the wood and the hollow, shallow sound disgusted her. She turned the button knob. "I could break down this door. It's cheap and ugly. I can't bear it."

"You want a new door?"

"Yes. I mean, no." Why should she have to explain herself? She started crying. "I hate this awful house. Us. You. I have to leave, I can't stay with you," she said. Now she had his attention.

"What's happened? What's wrong?"

"Our marriage is over, I think. I *know*."

Matt started laughing. She glared at him.

"Sam, what are you talking about?"

"I'm leaving."

Matt raised his eyebrows and lowered his chin to indicate disbelief. And irritation. The irritation came through in his voice as well, that familiar tone of his: weary, impatient, unenchanted. "What is this really about?" he said. He was standing at the counter, making some kind of post-workout smoothie. He didn't stop what he was doing.

Usually when he got home, she would tell him what happened to her that day. Who came to Clara Loomis House, where she worked (volunteered, practically), and what questions they had asked. ("One woman asked me if it was true that Clara invented abortions! I was like, most def! Sure! Like no one ever thought to terminate an unwanted pregnancy before 1895.") Sam would exaggerate the lameness of the questions to amuse, or try to amuse, Matt. He might laugh, but he would be distracted, occupied with his phone and finishing his post-workout branched-chain amino-acid supplements blended into his stevia chocolate-and-whey protein shake. That was her idea, these enhancing supplements, something she had heard about or read about and bought for him. He used them, and at least he didn't tell her she was being ridiculous, which she sometimes felt when she explained something she was excited about. Since the election, and certainly since the inauguration, when he came home from work she would go on about the president and the latest related drama. As she spoke, she lost her urgency or she increased her urgency as she realized how she would seem to him: like a person who had spent the day on the internet or watching cable news or listening to podcasts. She herself had done little all day; instead she reported from the edge of an unlived life. He would give her a polite nod, respond, but he was not really interested. He treated her the way someone would treat a talkative child or a needy dog: doling out just enough attention to be acceptable but not enough to encourage her to keep going. He tolerated her. Patronized her. Which she resented but also couldn't blame him for. She agreed with him, she was pathetic, she felt it as her words spilled out. But now, in this moment, she understood something new. His workouts, his distant looks, and his phone fondling aside, all those seemingly tolerant expressions served only one purpose. He was caring for himself, taking care of his needs, and it had nothing to do with her. She was the air to be got through.

"You've been gaslighting me, that's what this is about," she said quietly.

"What does that even mean?"

"What does it mean? It's a movie with Ingrid Bergman, *Gaslight*, in which her husband is trying to make her think she is going crazy."

"I know it's a fucking movie."

"He keeps dimming the gas light and when she notices, he lies about it. Tells her it's all in her head, her problem."

He had finally stopped making his smoothie. Oh how she hated that smoothie in this moment. The impossible-to-clean heavy grooved glass container and the whey-crusted blades. And that word, "smoothie," my god, how could anyone use that word, ever? The blender was full, but he stopped before he pressed the "pulse" button. Even he, the relentlessly efficient multitasker, knew that making a blender noise as your wife was leaving you would be tacky.

"You don't care about me. You aren't interested in me or what I think or feel or have to say. And you pretend this is okay, normal, a marriage."

Matt said nothing, looked at her. Really looked at her. Unnerving, that look.

"You don't love me," she said. "You put up with me out of loyalty and habit." Her voice cracked.

"You know that isn't true," he said. "You know that can't be true, Sam." His voice lowered.

"And maybe that is all I deserve. Maybe. But I don't like it," she said. He watched her carefully. She grabbed a tissue and held it to her eyes. Hot, swollen, the tears streamed down her face and stung her cheeks. The emotion seemed to build as she spoke, the anger (anger, that's what it was!) overwhelmed her. She was on the verge of fainting all of a sudden. She inhaled deeply, and on the exhale, she sighed. "I don't like you." The act of saying it made it so. "Not anymore."

"What happened? I know you aren't happy, but this is over the top."

"We are not happy," she said.

"Is this about the election?"

"No!"

"It is the election. You aren't the only one in the world who is upset over the election, you know."

"You think I want a divorce because of the election?"

"You do seem deranged. You took it very personally. But I'm stressed by it too. I think about it every day."

It was true that on election night they both were upset, but at some point during the unfolding disaster, he shrugged it off. She spent the night on the couch, actually cowering under a blanket, peeking at the TV. He drank beer and then scotch. She closed her eyes, tried to hide; then she opened the blanket enough to watch John King on CNN. He was pressing counties on a magic map of Florida, looking for unreported precincts full of Democratic voters. Michigan was too close to call. Pennsylvania was too close to call. She finally fell into a raw, fragile sleep as she watched. She woke up a few hours later. He was still sitting there, still watching CNN, no longer drinking.

"What happened?" she said.

"It's over," he said. "They are waiting for her to concede. And he's about to speak."

She stared at the TV for a minute, at the ecstatic celebrants. The feed underneath reported his electoral votes. Then she got off the couch and went to bed.

They were no comfort to each other. For days she woke in the early morning, ready to begin her normal routine, and then she remembered what had happened and felt the world shrink into a new, weird shape. It was very close to how she'd felt right after her father died and she would have some kind of sleep-propelled respite from her grief. What she realized—as the weeks went by and it sank in, until finally she woke knowing what the world was—what she realized was that the world had moved against her more than it had moved against Matt. To him it was the equivalent of watching his beloved Mets lose a closely contested World Series. To her it was much more than that; what exactly it was, she did not yet know.

On Facebook, shortly after the venting and the disbelief, she discovered that an online but also in-real-life protest group was forming. A Facebook algorithm suggested it to her, and she read the group's page:

> Don't give up. Don't just vent on Facebook! Take action IRL.
> Resist! Refuse! Organize! (Henceforth referred to as RRO!)
> Women Won't Wilt! (Henceforth referred to as WWW!)

Then she discovered the Syracuse offshoot of the national effort. One of the people she knew from her daughter's school posted about the local event. The description:

> **Syracuse WWWers!**
>
> Come talk strategy with other like-minded community members. We will begin with writing letters to our congressional representatives. We will not take this lying down. We will resist. Wine and light refreshments will be served.

The event took place in a beautifully restored stone farmhouse in one of the wooded and wealthy enclaves between Syracuse and Ithaca. The host was a Cornell professor. Her husband taught at Syracuse University, so they lived among farmers in this commutable-to-both area.

The professors' house stood on a hill with panoramic views in two directions. A large matching barn stood to one side, and Sam could see a wide, rocky stream behind the house at the bottom of the hill. She stood on the porch and listened for a moment. A sign was taped to the door:

> WWW GATHERING
> No need to knock. Come right in.

The large living room was filled with women, mostly her age. Already the mid-range New Zealand sauvignon blanc was being passed around, which she had to admit she appreciated (finally chardonnay and pinot grigio had become cliché and déclassé even in Syracuse). Crudités, cheese, and crackers as promised. The vibe was bright and cheerful as the women buzzed around, chatting and commiserating, each reporting her blow-by-blow election night story with the same boring annotated specificity with which women report their labor narratives after giving birth ("I sat on the sectional, incessantly switching between MSNBC and CNN, like that would make the news change. I finally went to bed at eleven after they called Florida. Michigan, Wisconsin, and Pennsylvania were still too close to call, but I knew by then it was a disaster and I couldn't stand to watch any more. When I woke up in the morning, my daughter came in and said, 'I am so sorry, Mommy.' It was then I burst into tears. We were supposed to have a woman president. I practically promised her. But she comforted *me,* can you imagine?")

After some mingling, the host shushed everyone and invited them to sit in a circle. She was trim in a blue wool sheath dress, sleeveless to show off her age-defying, sculpted shoulders and upper arms. Her bobbed hair fell to a face-framing point; it had been angle-cut from her ear line to just below her jawline. When she stood under the chandelier (antique stamped brass with bare incandescent bulbs), Sam could see her expertly balayaged highlights, the same gray-disguising ash-blond most of the women in the room had. The living room was very warm from all the people and a fire burning in the glass-windowed, cast-iron stove. Sam peeled off her black ribbed turtleneck. She already felt sloppy in her jeans, and now she wore a tank top that said "No Sleep Till . . ." in purple letters, which she had bought in Brooklyn for Ally, but Ally had never worn it, not once, so Sam wore it sometimes as an undershirt.

They were going around the circle, introducing themselves. It was then that Sam noticed two women sitting at the edge of the room. They were young—early twenties—and exotically beautiful. One had vivid cobalt streaks in her shoulder-length, thick hair. The other had a platinum buzz cut, her pretty skull shapely beneath the stubble. Both had copious tattoos and piercings, and they were clearly a couple.

One after the other, the women spoke, repeating the same lines of disbelief and resilience. As the icebreaker moved around, it stopped at a stout, sixtyish woman with gray braids hanging behind each ear. She sat in front of the two young women. Why would someone over the age of ten wear braids? An almost ostentatious display of not caring about her appearance. Why didn't Sam admire it, then? She didn't, though, the dull gray, coarse-looking yet thin hair repulsed her, which made Sam feel like a traitor, an age traitor. The gray-braided woman looked back at the younger women and smiled, deferring, and the rest of the room waited for them to introduce themselves. The young women made eye contact with each other and then looked down. The one with the buzz cut looked up at the rest of the women and frowned. Then she spoke, her voice shaky with emotion (which Sam could identify as fury, specifically, this despite the fact that her voice went up at the ends of her sentences as if she were asking questions. What is that called? Uptalk?).

"Look, I'm Larisa and this is Emma (?). We are from Ithaca (?). And I have to be honest with you all, I'm feeling pretty angry (?). At all the white women that voted for him (?)." This girl was, of course, as white as one can be, her skin made almost bluish and translucent by her platinum hair. Then Emma (black hair with cobalt streak) spoke, her voice low and somewhat adjacent to a hiss. "We had no idea this meeting would be so full of cis, straight, white, privileged women. You have a lot to answer for." It was funny to Sam that she didn't include "old" in her list of adjectives, or "middle-aged," but Sam understood that age was really the crux of it, nevertheless.

There were some awkward, audible exhales of disbelief. The hostess shook her balayaged head and held up her hand as if to quiet everyone. "You must know that none of us voted for him. That is why we are all here. We are as upset about him as you are." But the young, beautiful women shook their heads. Then Larisa pointed an emphatic index finger at the hostess.

"It was white women over forty (?), who voted for him, who put him over the top (?)." Over forty! The crux! The crux ansata!

"That is awful, shameful, but what about the much bigger majority of men who voted for him? Are they not to bear some blame?"

"All I know is that people our age, queer people, people of color—we didn't elect him (?)." And with a curt, frowny nod to each other, Sam watched as they lifted their lithe, elegant, plant-powered, bike-muscled bodies practically clanking with hidden piercings and scooted out of the house in a veil of righteous disgust. The remaining women exchanged shocked and outraged expressions.

"Un-fucking-believable," the hostess said. A person whose face Sam couldn't see suggested that the two women probably voted for Jill Stein and were actually to blame. Sam didn't speak, but something surprising came to her:

She agreed with the young women. In a way. Not that the women in the room were responsible for the election, exactly. But she agreed with how these young women looked at these middle-aged women. Although Sam was one of the middle-aged women, she too hated the smug entitlement that seemed manifested in their silvery haircuts, their Eileen Fisher linen pants, their expensive, ergonomic shoes. They reeked of status quo collusion, safely protected from it all. But it was worse than that. Sam hated their lumpish midsections and their aged necks, which she knew was awful, unfair. She slipped into these bouts of midlife misogyny sometimes. She did not feel solidarity just because they were all women; she felt estranged from them. At the gym she felt it when she saw the intense fifty-year-olds, yoga mats tucked under bony muscled arms, their faces lined and unmade-up, unsmiling and hard. Bikrami Bitches, she thought. Also the stupid pantsuits of the losing candidate, the ubiquitous highlights in the hair, the discreet eyeliner on the upper lash line, the scolding disposition, the postsexual benign vibe of her style and how she held herself. Ick, no. She understood why the world despised comfortable older white women. And age was the point—even if they didn't vote for him, they had been around long enough that the horrible state of things was partly on them, it was. Sam didn't want to garden or drink white wine or have anything to do with these women. Somehow, the disdain, the hate felt irresistible and also allowable, because, after all, she was one of them. She knew that wasn't quite right, that it was a problem, a mean reduction. And, after all, who is really safe? But she felt it all the same. Alienated from the well-off old women and the obnoxious young women. Plus, of course, all the men of all ages. Ha.

She didn't attend any more WWWers meetings after that. But Facebook kindly suggested some other local groups. One was CNY Crones, which was a "closed" group. When she applied to join—because who doesn't want to join something "closed" and exclusive?—she was sent these questions by the "admin":

1. Name two ways you have resisted youth-culture hegemony?
2. That was boring, and probably a lie. Give us two real ways you have resisted youth culture, and make it good.
3. What offends you?
4. And what have you done to offend others?
5. Rage much?

She responded in this way:

1. None of your business
2. Fuck you
3. Everything. Nothing.
4. See 1-3
5. Fuck yeah

She "got in," but she suspected it was only a formality. It was kind of a silly group, with a lot of posts about embracing your wrinkles, though only sort of ("learning to love my neck wattles, haha, scarves!"), and refusing to get plastic surgery on principle, but with posters often still obsessing—albeit through protesting

and professing the opposite—over how they looked. Sam reached
the breaking point when she saw this:

Delia West

I know you all will flame me for this, but I am newly divorced and
55. I lost a lot of weight recently (combo of boot camp, barre,
fasting). I really have trouble with being naked with my post
childbirth stretched stomach skin (post = twenty years later lol).
The skin is like a kangaroo pouch. No amount of exercise or diet
will fix it. I hate the way it looks. I can't live with it, I can't make it
work, it repulses me. Not for male approval, but for my own self-
esteem, I am considering a tummy tuck. Here is my question:
Can a crone spend money on looking good? I say she can. Isn't it
empowering to decide what you want to look like?

Susan Healy

Uh, no. If what you want to look like coincides with what
the culture says you should look like, you might want to
interrogate it.

Jill Blanchard

I disagree. I think you decide for yourself, that is the whole point.

Liza Winters

You do you, Delia.

Sam so hated that expression. Something arose in her, an almost
thrilling desire to post something nasty to Liza Winters. Whoever
she was. But then the desire passed. Inexplicably, Sam read on.
(But it was explicable, she knew that as things escalated, she would
feel a little touristic thrill. A posting meltdown was coming, and to
a lurker, it was a lurid yet irresistible entertainment.)

Antonia Luciano

I think "crone" is whatever you need it to be. I won't judge you.

Michelle Delcort
You are inspiring me, Delia. I might get one myself.

Liza Winters
What about cool sculpting? Less invasive and not technically surgery.

Susan Healy
Seriously, you are all on board for this? What about the money? Aren't there more useful things you can spend money on?

Michelle Delcort
I am reporting you for money-shaming!

> ***Admin**
> That actually is not a thing. Money-shaming.

Laci Cortez
I say burn this backsliding bitch at the stake. I mean, I am out.

Sam didn't post a comment, but she "liked" Laci's comment. It was the only one that seemed truly "crone-ish" to her. They friended each other, and after perusing Laci's page, her "likes" and groups, Sam ended up, or she found herself (because the path to the point is never clear in retrospect and also never-ending), invited to join a series of odd groups. Women-only, mostly, but also niche groups: Surviving the Anthropocene, which Sam discovered was a prepper group but on the political left, preparing for the climate apocalypse. The suggested Canning, Fermentation, and Preserving seemed to exist at the Venn diagram crossover of far right and far left, because if you are prepping for a racial Armageddon, a federal crackdown, or an environmental disaster and the consequent social meltdown, you will need a significant stockpile of preserved food. Although Sam did not can or preserve, she applied to join. Her admission to this group led her to myriad homesteading groups: urban homesteading (posts about the legalities of keeping chickens in a city and how to grow a vertical garden on your fire escape); off-the-grid (coed) homesteading groups focused on practical, *Whole Earth Catalog*–type skills from Morse code communications and well digging to sundial timekeeping, osmosis water purification, and first aid; and a plethora of (women-only) anti-tech homesteaders dedicated to living as if it were the past, with a specific cutoff date, such as 1912 or 1860 (interesting year choice on that). As far as Sam could tell, these tech restrictions involved a lot of posts about sewing denim, mastering hand-cranked washing machines, and the challenges of butter churning and molding, as well as many posts detailing the satisfaction and empowerment of "hands-on housekeeping," or HOH. Yet somehow living as a 1912 woman or as an 1860 woman involved being on Facebook a lot. Sam wanted to post a damning quote about the suffocations of housework from Elizabeth Cady Stanton or the *Feminine Mystique,* or just simply post, "Chosen drudgery is a form of feminist slumming" or "Out of the house and onto the ramparts, bitches!" but why pick a fight? Women join the groups to be with others who agree with them, to get tips, to post pics, to support their life choices. So what? But something about Facebook brought out truly juvenile impulses, which Sam had to actively repress.

It got worse. The ye olde homemaker groups led Sam, predictably, to some of the Quiverfull groups, explicitly anti-feminist and pro-huge families, because the Bible apparently has a metaphor about babies as arrows in a quiver. Since most of the participants were proselytizers (we need more and more quivers full of baby Christians), it was an open, even welcoming group. Sam didn't join, but she wasted a lot of time lurking and digging into the Quiver posts and comments. She learned that they were largely inspired by a book called *Mothering Is God's Career for You: My Journey from Lonely Businesswoman to Happy Mommy.* Sam thought of ordering it and "hate-reading" it, but then she thought, No. There was a bit of bad faith in smugly ridiculing these poor people. Posts tended toward selfies of rosacea-faced long-haired women in old-style prairie dresses and lots of pregnancy crowdsourcing about progesterone and wild yams. So what, if that is what they believe? Laughing at them was a shabby use of her time, but she knew part of what made Facebook—and the internet, really—addicting was simultaneously indulging your own obsessions while mocking (deriding, denouncing even) the obsessions of others from the safety of your screen. It was hard to resist, and indulging this impulse—even silently to yourself—made everything worse, made you worse, she was sure of it.

The Quiverfull people led to other fundy Christian groups, many closed (Sam was not interested in joining, but she felt compelled to read the public descriptions, parsing for dog-whistle subtext like they were society-in-decline word puzzles). On Instagram, Sam, to her surprise, also discovered a subculture of nonreligious groups dedicated to nostalgic ideas of womanhood via recovery of obsolete women's hand arts. Aesthetic fundamentalists, these women were drawn (in a sometimes ironic but also in a genuine and obsessive way) to hobbies in outmoded, old-fashioned "female" folk crafts: extreme pie making with stunt designs made of dough, pyrograph wood burning of boxes and wall plaques, macramé but also loom weaving, theorem painting of still lifes on velvet, daguerreotype copperplate photography, and Moravian-style wax star folding. Other groups went in for home arts but in more artisanal directions than the folk crafts women, with steam punk–looking excursions in beakers, copper stills, and bell jars, making hand-cultured vinegars and ciders but also shrubs, wassails, tonics, and bitters, which could be used to cure colds and doubled as craft cocktail ingredients. A further subset of these had a religious bent, albeit Wiccan and New Agey, with bespoke homespun potions, poultices, and other herbal remediations for illnesses, as well as plasters and pastes made from grinding seeds and oils by hand with a mortar. That led her to Twitter and back to Facebook, to wildly out-of-proportion, aggro throwdowns between various vegan groups and carnivore groups, omnivores and fasters. Diet had apparently become the major battlefield for all the dispossessed (i.e., all of us). There was something quaintly nineteenth-century American about it all: the focus on health, the zealotry, the desire for perfection, and the hot breath of impending Armageddon.

She clicked, she tapped, she followed, she liked. A few groups she joined, and always she lurked.

At some point after they were joined in declared "friend"-ship, Laci direct-messaged Sam and referred her to a secret group that was local. It was called Hardcore Hags, Harridans, and Harpies, and the description said it was a resistance group for women over fifty. A more extreme version of the crone group, it addressed things like perimenopausal, menopausal, and postmenopausal states and body (not beauty) strategies. Sort of an anti-Goop? Sam asked. u could say that, Laci messaged, and then added a string of stupid emojis. Sam joined, and by joining she got to know Laci, who also was active under the name Earl the Girl on Twitter and various other places that Sam was not that interested in. They started texting each other using the "safer" Signal app, which Laci/Earl insisted on. Sam discovered that the "Earl" moniker came from Laci's secret male identity, a sort of *nom de homme* that she used to impersonate a bro to "recon" incel and Men Going Their Own Way (MGTOW) boards on Reddit, 4chan, 8chan, and Gab (apparently some horrendous right-wing social platform). This Sam discovered when Laci called her one day.

"Hello?"

"It's Earl."

"Oh."

"Laci."

"Yeah, hi."

"Calls are the only truly secure way to talk," she said. "You aren't recording this, right?"

"Uh, how do you even do that? And why?"

"Never mind. I had to ask. Would you like to meet up IRL? I mean, off-book, F2F?"

"What is F2F?"

"Face. To face. We are all pledging to communicate—and operate—F2F, off-book, as much as possible."

Sam wasn't sure who "we" was, but she wanted to meet Laci in person. "Sure."

A few weeks before the inaugural, amid various discussions and plans for a women's protest beyond the march, they met at an empty diner in the city's Northside neighborhood. It was while waiting for Laci that Sam felt the first twinge of pleasure about what seemed counter to her life in the suburbs. She still thought of it as something she could tell Matt about at dinner, something she would make a joke about, just as she made jokes about the people who came into Loomis House. But she never did tell Matt about Laci/Earl.

A woman peered intently at her. This turned out to be Laci. To meet people in real life after meeting them on social media was always going to be slightly disappointing. Earl the Girl, a witty and fierce commenter online, was entirely ordinary in person. What did Sam expect? Sam hated her own shallowness, but she always wanted beauty on some level, or maybe a significance to the ugly, a deliberateness that indicated a sense of control. Laci's hair was undyed (good), but a coarse gray and blond that just looked dull, weirdly matted and nesty. She was in variously pocketed knee-length khaki shorts, despite it being January. Her oversized T-shirt said "Resist." Good god. The overall feel was sloppy and beige. Sam—lately kind of a slob herself—felt ashamed for being so harsh. She wanted to admire Laci's person, wanted her look to match her wit. Maybe her frumpiness was a form of resistance, rebellion? Sam tried to see it that way. She knew that she shouldn't always need to be seduced.

After they ordered awful but at least hot coffee and warm pie, Laci (again) explained her Twitter handle, @EarlTheGirl.

"Yeah, you told me," Sam said.

"It's a little joke because 'Earl' is also my seemingly male avatar when I rove the incel subreddits, lurk the pickup boards, troll the sad, self-pitying MGTOW posts."

"Why do you want to look at that stuff?"

"I don't know, honestly. I'm fascinated by them, by it. I mean, it's awful, of course. I want to know what men are really like."

"Some men."

"I want to see the male perspective."

"We are fucking living in the male perspective," Sam laughed.

"I mean, what they truly think and say when no women are around." Laci spoke through a mouthful of pie and ice cream.

"Right. Just go to Pornhub, you know? There it is in like very specific categories."

"Of course. I regularly scrutinize Pornhub."

"I was joking."

"In fact, between you and me, I get pretty aroused by some of the really not-positive stuff. Some real patriarchal bullshit. So that's confusing."

"Yes, I can imagine it is."

Sam began to drive out from Fayetteville to meet Laci at the diner once a week. It was through Laci that Sam met MH. MH (real name Devereaux, a.k.a. Mother Hubbard) was a sort of mentor to Laci. At first, Laci referred to her in a cryptic way.

"Who is this MH? What does 'MH' stand for?"

Laci would look over her shoulder before answering. "She started some of the groups, but she doesn't want to admit that. She doesn't think we should have specific leaders, you know?"

"Sure," Sam said. "Leaderless."

"No," Laci said. "We call it 'leaderful.'"

Sam groaned.

One day MH accompanied Laci to the diner. Laci might have disappointed Sam in real life, but MH did not. There was no mistaking her when she walked in. At sixty-five, she had the hard contours of someone who could do pistol squats and burpees. Her hair was silver rather than gray, and her eyes a high contrast, striking blue. She was wrinkled but beautiful in an austere, Walker Evans way. Sam guessed that MH was actually more glamorous as an older woman than she probably had been as a young woman. She didn't have that quality of a thing faded, a hint of beauty lost. She looked peak. MH immediately launched into a monologue about her "n=1" self-experiment in carnivory. She was eating nothing but meat and water for a month, "nose-to-tail," with lots of organ meat and raw suet.

"Only ruminants. No fish, fowl, or swine."

Sam nodded.

"The ruminants' stomachs' fermentation can alchemize any-thing into perfect human nutrition." Apparently, when MH was into something, or on to something, she was always deep in. MH also explained that she was part of a subgroup within the Hardcore Hags, Harridans, and Harpies group: Half Hobos, which was, Sam gathered, for hipster derelicts, those willfully itinerant, but a Half Hobo also encompassed the self-conscious resistance of a heretic or dissident. (Later Sam would discover that MH's Twitter profile "photo" was a painting of Saint Wilgefortis, a bearded female saint who was crucified. In the painting, Wilgefortis looked like Jesus with breasts. Sam laughed, but she couldn't quite tell how funny MH was being—she had to be joking about Messiah references, right?) Even though it was a group, Sam suspected MH was the only Half Hobo.

"Is a Half Hobo like a freegan, like those dumpster divers?" Sam asked MH.

"Half Hobos live at least half their lives as hobos." MH didn't have a permanent address. She stayed with friends around town and kept her possessions in a (very nice) leather duffel.

"A demi-derelict," Sam said.

"It's about having an optimal and deliberate relationship to the local, to the things, the culture, the people that surround you. To itinerate, and to use up—consume—as little as possible."

"Faux po'?" Sam said.

There was an awkward silence. Then MH laughed. Wow, were her teeth beautiful. Laci laughed after MH did. MH was very pronouncy, full of certainties, which Sam found both ridiculous and highly attractive. Seeing MH and Laci secretly in the city became Sam's main reaction to the election, her personal expression of "resistance."

It was true that the election had changed everything, had escalated everyone's anger and disease, but Sam understood it as a confounding rather than a causal factor in her defection from her marriage.

"I don't want to talk about the fucking election," she said to Matt. "And it has nothing to do with why I am leaving. The election was months ago."

"Yeah," Matt said.

Sam sighed. "Four months, two weeks, and six days ago. But no, that isn't it."

It took some time to get through to him. The more he insisted that her leaving was irrational and an overreaction, the more adamant she became. What she realized was that one person could unilaterally end a marriage. The more he challenged her, the more certain she felt. She had no real particular unhappiness this week, this day. But, she understood, it had been there for a while, waiting for a chance to breathe.

He acquiesced, finally. But he was pissed.

"You could have waited a year, until Ally graduated from high school, but clearly the urgency you feel precludes consideration for others."

"That's right," she said. "That's right."

"Then you tell her," he said. At some point he had abandoned his smoothie, and he was pouring himself a scotch. "I mean, tell Ally right away, as soon as possible. Don't try to make jokes or pretend that nothing bad is happening."

Ally. Good god, she hadn't thought about having to tell Ally. Ally would love that little house. They could fix it up together. Ally could decorate her room; they could go to estate sales like they used to on Saturday mornings. Ally always had an eye for a vintage find. She'd buy something for a few bucks, and then they would look it up on eBay when they were in the car riding home. Invariably, it would be collectible, valuable. But then Ally started doing indoor soccer on Saturdays, and then she had ice skating, and finally the increasingly demanding YAD meetings. ("Pitch simulations," Ally would say, correcting Sam. YAD was the hypercompetitive baby entrepreneur club at Ally's school.) When Ally got her driver's license, her weekends became her own, and that was the end of those early Saturday morning sorties.

"I'm taking a shower," Matt said. "I will come down when she gets home."

Sam thought she should reheat the chili from last night and put spoons and bowls on the kitchen table, but she didn't. Within an hour, Ally walked in, sweaty from her game, and dropped her backpack and duffel. She held her phone in her hand and had her earbuds in. Sam sat on the couch next to a newly clean Matt, waiting for her. He hadn't said anything as they waited, but he did pour himself another drink. They both must have looked stricken, because Ally glanced up from her phone, stopped, and pulled the earbuds out.

"What's happened?"

Matt took a sip of his scotch and looked at Sam, and she almost lost her nerve. If she spoke, her voice would fail her.

"What's wrong, what's going on, you guys are freaking me out—" Ally said. "Is it Grandma?"

"No! Everything is okay," Sam said, her mother voice returned to her. "We just need to talk to you."

"What?"

"Can you sit for a minute?"

Ally wiped her face with her hand. She stepped over her dropped backpack and her gym bag with her cleats tied to the strap. She was wearing her shorts and soccer knee socks still. Her face was pink, and her long hair was tied in a high ponytail. Even post-game, she looked held together, somehow efficient, to Sam. She might be sweaty, but that childish messiness was gone. Sam felt, as she sat on the couch, a sense of her own disheveledness: she hadn't bothered to blow out her hair or put any lipstick on in weeks. Sam barely even looked in the mirror when she washed her face. She wore the same jeans and sweater she had worn yesterday, and her fingernails and cuticles were ragged from not wearing gloves. Ally, Sam noticed, had clear polish on her perfect ovals.

"Ally, Daddy and I wanted to talk to you, but first let me say this has nothing whatever to do with you. We love you."

"Oh," Ally said.

Sam felt her throat constrict. Ally was so tough. There was a thick pause.

Ally's eyes flared at Sam. "Just say it."

"We are splitting up," Sam said. Ally, to Sam's surprise, started blinking back tears. Ally never cried. Sam believed, because of the oval nails and the neat ponytail, that Ally somehow knew everything, that she had figured it all out. But no. Sam's own eyes began to blur again. Sam knew not to touch Ally, but she moved to do so anyway. Ally's hand went up, her fingers spread, and her palm pressed the air. *No. Stop.* Sam sat back down. Matt made some odd throat-clearing noises, which Sam knew he made when he was trying to get a grip on his emotions. No one spoke for a full thirty seconds.

"Daddy, how can you leave?" Ally said to Matt. Then she shook her head.

"I'm leaving." Sam's mouth was dry. She could hear herself swallow. "It's me. But I'm not leaving you, I am leaving Daddy."

"What?" Ally said, looking at Sam as if she were insane. (Which, Sam would discover, was what everyone would wonder. Everyone would think Matt had to be the leaver, not Sam.)

"I bought a little house in the city. You will love it. Once I fix it up, you will love it. The windows in your room, the view. You can help me fix it—"

"Are you kidding? I mean, really?" Ally said. "I'm not moving. This is my junior year. I have to stay right here." She said this with such bitter emphasis that Sam simply nodded.

Matt said he would stay in the suburban house (which was "his obligation" he said, meaning to Ally, said in such a way as to gently remind, to upbraid, or to scold Sam about all the obligations she had apparently abrogated, meaning to Ally and to him). Sam watched Ally, who was staring at the floor. Ally stood up, reached for her backpack. She finally looked up at Sam.

"Ally—"

"I have to do my homework," she said. "A lot of work. Just leave me alone."

Sam nodded. She sniffed and wiped at her eyes. "I'm so sorry," Sam said, which definitely made them all feel worse.

Ally started to leave but stumbled into the arm of the couch. At the door to the living room, she looked back at Sam. And then she left.

Sam did not go after her, although she wanted to. She wiped her face again.

"What have you done, Sam," Matt said. But it wasn't a question, or it wasn't stated like a question.

The next day, Sam slept until six, which was very late for her. She glanced over at her husband. Matt didn't get up until six-thirty, and when he was asleep, he looked peaceful and young. He was good in sleep. Not everyone was. Matt didn't snore, drool, or mouth-breathe. Sam went down to the kitchen, and she could hear the coffee already brewing. Ally was at the kitchen table, earbuds in, studying her Latin.

Ally looked up, and Sam waved. Ally pressed pause on her music.

"Good morning," Sam said, at once amazed and alarmed by how her child had become so self-sufficient. Ally pressed her lips together, shook her head slightly—she was, it seemed clear now, livid—and then she spoke:

"Go to your stupid house. I don't care what you do. This is better anyway. I don't want to live with you."

Sam nodded.

"Or talk to you, or have anything to do with you."

"Come on, Ally. I know this is upsetting."

"*This* is not upsetting. You, *you*, are upsetting."

Stupidly, Sam reached out to Ally, touched her shoulder. Ally whipped away from her.

"Do not!"

In the awkward days that followed, Ally wouldn't look at her or talk to her. Who was this girl, this tough, hard woman?

"Don't push her," Matt said, and Sam knew he was right, knew how it could backfire with Ally. The truth was that these days, Ally got along better with Matt than Sam. This had been true for a long time despite their being "as close as a mother and daughter could be" (as Sam once bragged to other adults). Sam thought she had escaped the rebellious teen thing, the whole "I can't stand my mother" drama that other moms complained about. But then there was the fiasco at the hospital, and, even before that, things had begun changing once Ally hit puberty. Sam could feel Ally separate, almost like a membrane ripping, except Sam didn't believe it. Ally became more distant, more self-sufficient, more of a mystery to Sam. Of course, whatever Sam had lost, Matt gained. Sam wasn't an idiot; she knew these things change and change again. She worked to not be too hurt when she walked in on Ally and Matt snickering and no one could explain what was so funny. So now, when Ally shut her out, Sam relied on Matt to be her conduit. He was good with parenting, albeit less passionate than Sam. He was practical and constant. So Sam longed for her, but she was used to her mother love being unrequited. Even now she told herself this was temporary, that she and Ally would be close again when Ally was in college, just as Sam was close with her own mother, Lily. She persisted in believing that Sam and Ally would be like Sam and Lily, despite many differences. For instance, Sam had never had a falling-out like this with her own mother. Why draw analogies between herself and her daughter? Ally was not her. (Which was good, wasn't it?)

Sam waited for the closing, called her lawyer every day to speed it up. It was an all-cash transaction, after all. Matt pulled the money from their "emergency" savings. She thanked him, and he replied that it was her money too. After it had become clear that

Sam was still leaving despite Ally's anger, he had changed tactics. He became supportive, almost sentimental. Not a trace of anger or sarcasm in his tone. He even flirted with her and made her laugh. A performance of his capacity to be a generous, attentive husband even when wronged. Was this performance for her or for himself? Yet his accommodations were seductive.

Sam had to get the hell out of there as soon as possible.

She tried to sleep in the guest room, but Matt begged her—begged her!—to stay in the bedroom. "These are our last nights together," he said. They didn't have sex, she made it clear that wasn't happening, and he said, "I know." She slept turned away from him, and he pressed his head against her shoulders. She could feel the warmth from his body behind her. His breath slowed and he fell asleep like a child. Warm bodies in bed felt totally different when they touched, even slightly. Anyone would find him appealing when he was asleep, which she realized was such an inadvertent slam that she snorted into the dark room. Matt didn't understand that he was only one part of it; clearly Ally didn't understand what Sam was doing. All Sam knew was what she knew. She no longer wanted to be in the suburbs (that had always been his preference, because he liked having land and trees and privacy, and she had thought she liked that too). Or, rather, she could no longer live in the suburbs. "Wanting" sounded volitional, and that was not what this was. She had always disdained people who left marriages by saying they had no choice, as if it were out of their hands. Yet that was how it felt to Sam: a force in motion that couldn't stop once it started.

The morning walk-through before the closing elated her despite the April damp, the evidence of pests, the cold everywhere. There were so many papers to sign at the closing, and each time she signed or initialed, she felt her certainty harden. The key in her palm stunned her; the first step across the threshold, by herself, as the owner, gave her focus. Purpose.

Once they drew up the separation (but not the divorce, not yet, he insisted), he gave her an additional fifteen thousand dollars (dipping well into their savings but not Ally's college fund). After the closing, she fixed the house enough for her to move in. She got the basics updated: plumbing and electric (even though the copper crisscross of porcelain knob-and-tube wiring in the attic appealed to her). Sam opened her own bank account with the little leftover money. She said she wanted nothing more, but he just laughed. "You pay our bills. You must know that your job won't cover it."

"I can be very frugal on my own."

"It's your money too," he said. He kept saying that, but it didn't feel like it to her. She agreed to a minimal monthly amount until they settled everything, just enough to cover her property taxes, utilities, and her food. He smiled, and there was a twinge of victory in the corners of his mouth. "Good. Let's not worry about the rest now," he said. It was truly helpful, she had to admit, that he was being so nice to her. Gentle about everything. But she knew Matt, knew how under the veneer of patience he was simply waiting her out. It was more than a little condescending that he viewed this as temporary, that he imagined that if he behaved, she would come home once it was out of her system. Sam was glad for the ease anyway.

When at last the house was minimally habitable, Sam took only her chest of drawers, two cane chairs, a round wood table, and some kitchen items. She had bought—with a delight that shocked her—a twin-sized mattress and frame. She set the bed in a corner of the living room until she fixed up a bedroom on the second floor. She could fall asleep looking at the fire. The plain iron frame by the window looked like a nun's bed. Or a saint's. Good. The mattress was quite expensive—a concession, a signifier really, of her faux poverty (faux po'/demi-dereliction), despite her renunciations and her almost ostentatious austerity. She liked to imagine herself in voluntary poverty (living among the involuntarily poor) like Dorothy Day. But her back hurt sometimes, and she couldn't have a bad mattress and end up immobile at some point, pinned to the floorboards moaning.

She thought of the old movie where the rich guy pretends to be poor and lives with the hobos in order to suffer and feel authentic things. It goes awry. (A really good movie, except for the ending, in which he has an epiphany about solving everything with laughter.) Sam didn't want to be like that movie. The title of which lay behind some muggy hormonal veil, not brain fog so much as a muslin sheet she could almost see through.

As soon as the bed was installed, she mouthed goodbye to Ally's closed bedroom door and left the house in the suburb for the last time. Three weeks after the closing and with much work not yet finished, Sam moved into the house in the city. Scarcely an hour had passed before the doorbell rang. Flowers sent by Matt. Oh for god's sake. Dusty peach-colored peonies, her favorite. Her leaving had made him attend her, but he didn't understand that wasn't her intention at all. Sam just wanted to be alone in her house.

That afternoon, Sam deep-cleaned every surface of the many-surfaced space, and in cleaning, she felt a deepening of her love, an intensification (if that was possible). The dark oak floorboards, mantel, and moldings glowed after she rubbed them with oil. She used a fingertip swathed in cotton to dust the notches carved into the beveled corners. The details emerging pleased her so much that she thought she might cry. What was wrong with her, feeling so happy about cleaning old wood? It was solid beneath her hands.

She looked up all the available paperwork about the house at the county historical association. She color-copied the ink-on-vellum blueprint templates, and she even read through the contracts the architect Ward had made with the artisans who worked on the house. Every voluptuous detail enchanted her. The stucco was to be of "Portland cement," "hydrated lime," and "clean, sharp sand," with a liberal allowance of "cow's or goat's hair," all thoroughly mixed. What a house, what a sturdy, well-made thing.

The peeling paint on the elaborate windows was a little daunting, no doubt full of lead (but it was "Brooklyn White Lead" mixed with French zinc and the "best raw linseed oil"). Why should she care, at fifty-three, about lead? Was she pregnant, did she have small children? She was invincible in her way—a few IQ points shaved off by toxic exposure meant nothing to her. Letting go of the lead fear elated her, made her buoyant, although she also knew that she might wake up at three a.m. imagining the lead dust she had kicked up in her lungs and in her blood making her ill. This was the problem of the Mid: the part of the night, the mid-night, that gave the lie to all the fearlessness.

That first night alone in the house, as the light faded, she heard things. But it didn't exactly frighten her. So what if the world was filled with ghosts? Ghosts would be great; anything more than this life would be great. But maybe it wasn't ghosts, maybe it was hungry junkies from the streets, the pale opioid zombies with the vacant eyes and the bad skin. They frightened her. And maybe some of the neighborhood denizens had seen her move in and probably figured her for an easy target. This house with its endless windows was fucking porous as hell.

Just stop, please, with these thoughts, these fears.

Also: why was she afraid of poor people?

And: what was she doing in this lonely place?

Sam reached for her phone, touched it until it came alive, and then texted Ally.

> Hi, Ally-oop, I am in the new house. Pretty but lonely. (I mean the house, not me . . . ha.) Love you.

Her phone suggested an emoji in place of "Love you," and Sam complied. Keep it light. Since Ally had stopped talking to her, Sam allowed herself one text a day, at nighttime. Ally ignored it, as Sam knew she would. But the phone showed that the message had been read, and Sam took her leaving read receipts on as an encouraging sign. Ally hadn't blocked her, which she had feared. Sam must hold back, not send dozens of texts, or she would be too much and nothing would get through. Besides, wasn't everyone more favorably disposed to their mother at night? Sam had texted each night even when they were still in the same house. The closed door of a teenager's room may as well be another continent. So she sent a text before she went to bed. Ally read it and didn't respond. It was still a connection, and maybe it would soften her over time. Sam couldn't do nothing.

Sam wanted suddenly to call her own mother, but it was nine, and her mother was asleep. Sometimes she went to bed before eight, her elderly, weary mom.

Just, god, just don't. Don't think about Mom. And not right before bed.

Cognitive behavioral therapy involved redirection, recognizing and short-circuiting dangerous/self-defeating/habitual lines of thought. Or at least that was how Sam had understood it when she'd listened to a podcast and then read (skimmed) some self-helpy quickie articles on CBT for insomnia (CBTi). But it was so much work, so hard to do. She started a new toxic line of thought about how lame she was at implementing CBT or any other disciplined solution. Meditating. No screen time or eating or drinking for hours and hours before bed. The finest calibrations of mind and body, as if sleep were an elusive miracle to be conjured rather than an ordinary function of human daily life. What did it mean to lose your natural connection to sleeping? Thinking about it made it impossible, moved what should be autonomic to somatic. Sam should take sleeping pills like everyone else. Or just submit to the crap fitful tailspins and see what happens. At some point, sleep had to come.

She texted Laci and MH on their group chat and told them she was spending her first night in the new house. She had surprised herself by keeping them in the loop: I left my husband, I bought a house, I moved into the house. But always after the fact, because she didn't want help or company or advice. She just wanted to declare herself, remind herself of what she was doing.

Laci wrote back in seconds.

Good 4 u! Housewarming??

Instead of answering, she texted her a photo of a candle glowing on a ledge built into the oak wainscoting.

She was tired. She should get in her bed.

It was then that she discovered that she didn't have sheets for her bed or a pillow. How could she have forgotten that? She brushed her teeth and then lay upon the bare mattress. As soon as she did, she lost her sleepiness. Sam tried to push into sleep, fully clothed on the bed, and of course it didn't work that way, pushing it. She let herself go; she returned to lead poisoning, but then moved back to the avoidance/unavoidance of catastrophic mother-loaded fears (what if her mother died in her sleep tonight, what if Sam never got to see her again, what if Sam had called the doctor she heard on that podcast and talked her mother into his protocol, something about push-pulse, she should remember to read about the Wurburg or Warburg effect), then Ally (just the song "Once upon a Dream," as sung by Ally at age twelve, in the delicate soprano of prepubescence, how Ally used to beg to sing for Sam in the car, *But if I know you, I know what you'll do, you'll love me at once, the way you did once,* Ally pausing, Sam glancing at her in the rearview mirror *upon a dream,* a smile and then Ally waited for Sam to say "Wonderful," which she always did because it was a wonder, the girl, the voice, in the back of her car). And then back to the neighborhood, the zombie junkies and Sam's disgraceful fear of the poor people who had seen her move in. Then disgust at her own monstrousness, now exaggerated and abstracted: her lack of compassion, her need for safety. Why does she get to have safety? What has she done to deserve that. But everyone should be safe—the desire for safety is just human, maybe she was too hard on herself. (Reprimanding herself, arguing with herself. These are the deeps found in her wretched, exhausting wakefulness.) The fears are not discarded by sheer will; the fears are myriad and persistent. It was only human. She was human. Fall asleep.

And, somehow, this time, she did. Until she woke later, in the Mid. Somehow the Mid always seemed to be precisely 3:00, very seldom 3:10 or 2:55. Uncannily on the dot of 3:00. This was worse than the sleepless slow period at the beginning of the night ("latency insomnia" it was called), because Mid-waking was disorienting, a shock to Sam. Her eyes would open into the deep black of the room, and her body would wake up. Tired yet fully awake. Lying next to sleeping Matt, she would feel a tremendous isolation at these moments, a dread and then a kind of vacuum.

During most Mids, the vacuum would not last, it would again fill with all the worried things, worse things than nothing. Sometimes a wave of heat would have woken her, something from inside, an endocrine-stoked furnace, and she would throw off her portion of the blanket and let the night air cool her body. Other times there was no discernible reason for the wake-up, and she would press her eyes shut, pull her portion of the blanket tight, and try to go back to sleep. Either way, she knew pretty quickly if a prompt return to sleep was lost to her. She might be awake for an hour, or more. On really rough nights, maybe even for the duration. Then she would take her phone off the nightstand, shield it with the covers away from Matt, and press it awake. The light, of course, would leak into the room anyway, that cold, bluish, painful light. You shouldn't look at a screen, but it was her clock, wasn't it? She needed to know the time, to orient herself against the night. Who had resistance and discipline at three a.m.? It was a vulnerable state. She wasn't stupid, wasn't totally reckless, though. She didn't let herself, for example, scroll through the president's Twitter feed. But she had the impulse, which she had to will away, fight. That was the typical Mid.

Somehow Sam had imagined that she would sleep better once she was in her new house. But that very first night, she burst awake with the odd certainty, not driven by a clock or darkness, that it was not morning. She started a little, made a sound into the dark, a gasp, as she realized where she was. The room took strange shape around her. But then, like a switch turning on, she realized that she was alone, and she didn't have to concern herself with Matt. Waking him, disturbing him. She was surprised to discover what it felt like, this not needing to do anything. She could go back to sleep or not; or she could just sit here looking into the dark. She could get up, turn on all the lights. She could cook dinner, if she wanted, watch a movie, make noise, not have to explain to anyone that *nothing was wrong*, while also meaning *everything was wrong*. How much of this night-waking problem had related to him, to them, to the pair of them in the bed?

She sat up. The multipaned windows glowed for a moment, illuminated. Car passing.

And, for that matter, what a ridiculous thing, the daily arrangements of a marriage: sleeping in the same bed side by side, when even children learn to sleep alone. Throughout her early years, Ally would try to make a nighttime end run into their bed, and Sam would be torn, wanting Ally to come into her arms, but wanting, just as much, to sleep. She knew that allowing Ally in would mean a restless night of limbs crossing, blanket pulling, and constant waking. And that it would, as the experts said, make for a bad habit. Fuck all of that—why didn't she just enjoy Ally in her bed with no equivocation? It wouldn't have been forever. Why had she wasted so much time, expended so much energy on this endless, fruitless, pointless questioning of her parental inclinations? Time that could have been spent clutching the little body to her, comforting her daughter while she could still be comforted, before she grew up and they both become, well, uncomfortable?

One night, during Ally's sleep-wandering years, Sam went through the usual bedtime routine. After the bath and the teeth brushing, she always read to Ally. Several whole books when she was really small, and then portions of chapter books later. Ally could usually get two chapters out of Sam, and by the end her eyelids would be nearly closed, her breathing slow and steady, her pink-ribbon lips slightly parted. But this time, when the second chapter was done, Sam looked over at her and Ally stared back at Sam, awake, not drifting at all. Sam went to turn out the light. Ally sniffed, her mouth a hard, narrow frown.

"What is it?"

"It isn't fair," she said, a tearful jagged blurt.

"What?"

"Grown-ups are never scared, but they don't have to sleep alone. Children are scared, and they have to sleep alone," she said, exasperated, the injustice of it becoming more and more outrageous to her as she spoke the words. Sam smiled, which was the wrong thing to do. She shouldn't condescend to her daughter, really. Sam corrected her face.

"It's true, it does seem silly," Sam said. "I never thought of it that way before."

Ally nodded, accepting this concession.

"But grown-ups do get scared, everyone does." Sam always made the mistake of thinking of Ally as a person she could be totally frank with. Be the way she was with everyone, always hedging everything, always admitting weaknesses and doubt. But Ally didn't need to hear about adult doubt. She wasn't Sam's confessor. She wasn't an adult. Ally needed security, sleep, constancy. Sam should have smoothed her brow and soothed her the way Lily had when Sam was small. When Sam got spooked as a child, she would run downstairs to where her parents were watching TV. Her mother would hold her hand and walk her back to bed. Then her mother would rub her back as she lay there. Stroke her cheek. Her mother would let Sam state her fears (I dreamed you were gone and I was all alone in the house). Lily would tell her, "Don't worry. I will never leave you. I will always take care of you." This may have been a lie, but it was exactly right. Such glorious certainty and assurance. Sam, in those moments, felt a profound security and deep peace. Remembering her mother's hand on her face, her mother's voice, all these years later, brought that peace back, made Sam feel calmer. In your whole life, only in young childhood, and only if you were very fortunate, could you get a measure of innocence—a time free of knowing what will come, of what must come. Those moments, that simple engagement of only what was wonderful about being alive, that *love*, really, would be at the center of you forever; deep inside, you would have this tender core that believed everything would be okay.

Sam should have done that with Ally. Told her they would be together forever. But Ally would have seen through it. She was always too smart to be lied to or brushed into calm. Sam would have betrayed her own lack of confidence, it would have been in her face somewhere, and Ally, smart Ally, would have noticed it. Ally was such a force, is such a force. So particularly herself. Even when she'd been scared of sleeping alone, Ally had marshaled logic and made her case. It wasn't about her fear; it was about the inequity of sleeping arrangements. And the frustration of not having a say in these crucial matters.

Ally, by age seven, had reached the pinnacle of a phase in which she sharply decried and enumerated the differences in how children were treated versus adults. She noted all the differentials in power and agency, and she found her own lack of freedom a chronic source of irritation. One day Sam was called in by Ally's Waldorf teacher, who, with slight-but-deliberate frown, showed Sam a drawing Ally had made at school. The teacher, usually a bright, felted, fairy type, seemed to want Sam to find it disturbing, but it made Sam laugh so hard that she had to cover her mouth. Magic Marker on butcher paper, the title at the top said, "Things I will do when I am a Grownup." Beneath it were several drawn objects: a knife, some pill capsules, matches and fire, a car, a toothy open mouth. Under each drawing, captions: "Knifs. Pills. Fier. Driving. Gum." Funny, precocious, tough girl.

At some point, gradually and then definitively, came the extinction of Ally's middle-of-the-night visits to their bed. Only a few scant years of peaceful sleep followed. Soon Sam's body—at first occasionally and then in a nearly nightly fugue of climacteric hormonal fluctuations—would begin to wake her during her deepest sleep.

Then, the same as now, her thoughts would turn, and return, to Ally. Always there was a thing she needed to work out regarding Ally. One thing you discover in motherhood that you never understood from being a daughter and loving your mother—the mother end of things went deeper. After you gave birth, no sleep ever again would take you far from your child. The particular sound of Ally's cries, the pitch and tenor, was keyed to unlock Sam's sleep. Sam used to think this was a baby thing, that she had to wake to hear her child's cries. But sometimes in the middle of the night, years after the night crying had ceased, she would imagine she heard Ally cry out for her, or heard Ally simply cry out, which was also always for Sam. It was a muscle that remained ready. Sam remembered jumping up and going to her, and how it gave Sam a wonderful sense of purpose even as she felt a terrible fatigue. What you don't get from having a mother versus being a mother is how consuming it was, how profoundly one-sided. The child's job was to need her mother less and less, a progression toward independence. But the mother's job was to always help, always be there when needed, and never, ever stop worrying. Was that true? She knew that her mother still worried about her, even when her own body was failing her, even when she was—

But she shouldn't think of her mother's body now.

Ally.

Ally out of reach like this was an entirely new situation. Sam missed her, and she would almost give up everything to be back in Ally's favor. Almost. Except if she went back for Ally, Ally wouldn't want that either. A needy, depressed, overmeddling mother. Ally needed—preferred—for her to be gone, even as she was angry that Sam had left. Was that true or was that just something Sam told herself so she could do what she wanted, leave Matt and the life she had been stuck in? She wasn't sure, but in any case, she missed Ally and longed for her—seeing her, hearing her, being in contact with her—with a visceral intensity. Sam wouldn't go back, but she also wouldn't let go.

What could she do? Every night she would continue to text Ally. Just one text. The unanswered dailiness of her texts was devotional, humble, a sign of her unconditional love. Probably Ally just found her pathetic and that's why she didn't block her.

The Mid was the time when all her gestures felt unbearably sad and futile. And when heat suffocated her. Sam pulled at the neck of her T-shirt, pulled it down and away from her chest. Her body knew what was coming. Her heartbeat picked up speed. And then the hot. A sudden interior flame had bloomed in her. Her heart beat so fast she could hear it in her ears.

She went to the built-in window seat, cranked the handle of the casement window, and with some splintering of dust and paint, the window opened and cool air rushed in. Bright, sharp night air, bracing. Even by the open window, she was hot. She looked at her phone. No texts. Of course she would still have trouble sleeping in the new house. Tonight it was the blast of heat, not merely the worries, that tormented her. Body-driven. The erosion of sleep was a gradual but escalating consequence of physical symptoms. There was nothing wrong with her; Sam simply woke because she had what she supposed was a "hot flash." But it didn't feel flashy, just hot. Her doctor had explained that the night wakings were a natural and common aspect of her menopausal journey. Oh well, if it's natural, then no problem, right? Natural or not, she knew she was doomed. No matter how she looked at it, she knew that tonight her fight against wakefulness would lead not back to sleep but, instead, to rumination. (That was the right word, like a ruminant's stomachs going over and over the same material, a dreamful distortion darkening it further each time. It would move from the specific, like Ally's face when Sam told her she was leaving, into more sweeping things, like the president, wars, the environment, her own nascent cancers, her whole ruined life.)

That first Mid waking that first night on Highland Street, in her new old empty house, she sat in the living room and peered out the half-opened window. She could see the lights of the city sparkle and the old parklike cemetery glowing with streetlamps. No one around. She reached into her purse and pulled out a pack of cigarettes. "Who," she said, "bought these?" And she laughed. She smoked, looked out at the city, and decided she wouldn't try to go back to sleep. At four o'clock she made coffee (a single-serve pour-over), opened her laptop, and scanned the *New York Times'* front page, then the *Washington Post'*s. She clicked over to the *Post-Standard'*s site, Syracuse.com. The first four articles were sports coverage; then various arrests and mug shots. She read the police blotter. The streets near her house on Highland, in the Northside, came up frequently. (Petit larceny; criminal mischief, third degree;

assault, second degree; burglary, second degree; criminal con-
tempt, first degree; criminal mischief, second degree. Rape, first
degree, two counts. The website even had a database searchable
by name, crime, or location. In the suburbs, the blotter was mostly
DWIs, but the city didn't have time for that.)

At six, when sunlight had barely begun to pinken the sky, she
brushed her teeth, got dressed, and went for a walk past the cem-
etery park, down the hill, past the crumbling AME church and
under the damp, black concrete overpass, and into downtown and
the blocks lined with grand old city buildings.

Later that morning, MH showed up at the house with an aloe
plant. A medicinal, of course. Sam fondled the slick leaves. Maybe
useful but also pretty. They drank very strong coffee from her
French press. Sam's third cup of the day. "I have been up since
three," she said, and it half-sounded like a brag.

"Night wakings are features of midlife, not to be squandered."
Sam laughed when MH said this, but MH was serious.

"You wake for a reason. It is time for a special kind of thinking,
middle-of-the-night thinking. Don't fight it. Wake for your night
office, your nocturna. Get out of bed, fall to your knees, attend the
moment."

Sam shrugged. "Whatever. It will still be my sad, addled brain
drowning in the same material. My stagnant yet churning pools."
MH wore a shiny metal ring on her index finger that looked like
the business end of a lug wrench or a bolt nut.

"No, let go of that expectation. Recast this problem as a gift.
You are a desert mother. You don't need sleep. You have things
that need the contemplation that can only happen alone on your
knees at three a.m." She spread her hands emphatically, and she
caught Sam staring at the ring again. MH touched it. "It's a wear-
able. Made of titanium."

"Aren't all rings 'wearable'?" But Sam was just messing with
MH. She knew from lurking around MH's n=1 Hag Hacks group
(another sub of the Hardcore Hags, Harridans, and Harpies group)
that "wearables" referred to smart tracking devices. MH was a bio-

hack obsessive, and she was into all the gym-bro self-tracking and quantification, from food to sleep to activity.

"So it counts steps?" Sam said.

MH snorted. "No. It's a Scandinavian device. Tiny sensors inside the ring track heart rate variability, beats per minute, sleep stages, body temperature, respiratory rate. Which are uploaded and analyzed via an app." She waved her phone at Sam by way of illustration. An accounting of MH's sleep appeared, with graphs and analysis of every micrometric involved.

"It's like you're stalking yourself," Sam said. "Does it send you push notifications when you aren't breathing correctly? Mis-respirating? Contra-haling?"

"Actually, it does."

"What do you do with all that . . ."

"Data?"

"Yeah."

MH shrugged. "Optimize."

"Potentiate?"

"The promise of total control, even when you sleep."

"But you just told me not to resist the sleep disturbances."

"We all have our own contradictions. It is embodied in us, we are built for it. For example, stress is bad, but then if it is pulsed in the right dose, it creates a hormetic, adaptive cellular response. It makes you stronger. It takes a huge effort to control your physiology. Once you have dialed in all the variables, calibrated your potential optimization, only one avenue remains."

"What? Acceptance?"

"No. Beyond mere acceptance. Bold surrender. Defiant gratitude. Perverse celebration."

Sam legit tried to embrace the wakings, if not celebrate them. The very next night, she woke in the Mid. She got up from bed and kneeled on the bare floor. It felt mildly ostentatious, foolish, performative. Plus it hurt her knees. She sat cross-legged on the floor. This also hurt. How can a body in middle age become so determined to acquire excess fat and yet that padding offered no protection from the hard surfaces of the world? She put her pillow on the floor and lowered herself to her knees again. Her mind wheeled and whirled. Maudlin, self-pitying, reductive, hysterical—hardly the stuff of a desert mother.

"Keep trying. It's a practice," MH said the next day when Sam explained how it went.

"Yeah, okay," Sam said. It was better than trying to sleep and failing. MH was all about the gift of middle life, of menopause, of "super-exaltation," as Eliza Farnham called it in the 1860s, a secret joy, freedom from childbirth and housework and, presumably, the demands of men. MH, however, took hormone replacement therapy. Which didn't mean she was trying to stave off anything, she explained. (And not that natural/bio horseshit either: real pharmaceutical-grade hormones. Progesterone, estradiol, and testosterone. "T," she said, was "dick in a bottle. The man within.") She also manipulated her body with time-restricted eating, with exercise, with sleep training (including lucid dreaming, dream fasts, staged rapid eye movement waking), and with lab-tested and third-party-verified supplements. Yet MH firmly believed in the gift of menopause.

"Historically, only for women of a certain class, of course," MH said.

After MH left, Sam enacted her own "n=1" biohack. Drink a ton of coffee and don't sleep. Then do her weight routine at the gym. She ran to the Downtown Y feeling virtuous, invincible. Sam wondered what testosterone, a jolt of it, would feel like in her body. Would she finally be able to do a pull-up? Would she get tattoos and want to wear motorcycle boots? (But she already wanted to wear motorcycle boots. Would testosterone make her feel entitled rather than pretentious if she wore them?) Would a hormone change what she did, how she thought? Wouldn't that change who she was? What if what she thought of as her "self" was a matter of endocrinology? As mutable as the house you lived in or the clothes you wore?

A week after Sam moved to Highland, MH invited her and Laci to the Smiley Face, the sad chain stand-up joint at Destiny mall. Sam's move into the city seemed to signal some new trust, a closer embrace, even some potential at intimacy, with Laci and MH. Sam was no longer a suburban tourist. But the Smiley Face was not the setting for the sort of rad hangout Sam had imagined.

MH had recently taken to going to open mics, to comedy clubs in particular, to test herself in the "real" world.

"I hate comedy clubs, hate the people who attend them," MH told her as they found a banquette table in the half-empty club. "And a chain comedy club in Central New York? It ain't the Groundlings, you know. This is some middle-America shit right here." Sam looked around at the other customers. They did look like frat boys approaching forty. They had that bloated, doughy look that men get in their thirties if they keep drinking beer the way they did in their twenties.

"So why do you come here?" Sam asked.

"I come to stand up," MH said. "Not funny stand up. I come to make them look at me, to make them see me, even if they boo me. And I come because I am scared of it, and I want to do what frightens me."

"It's her method. Her philosophy, really," Laci said. "It's why she started the Hardcore Hags."

"Who says I started it? It's a secret group," MH said.

Laci smiled. "Yeah, it is."

MH turned to Sam. "When I turned fifty, I was divorced, my son was grown up, and I realized I still had decades to go. It was the oddest thing—just as the culture began to lose interest in me, just as the world decided I was irrelevant, I began to feel more myself than ever. Louder, smarter, stronger. It felt truly adolescent, like I wanted to take drugs and drive fast and shave my head."

MH ran her hand through the bristles on her head. "I didn't want to be quiet and supportive. I didn't want to be dignified, and I didn't want to take care of anyone for a while. I wanted to be a little selfish, a little eccentric."

She looked around the room. "And once I hit sixty? Rather than mellowing, it intensified. I felt wildly unleashed. There is something about not pleasing people that interests me. About provoking people. About failing to meet expectations. It might be the abasement in it, I admit that. There's something revelatory and liberating about being an object of contempt."

MH looked back at Sam and held her gaze for a few seconds longer than Sam felt comfortable with, so Sam nodded and looked at something on the table. MH's blue, heavy-lidded eyes were set off by the glittering silver of her gray hair. Sam snuck a glance at her eyes again, when MH wasn't looking back at her—the blue was so deep, it almost looked fake, like contacts. But that seemed unlikely.

"I like being grotesque," MH said.

But MH wasn't grotesque, so, like with so many MH comments, Sam didn't know how to take it.

It occurred to Sam that they were the oldest people in the room. Really? The doughy men and their wives, the doughy men with other doughy men, and even a few college-age girls at one table. Yep, the oldest by ten years or so. And all three of them with short hair and no makeup. They stood out already.

Sam ordered a glass of wine: a sugary, thick, revolting Malbec. She sipped and grimaced.

"What?"

"I think they added sugar to this wine," Sam said. Laci and MH laughed.

"'Wine,'" Laci said, making air quotes with her fingers.

"You don't come to places like this and eat the food or order wine. It all comes out of a giant vacuum-packed Sysco bag of chicken breasts, including the wine," MH said.

MH and Laci were drinking whiskey on the rocks. Laci ordered Sam a Maker's Mark, and then they were being quieted for the show. A local comedian warmed them up with jokes that amounted to "kids today, amirite?"

MH was the third to go on. Each person had five minutes.

MH spoke in a low voice. Always a bit too confident, and declarative, she now read as charismatic. Sam could see her clearly, and there was a shiny appeal to her onstage: broad but muscular, short-haired, makeup free, yet glamorous in her way. Her jeans were cut narrowly and cuffed; she wore expensive motorcycle boots that folded back at the ankle. She didn't look like the itinerant (the "Half Hobo") that she apparently was. MH began her set with the story of getting her first period at twelve. "The dictionary defines a period as 'a flow of blood and other material from the lining of the uterus, lasting for several days and occurring in sexually mature women who are not pregnant at intervals of about one lunar month until the onset of menopause.' Let's follow that line." She then described her abortion at age eighteen, her pregnancy, her miscarriage, and her birth experience, until she finally detailed her perimenopause and menopause. People sort of laughed in discomfort, but there were no jokes in there, not one. There was, however, a kind of arc, or at least an intensification to her set as she moved through time. MH then described her aging physical changes in clinical detail, the experience of discovering her postmenstrual body.

"If you accept this new body, you have a period of freedom from fertility before you really begin to decline. It is an adjustment: your waist thickens and your jawline softens. Your ass becomes both lumpy and flat. You chafe against the world. Yes. Everything—everything—becomes drier and rougher. And worn down—like sprung, stretched-out elastic on a pair of granny panties."

Her set had a clarifying effect on the room. People got up and left. Others conversed and ignored the stage. One guy—alone, naturally—stared at MH with a look of concentrated disgust. There was always going to be one guy who could meet the moment, bite on MH's provocations. MH sat back down and looked over the room with a huge grin, apparently not just unfazed but energized.

"You should try it, Sam," MH said. "Open-mic night is the last Wednesday of every month. Don't overthink it—just get up and talk." Maybe she would. Could she stand to be groaned at, unliked, misunderstood?

After, Sam paid their bill while MH and Laci studied their phones, scrolled their feeds, tapped their responses. This despite their mutual pledge to move themselves off social media. Only Sam stuck to that goal. They swiped and clicked. Sam took out her phone, pressed it awake, and sent Ally a long text, but only one:

Hi, honey! How did the YAD conference go? I am sure you won a citation. You would never believe it, but I am at the Smiley Face, the comedy club at the mall. Awful but also pretty interesting. Love you!

Like notes in a bottle. It had been almost a month, which was getting serious, wasn't it. She instantly regretted the length, the exclamation points, the markers of her neediness.

Spring progressed, but Syracuse was still damp and cold. After a week of daily rain, it was finally clear. Sun streamed in everywhere throughout her elaborately fenestrated home (Sam felt a marvelous drunken awe, gazing at all the types of windows, her house a festival of inflected light). She spent the day waxing the red oak floors upstairs, then fell asleep at three p.m. She woke from a startling noise at five p.m. Or she woke, but had no memory of what the noise was, just a feeling of having heard something. She ran to her window. A car had pulled up to the corner. The bass from the music boomed out. Was that what woke her? She washed her face, brushed her teeth, and decided to explore her new neighborhood on foot. She discovered a small bodega as well as a butcher, a liquor store, an old Italian bakery, a dollar store, a Rite Aid, and a noodle shop. Sam could smell the steamy salt broth as the door to the shop swung open. She was, she realized, very hungry. In all the excitement of the house, she hadn't consumed anything but coffee and water for twenty-four hours. Actually, more like thirty hours.

Roaming the neighborhood, she bought some groceries for the week, and she also bought some items for a feast tonight: a wedge of powdery tiramisu, a bottle of red wine, a triangle of aged provolone, and a large container of beef pho. She marveled that everything she needed was within walking distance. It started to rain again. She hurried to get back to the house, to get out of the damp, to sit in solitude in her little kitchen alcove and eat the warm soup. Then she could make a fire, have a glass of wine and the cake. She imagined taking a bite, devouring it slowly and completely. The pleasure would be deep and totally satisfying. Deprivation and indulgence—was the deprivation really a kind of decadence, a way to underline the intensity of surrendering to indulgence? Maybe she was going to be one of those menopausal women who developed an eating disorder, binge-purge or anorexia. The whacked-out hormones and the fixation on food—it was a thing at fourteen and a thing at fifty. But really, who cared? (Who cared if she had some dysfunction, some disorder, and who cared what caused it. She didn't.) What she did care for was the sight of her house in the dusk glow, waiting for her. And the coming simple pleasure and satisfaction of her plan. She crossed in front of the dormer windows and turned toward the doorway. She'd forgotten to leave her entry porch light on.

A figure was sitting in front of the door.

Sam stopped, tried to see who it was. Rain clouds made it dark. She tightened her grip on her packages and took a step closer. "Hello?" she said. Her heartbeat ticked up, her eyes focused. It was a woman, about her age. Under a blanket, crouched on the brick entryway, with her head against the door. She had a watch cap pulled over her ears, but Sam could see her face.

"Excuse me," Sam said. The woman woke, startled, and jumped to her feet, but she was still partly asleep, so she almost fell. The woman steadied herself against the doorjamb, looked toward Sam with blinking eyes.

"I live here," Sam said, moving her chin toward the door. The woman looked at her, nodded. Rain started to fall harder, and Sam leaned under the eave, closer to the woman. Her eyes were enormous, with dark circles. Her skin had red marks, blemishes. She was thin. She smelled like old vegetables and wet wool.

"I thought nobody lived here," she said. "I'm sorry."

"I just moved in. It's okay," Sam said.

The woman looked at the rain. "I'm gonna go," she said, but she didn't move. She looked at Sam.

"Are you okay?" Stupid question. The woman started gathering her stuff, tucking the blanket into her belt and over her head, preparing for the rain.

Sam put down her bags. She reached for her wallet in her jacket. She thought she would give the woman twenty dollars, but then she just took all her cash out, a handful of twenties, and held it out to her. The woman, astonished, took the money. She didn't look at it and shoved it into a pocket under her sweatshirt. "God bless you," she said. And then she started crying. Even in the dark Sam could see her crying. And hear her. Sam didn't know what to do.

"Is there a shelter you can go to?" Sam had seen the Rescue Mission downtown, not far from here. What happens to a woman who sleeps there? Or who sleeps on the street? Are they raped and prodded and beaten?

"Yeah, I'm good. Thank you," she said. She sniffed, wiped her eyes. She moved away from the door so Sam could pass. Now that Sam was closer to her, it was clear that she was younger than Sam, also clear that she was fuzzy with something, out of it. She was probably an addict, looking for a place to nod out. So dangerous it must be, how desperate you have to be, to get that way with nothing to protect you.

The smell of the hot soup was impossible to miss. Sam held the bag out to the woman.

"Do you want this soup?" Sam said. She should give her the groceries too, and the cake. That's stupid—what would she do with groceries without a kitchen? With coffee grounds and eggs?

"Thanks," the woman said. She took the bag with the soup, then hurried off the steps and down the rainy street. Sam could have let her stay on the porch to eat the soup. She even could have invited her into the house until the rain stopped. Why didn't she do that? Because she didn't know her and she was scared of her. Sam stepped inside, flipped on the overhead light and the porch light. Why scared? That she would attack her? It would be different if she were a man, of course, but she was a tiny woman. So scared of what? Sam unpacked the groceries, put them into the fridge. Gave her the soup, and she probably didn't even want it. Just took it because. Because Sam had given her money and it was what Sam wanted, for her to take the warm soup. Maybe she did eat it, at the shelter. Sam scrambled three eggs with chopped onions and garlic. It smelled delicious, made her ravenous. She ate it with the wine, by herself, at the kitchen table.

She hadn't invited the woman into her house, despite the awful weather, because she was scared the woman would want things from her, would need things, that the interaction would extend out into forever, that this person and her problems would become Sam's responsibility: what had gone wrong, where she slept, what she needed. Responsibility, that's what Sam didn't want.

Then Sam spotted a white flyer that had been tucked under the front door. She stooped and picked it up. Another rectangle of impressive card stock with letterpress words in blue:

BEWARE THE COMING "SMART" CITY;
BEWARE THE SYRACUSE SURGE.
SMART FOR WHOM? SURGING WHERE?

Oh for Pete's sake. A grammar stickler giving urgent cryptic warnings. But she couldn't throw it away. She placed it in a drawer with the other one about the NTE, whatever that was.

Sam made a fire. The flames brightened, and she could see the ceramic glow of the pink tiles. So old, so beautiful. She began to feel the warmth of the fire on her body. She pulled off her socks and felt her bare toes get warm, then hot. Sam flexed them and did not move, like a cat hypnotized by the heat and the flickering light. She could see and hear the city outside her windows. Rain and wind beat down, and she was inside, in this beautiful old inglenook, warm. After some time by the fire, she went into the kitchen, opened the white cardboard box with the pink string. She put the wedge of tiramisu on a plate and went back to the hearth bench. The cake smelled eggy and sweet. She sank her fork into it. It gave with a little pull, the layers of marscapone and espresso and ladyfingers. She put it in her mouth and felt a melting back, a dissolving of sweet flavors and different textures, her body almost gathering to a point in her mouth. The swallow, the next bite, and the street and the rain fading back. She was warm and full.

She texted Ally.

Sam was walking to Schiller Park (built in 1901 and named after the German poet Friedrich Schiller back when it was a neighborhood of German immigrants). It was late May and warm weather had not quite arrived, but it was spring nevertheless. She walked past the boarded-up house next to her house and then past the quiet, ugly apartment miniplex on the corner. She crossed the street and looked ahead toward a green one-story bungalow. An elderly woman named Tammy lived there with her dog, Lucy. They often sat out on the porch, even in the cold weather. Sam had begun smiling whenever she passed them, then waving hello, and eventually stopping to pet Lucy and discuss the weather. But they weren't on the porch today.

In the next block, she saw a man standing on a street corner. He was wearing a hand-lettered sandwich board that said, "OGs Against Gun Violence." Sam had read about a teenager getting shot by another teenager two nights earlier—she hadn't recognized the street names or realized how close the crime site was to her street. The neighborhood had a high rate of burglaries and petty crime, but being shot on the street was starting to happen more and more. The paper blamed gangs that had expanded from the Near Westside into the Northside.

He stood with his signboard and handed a leaflet to her as she passed him.

> KEEP GUNS OFF THE STREETS.
> KEEP OUR KIDS SAFE.

"Right, yes," she said.
"Thank you," he said.

She looked at the concrete sidewalk where the teen had fallen and the houses that stood near the corner. Lots of peeling paint. Older homes subdivided into multiple apartments. One had waterlogged furniture and stacks of magazines on the porch. But another house had recently prepped and tended flower beds, a bird feeder, and a kid's Big Wheel bike. No one was around. No police tape. Nothing but quiet now. She walked to the park and then back home. What you could see and what you couldn't. Who lived in the houses next door to her? One was boarded up with particle board, but that didn't mean no one lived there. The other side was a once-lovely Victorian split into two apartments. Despite the insult of vinyl siding and replacement windows, it retained an impressive profile against the evening sky. A young man lived in the upstairs apartment, but Sam hardly saw him. Two women, three toddlers, and several cats lived on the first floor. The children waved when they saw Sam, and she would smile and wave back.

Sam ate an early dinner, then poured her one drink. She took it to her side porch and smoked her one cigarette. She wanted to see her neighborhood, her neighbors, but no one was out. She made sure she was done with the drink and the cigarette before calling her mother. Her mother would be listening for sounds and clues, things to mention to her.

"How are you feeling?" Sam asked. She wanted to say, When will you tell me what your doctors say? But she should not push her mother.

"Nothing to report here. But are you okay in that house? Is it safe to stay there?"

"I told you I got carbon monoxide and fire detectors upstairs and down."

"That's not what I mean. I saw on the news there was another shooting. Isn't that close to where you live?"

How did her mother know that the shooting was so close by? Did her mother have a map of Syracuse?

"It's fine here," Sam said. "When are you going to come here and see it?"

"Maybe I'll come for Ally's concert—that's in a couple of weeks."
Ally's viola concert. Would Sam be welcome or a distraction? Just
showing up probably was a terrible idea.

"Good. I'll come get you. And you can stay with me here," Sam
said. It was a bluff. She had only the one bed. But she would get
another one. For her mom, for Ally. There was a pause.

"If I come, I think I'll stay in a hotel I found. It's very close to
you, but also close to Ally and Matt. But I can't wait to see your
house."

"Okay," Sam said. "I want you to be comfortable." Which was
true. She almost started to cry, but she stopped herself. Just the
idea of seeing her mother soon was making Sam miss her. Her
mother sensed it somehow.

"You're welcome to come here, darling, if you need a visit."

"That would be good, Ma. I might do that." She liked to be
called "darling." After the call, she wrote a text to Ally. She wanted
Ally to know she was darling.

Sweet dreams, my darling child.

She tapped the delete button, the one marked with a boxed X, and
watched the words disappear. No way. Ally was never called "dar-
ling." She would think that was weird.

Sweet dreams, Ally-oop.

Send. The send sound.

No reply, of course, but at least Ally knew she was thinking of
her dreams and wished them to be good.

The next day was Sunday. As she had done many times before, she
drove past the beautiful Lutheran church on James Street (built in
1911 and designed by Archimedes Russell, one of the top architects
working in Syracuse). She had read in the paper that it was closing

at the end of the month because the congregation had shrunk so much in the past ten years. People objected because it was used so heavily by the neighborhood as a meeting space: food bank, thrift store, activist groups, AA, NA. But the building's overhead was too much to sustain without an infusion of city and community money.

As always, she admired its sandstone bell tower with cast-iron cutouts at the top. As always, she wondered what it was like inside. But this time she went around the block and pulled into the parking lot in the back. Maybe there was a late afternoon Mass—there were a number of cars in the lot. She wanted to see the beautiful church from the inside, and this might be her last chance. She wanted to sit in its pews and look up at the stained-glass windows. She stepped inside, and the sound evaporated from busy street sharpness to the hushed reverberations of a tall-ceilinged space. Church sounds. Not a Mass, but the church was half-full with a community meeting. Sam sat in the back. She loved pews: the polished dark wood, the smooth hardness of the seat, the red leather cushion on the pull-out kneeler. She could smell lingering incense as she listened to the speaker at the podium. She gathered that the meeting was for Syracuse Streets, an activist group that tried to hold the local police accountable for targeting people of color. This particular meeting was to plan a response to the arrest of an unarmed man who'd ended up mysteriously bruised and beaten. As she listened, Sam sank down a little in her pew, her age and whiteness everywhere on her. She waited for someone to point to her and say what the girls had said at the white liberal party: You have a lot to answer for. There was a break while someone fixed a microphone issue, and while she waited, she looked up.

The inside of the church was striking but austere, just white molding against yellow plaster. The vaulted ceilings had very little decoration. But the stained-glass windows! They were lush, ornate. She had read about them. They were made in Rochester by the Haskins Art Glass company. The afternoon light made them glow. The depictions were more art nouveau modernist than church-glass traditional, with big abstract horizontal waves of cobalt-blue sky in the upper windows. Thick leaded divider lines between panels. The figures in the lower half were done in stylized bold outlines. Lots of voluptuous curves and deep colors. They were the perfect contrast to the plainness of the yellow vault.

The meeting resumed and grew more emotional. One by one, incidents were recounted. Being stopped and warrant-checked for no cause. Being searched. And those were the easy outcomes. The cops looking for reasons to stop people of color and the inevitable escalations that often followed. Lawsuits were discussed. The problem wasn't the mayor or even the police chief. The problem was the police culture. The problem was the district attorney. The police union. Recourse was what? The Citizen Review Board, and its toothless frustrations. Worthless Office of Professional Standards investigations. The only successes were increased visibility to the issue, more transparency, and a couple of civil suits. The possibility of requiring body cams because of community pressure.

Sam noticed the OG sitting a few rows from her. And some other people in her age range. She worked up the nerve to go to the basement, where the subcommittees met after the big meeting finished. No coffee or other refreshments: all business, which impressed and intimidated her.

"Where do you work? I mean, do you have a job?" a young woman asked her after she had been assigned to a group. Sam had written "unaffiliated" by her name on the sign-up sheet.

"Of course," Sam said. She must still have a housewife aura, a cosseted vibe, despite her newly hacked-off hair and her old jeans. The woman shrugged and handed her the pen. Everyone had to come clean here, admit origins and affiliations. Everyone had to trust that other people were not infiltrators. They all even had to remove their mobile phones and put them in a microwave.

"What if someone accidentally turns on the microwave?" Sam said, half-joking. No one responded. She threw her phone onto the spit-stained, finger-smeared pile of smart devices. But Sam should be here, she should be supportive if she wanted to live in this neighborhood. Be a good citizen and clearly show her loyalties. It seemed

important, and it felt very different than Facebook posting or talk-
ing to MH and Laci about resistance.

She wrote "Clara Loomis House" by her name, which was where
she worked three days a week. The girl read as Sam wrote, and then
she snorted.

"That place?"

"You know it?" Sam asked.

"She's a problem. She is problematic," the girl said. Sam nodded.
Yeah. It was true. She was.

"Welcome to Clara Loomis House," Sam said with a smile. It was unusual to have anyone come into the house, but especially once the weather got nice and more outdoor activities were favored. Loomis House was a large, boxy square with a Greek Revival–style portico complete with four oversized white pillars. Doric, maybe? Sam always confused those names, which was another reason why she suspected she could never have made it as an architect. She nevertheless felt very affected by the building where she worked, because honestly, she did not like this house. The pretentiousness of the portico seemed provincial to her, like they blew the big bucks on the front of the house even if it was ill-proportioned to the rest of the house. Greek Revival in general was a bit kitschy, one of those styles, like Tudor Revival or Gothic Revival, that we admire now because they are old, but at the time must have seemed as ersatz and corny as the fake colonials that are built today in housing developments. This was not quite fair—unlike those houses, the nineteenth-century houses were well built, full of crafted, hand-finished details. They had no choice. They would have used cheap shit, like hollow doors and drywall, but all they had was plaster and wood. So Sam didn't entirely mind being in the old, ridiculous house. At least it was intact. Many people worked under dropped ceilings and corkboard. She was lucky. She knew that. But still, when she gazed around, it felt soulless and unimaginative compared to some other houses. Compared to her own soulful house, for instance.

Today would be busy. A high school group was coming in—overachievers who attended the summer precollege courses at SU. This was a women's studies course. Sam ushered them in and began to give her set spiel on Clara Loomis. She was used to kids

and retired folks. It felt good to have some young adults to talk to.
Sam began to improvise, pushing hard on the most radical telling
of the Loomis story. She wanted to impress them.

"Clara Loomis, in her middle years—after menopause, when hav-
ing children and rearing children were no longer considerations—
started what she called her true life." Sam emphasized the word
"menopause." She didn't know why, but she felt the urge to scream
it at young women sometimes. She imagined herself shrieking
"Menopause! Menopause! Menopause!" but settled for merely
enunciating it, because she wasn't a total psycho, not yet. "Loo-
mis wrote, 'We women are not oppressed by distant men in con-
gressional chambers, but by our own physiology as child bearers.
God makes us not only give birth and suckle, but he makes our
hearts weak in devotion to our children. We spend our youth keep-
ing our children whole and happy. Yet in the few quiet moments
between nursing, washing, and tending, we secretly yearn for a
bigger, deeper world. We must hide how we grow weary of child-
ish games, books, songs. Then our children grow up and leave, but
only if you are very fortunate, because, occasionally but not rarely,
a child will die. In either case, our bodies grow older and uglier,
until we are finally liberated.'" Sam paused and walked to a wall
of framed formal portraits. "Here you can see photographs of her
children. Loomis had four, two of whom died. One, little Amelia
May Loomis, was born with a genetic disease. She was, by Loo-
mis's own account, her favorite, and when Amelia died, Loomis fell
into a profound depression, which at the time was called excessive
grief or melancholia. Grieving in Victorian times was already a
mannered, endless performance for women, but even among Vic-
torians, Loomis took her grief to extremes. She was treated with
laudanum, an opiate often prescribed to women. She eventually
renounced laudanum and all 'mind and soul distorting substances.'
Instead she treated her depression, which she called 'her depthless
burden,' by pursuing spiritualism, which was quite prevalent in
this part of New York." Sam noticed that the students' attention
pricked up when she mentioned death and opiates. "Loomis had

several séances performed here, in this room, so she could talk to her daughter." Now she had really piqued the students' attention. "At this big table, in fact."

The young people looked at the table. Sam could feel their imaginations moving back in time. "Some people say this house is haunted." A few of the students smiled and laughed. Two girls grimaced comically at each other, bug-eyed, like scared emojis, and grabbed each other's arms. Sam wasn't supposed to talk about the ghost crap, but she was drawn to the attention the subject aroused in visitors, especially teenagers. Sam needed their interest. She wanted them to like Clara, really, and not being boring was part of that. "Sometimes, when the caretaker is here at night, footsteps are heard upstairs. And a girl's cries can be heard coming from the area at the top of the stairs. Here, let me show you." Sam gleefully led them upstairs to the little landing, where there was a small sewing table and a rocking chair. "The sound seems to come from the nursing chair and sewing area. This little room connects to the children's room via this cubby passage." She opened a cabinet that was, in fact, a passageway between the rooms. "But when the cubby is opened, the cries stop. Little Amelia was so often sick that she spent many afternoons home from school, reading by her mother's side as her mother sat here sewing."

"What was wrong with her?" asked the one young man in the women's studies course. He was, Sam speculated, maybe not a "he" but a "they," as their presence appeared deliberately nonbinary. This was indicated by their earrings, their makeup, and their jewelry, all femmy. Black fingernail polish on short, manicured nails. But their hair was a kind of shaggy boyish cut, and their clothes were not feminine: Carhartt jacket and Timberland boots. Their nonbinariness was not the androgyny Sam thought of from her own adolescence. This was something different, a deliberate, stylized confounding of gender, non-masculine and non-feminine, that made it more surprising, unsettling, unclichéd. There must be a name for it; it impressed Sam, but maybe she overthought these matters. "Do you know?" they said, because she was staring at them, distracted and not answering. They must be used to upstaging their own questions.

"Oh, well, from what we can tell, Amelia had Huntington's disease, which is a fatal inherited genetic disorder. In early childhood she showed symptoms, and they grew severe over her short life. She used crutches, and she had seizures. Going to school eventually became impossible, so she stayed by her mother's side and was tutored by her, even as her memory and cognition were degraded by the disease. This obsession with Amelia, both during her affliction and after Amelia died, lasted Loomis's whole remaining life."

One of the scared-emoji girls opened the cubby and looked in. She pulled out a doll. "That's so creepy," she said, and laughed. Sam wanted to smack the girl's hand. Shouldn't she have asked if she could touch the doll? But, but at least they were interested. She waved them into another room. "Clara's bedroom, which was also her study."

Half the students were looking at their phones. Sam pressed on.

"The Loomises, like many married couples of some means, each had their own bedrooms. You can see all the books and the desk instead of a dressing table in here. It became her study even though there is a library downstairs. That was her husband Henry's domain. When her last child left for boarding school in 1895, Loomis enrolled at Syracuse University, which had been coed since its founding in 1870. In fact, the university had female undergraduates at parity with male undergraduates, which must have made it feel very modern to Loomis. She was forty-five, and she took to the classes with a profound devotion. No youthful glee clubs or other distractions for her. The middle-aged student is focused, and, as you can imagine, quite formidable."

Could they imagine? Sam thought not, but she gave them the benefit of the doubt.

"She studied science, her passion. She graduated top of her class, even above the male students. She attended the SU medical college, one of only a handful of women matriculated. At the same time, Loomis led the local fight for women's suffrage, and she founded the Central New York Society for Temperance. She also pioneered a kind of proto–Planned Parenthood, the League of Deliberate Population."

A smiling, poised sixteen-year-old girl raised her hand. She was very Ally-like. Sam smiled back, but then saw the eyebrow of the girl veer up with disapproval. Also Ally-like.

"What about her letters to Elizabeth Cady Stanton? The Loomis letters?" Those goddamned letters. Elizabeth Cady Stanton was just as bad, worse maybe, but around here Stanton was a local hero, the saint of Seneca Falls, untainted by criticism.

"The letters, yes," Sam said, frowning. "Loomis was impressive, extraordinary even, in some regards. But in other areas she was, sadly, a woman of her time, with many of the failings and blind spots of her time." Did that really excuse her? Those stupid letters. And some of her pamphlets.

Sam had, she admitted, some historic-house envy. She thought of all the local women she could be working to promote: Amelia Jenks Bloomer, who invented—or at least popularized—women wearing pants, "bloomers." It gave you something concrete to show people. Here, look, some blousy-ass bloomers, the closest thing to pants that any women got to wear. She could talk to the little fifth graders, and it would be very clear to them, shocking even, how unfair and ridiculous this was for women. That physical clothing oppressed them, defined them, limited them. Not complicated, and the arc of history felt like pure progress from there. Bloomer's house was a bracketed Italianate with a multi-windowed square tower rising in the middle of the roof.

Or Adelaide Alsop Robineau, Syracuse's Arts and Crafts ceramics genius and editor of *Keramics Studio* magazine. Her house, Four Winds, included her art studio and sat on a street named after her. Sam could usher this Ally-type around the shimmering but earthy glazes, she could talk about the Arts and Crafts movement, artisan culture, and it would be tactile, beautiful, and undeniably a good.

Harriet Tubman's house was thirty miles west of Syracuse, in

Auburn. That would be a good place to work. Sam wouldn't have to overcome those skeptical looks like she had to with a more obscure, compromised figure. Austere unpainted brick with beautiful six-over-six double-sashed windows.

Or Mother Ann, the visionary Shaker who founded a settlement near Albany. A unique, woman-focused utopian leader. So much did she want to liberate women, she canceled sex. Just imagine being in that building: all the dovetailed joints and clean lines on the Shaker furnishings. None of the cacophonic style of this pillared, cluttered house.

But instead she had Loomis, with her creepy eugenics bullshit, her loquacious (and not ironic) advocacy of "controlled genetics." The whole thing was euphemistically described in a plaque as Loomis being an "innovator in family planning," which was not all that was covered by her suspicious-sounding League of Deliberate Population (but another group she founded was worse, Society for Horticultivation of the Species, yikes). And to be fair, Loomis did actually help women get birth control in the form of primitive diaphragms (referred to as "thimbles"), and she even performed abortions, which was remarkably brave. Sam wasn't supposed to bring the abortion stuff up, either, but she did. No ghosts or abortions. But Sam thought it would make Loomis much more interesting (and relevant) if they owned up to who she was in her totality, not just one isolated odd issue. She was no Margaret Sanger, but she was ahead of her time in understanding how freeing sex from birth was the key to women's liberation. (Besides, didn't Margaret Sanger write something like "Why Poor Women Should Not Have Children"? But maybe that was Emma Goldman? One of those birth control/socialist/revolutionary women. It too had a whiff of eugenics to it.)

"She was into white supremacy, Nazi stuff about pure genetic lineages," said the girl, who was starting to seem familiar to Sam. This city was so small. Did she go to Ally's school?

Sam sighed. "Genetics, yes, but not tied to race or ethnicity. She hoped that diseases, like the one that killed her daughter, would be eradicated. And early on she followed some ideas about being, uh, God-struck—'spiritual clarity' was how she described it."

Sam had trouble explaining it because it seemed nutty to her too.

"She did think that a talent for religious faith was heritable, and that genes were something you could prune for ideal outcomes, like in horticulture. In fact, that was the precise metaphor she used."

"So she thought people should be mated for selected traits and those without those traits should not reproduce."

"Yeah," Sam said. "Pretty much." The other kids were getting bored of their conversation, looking at their phones.

"That is some Nazi bullshit."

"To be fair, this was pre-Nazis, so the logical end of cultivating humans was not as evil-seeming then as it is now. Sort of."

This girl probably didn't know some of the worst of it. How after watching her older sister die in childbirth, teenage Clara ran off to live in a nearby Perfectionist commune, the Oneida Community, as an underage acolyte of fifty-seven-year-old John Humphrey Noyes, advocate of spiritual eugenics and complex marriage. Given his spiritual superiority, his clear duty was not only to be the "first husband" of the young women, but to father many of the planned children, while other less spiritually advanced young men were not allowed to procreate. Loomis's first child, Margaret, was rumored to be fathered by Noyes, although Margaret was raised by Henry Loomis, another former member of Oneida, as his. They left the commune and had a conventional, no-longer-complex marriage, but apparently, judging from the letters, she had retained some of Noyes's sketchy ideas about intentional "cultivation."

The students filed out. Sam's phone dinged. She looked at it, hopeful that it was a text even though it had a different sound, more *ping* than *ding*. It was an AirDrop image from someone (user name "Bra Tart") as they left the room: a photo of Hitler with a white paintbrush dragging up the side of it. It said Decline / Accept. Sam shrugged and pressed Accept. The full image had text under it: keep on whitewashing. Sam nodded.

Even Elizabeth Cady Stanton, clay-footed, racist Stanton, with her pissy renunciation of Black men as "low" after they got the vote before women did, would be better than Clara Loomis. For one thing, she did pretty much start the whole suffrage movement. And at least her big plain Seneca Falls farmhouse would be better than Clara's tainted, wacko reformism framed in pretentious Greek Revival.

A notification woke Sam from her reveries. Yelp alerted her to a newly posted one-star review of Loomis House.

Marlee S.
It was creepy, but the difference of the past is creepy. History is creepy. Like it is humans, but it isn't. Photographs, ghosts, smelly old spaces. Clara Loomis was a female doctor, that's kinda cool. She performed abortions, but eugenics is why she did it. Not cool. And she was in a sex cult. Loomis House, high-key sketch.

Sam posted right away:

Comment from Sam R., of Loomis House
Thanks for visiting. Yes, the hint of eugenics is creepy. But women's rights, the abolition of private property, advocating for individual choice about reproduction? Can we tease these things out from the misguided stuff and salvage rather than savage?

Sam closed her laptop with an emphatic snap. That inquisitive girl? Sam now placed her in Ally's class at school. Though not a friend of Ally's, no doubt she'd recognized Sam as Ally's mother.

"So that's the Ally update," Matt said. Sam had listened as he'd told her that Ally was busy studying, planning college visits, and working on her YAD start-up papers. Sam sat across from him at their kitchen table. No longer theirs, *his* table. It was an odd thing to go back, to be in that house. It was hard to believe that their lives went on without her.

"The college counselor is pushing her toward early decision at Carnegie Mellon. But her reach school, the one she really wants—"

"I can't talk college admissions right now. I really can't."

Last year Matt had suggested that they hire a very expensive college counselor. He, the counselor, was all about gaming it out ("leveraging her strengths," as he put it), which Sam felt was a mistake; it encouraged a sleazy grubbiness in their daughter, who, Sam told Matt, had a precocious and distinctive amount of dignity and gravitas that they might want to respect. They were eating takeout in their den and talking in hushed voices while Ally did homework in her room.

"But she agrees with the counselor," Matt said, as if that hadn't been manufactured by the school culture or by the counselor or by them.

"Then I will go on the record as a contentious objector to this process."

"Don't you mean 'conscientious'—" But then he stopped himself. Sam smiled.

They finished dinner without more discussion. Sam didn't care what college her daughter got into; it just didn't matter. The kids and parents were gripped by a whole psychosis, a terrible desperation, a deep anxiety beyond what was rational. Everything, the whole life of your child, seemed to get reduced to this one goal. At the meeting with the counselor, Sam had wanted to scream, College? Reach schools? Do you realize how fucked our kids are, what they will witness in their lifetimes? But then Sam understood what it was all about, the unspoken agenda. It was all about getting them a place on the lifeboats. On some level, they all knew what dire things were coming. And they also knew that those spots on the lifeboats were for sale, were reserved, really, for the ones who made the cut. As chaos descended, as the coming catastrophe unfolded, to be poor or even simply middle-class was to be washed away in a horrible conflagration of floods, hurricanes, fracking fissures, earthquakes, extreme temperatures, pandemics, droughts, fires, mudslides. Everyone with money will have an environmental panic room, like a bomb shelter, or they will have an escape hatch to the few remaining habitable realms. That was what was at stake in the college admissions Hunger Games. But—much to Matt's relief when she later told him what she really thought—Sam had not said all this to the very expensive college counselor or to Ally. She regretted that now. She'd restrained herself from speaking because she knew Ally was on a trajectory that Sam couldn't stop. Sam wanted no part in it.

Maybe that was why she'd left—so she wouldn't have to participate in the distasteful work of slyly encouraging hard-grabbing in their daughter.

"You know I don't want to hear about college strategies," she said.

A flash of irritation crossed Matt's face. Uh-huh. "Whether you hear about it or not, it continues to matter to Ally. She has to decide where to apply, and although it might be convenient for you to think so, it isn't some nefarious conspiracy of the privileged but, rather, our daughter trying to figure out the best place to spend the next four years of her life, which I think you might care about."

"Has she mentioned me or the breakup?" Sam said.

"No," he said. He seemed to catch himself, to soften. "I'm sorry. She hasn't asked me anything. Have you two been in contact at all?"

Sam shook her head. "Not really. I text her, and I guess she reads them. But she doesn't respond. I think—or I imagine—that I am slowly building my case to her."

"Sam, has the issue ever been that you didn't talk to her enough?" he said, which wounded her. He thought she talked things to death, and he assumed everyone must feel that way. Just like that, she felt her anger toward Matt bristle through her body. She even leaned back, away from him. She imagined Ally and Matt discussing how much Sam talked, how nice it was to have quiet at home. Without Sam, they probably had hours of silence. Silent dinners, silent breakfasts.

"What choice do I have?" Sam said. "She won't talk to me."

"I know, I know. That will change eventually."

Sam nodded.

"Just let her—"

"I know, I know," Sam said.

"How is the house? Did you put up the carbon monoxide detectors?"

"Yes," she said. She hadn't, not yet.

"Is it cold?"

April and May had been awful. Ugly snowmelt lingered in dirty lumps. Mud, freezing rain, vicious wind. The coldest, dampest spring in Sam's memory, still dipping into the thirties at night.

She shrugged. "I have a cord of wood. I burn a fire every night. It's drafty, actual outside cold air blows in at some spots, but as long as I have an open flame to huddle by, I'm good. And it's June—it's getting warmer."

"That house has very little insulation," he said. "It will be cold and then it will be hot." He snapped his fingers. It was true. Already at the height of the midday sun, it had felt hot.

"Yep," she said. In the heat of summer, Matt loved central air and a constant sixty-eight degrees. Like a sealed pod. She would do what people used to do: keep the windows shut against the sun during the day and open them at night. Drink ice water and not exert herself.

"Did the exterminator come?"

"Yes, it was pretty expensive. There are a lot of entry points."

Matt looked horrified. It was true that Sam could hear the scuttling of creatures at night. This too was not bothersome to her.

Then he reached into his interior jacket pocket and retrieved a gold Cross pen. She used to love how he looked in a suit, and rather than regret the fact that he embraced a "straight" life so completely, she found it alluring, as if he were grown-up and in the real world, and she was his connection to the left behind, young world. She used to like undoing his tie and bringing him back. When did she stop doing that? Instead of bringing him back, she somehow followed him.

Matt took out his wallet, found a folded check. He spread it on the table and filled it out. Then he handed her the check. Again he was plying her with support, and again it was working.

"Thanks," she said. "This is more than I need."

"Well, it's our money. You don't have to thank me."

She nodded, keenly aware that he was stalling things, assuming they would reconcile. But she didn't feel like pushing back today. She was weak. Phony poverty, fake independence. She told herself she just needed time to adjust, to get more days at work or to find a second job.

"I mean, just until we sort it out, I want to make sure you have everything to equip the house." He smiled. "Whatever you need, Sam, to be comfortable and safe."

But I don't want comfort, can't you tell? She thought this but didn't say it.

"And even if you don't care anymore about your own comfort or safety, do these things for me. For Ally." He put his hand on hers. Matt used to be good at reading her, imagining her thoughts from her expression. Apparently, he still could do it when he tried. Goddamn him, he had to turn caring and easy just when she needed to stay mad at him. He put his pen back in his jacket pocket, and he looked up, into her eyes, and then looked down, exhausted. His sadness made him look old, his face too thin from all his running. He was a middle-aged man in a movie about a midlife crisis. A cliché. But in such a film, he would be leaving her, right? So not a cliché. Matt, Matt, Matt, she thought.

When they'd first moved in together, there was very little money. He was still in law school, and she worked as a waitress. They would carefully put her tips in envelopes labeled with various expenses, like "rent" and "groceries." One was marked "treats," and every few weeks they would use this money for a night out, a cheap dinner and a movie. Afterward, heated discussion of the movie (they often disagreed), then wine (occasionally pot) and sex (they were in their stride). Followed by more talk, often about the future. She never wore him out. He would laugh even (or especially) when she made silly jokes (sometimes involving stupid puns). It was easy, then, to make a lot of very little. They were so far from that now. Partly because so much of their future had already unfolded. But not only that.

"We really fucked this up," she said, moving her hand in the air between them. He pursed his lips, nodded at her. She looked away. Now he was tender, vulnerable, attentive.

Too late.

Syracuse was the inspiration for the Emerald City (though people don't believe it). L. Frank Baum grew up with Syracuse as the big verdant city in the distance, so green it was emerald. It used to be called the Salt City, when salt harvesting was its reason for being. But the chamber of commerce rebranded it, officially, as the Emerald City, which was supposed to counteract the city's rep for all snow, all the time. And this time of year, late June, it truly was emerald. Sam ran from her house to the lake, then headed back along a different route. She noticed the long-matured parks and triangles of green spaces everywhere, lush artifacts that remained from a more prosperous era. The endless spring rain and snow-melt fed the trees, lawns, and bushes in the summer. Sam loved the peak density of June, but she preferred the city in the weeks before it reached its full summer green. By the end of May, the flowering trees had popped in variegated pinks and whites, from deep coral to the palest blush. Sam inhaled these trees, noticing them on every corner, in front of faded and ugly wrecks as well as neatly landscaped, tidy houses. They seemed to thrive despite neglect, as if the winter itself made them stronger, deeper, pinker. Each year the spring came slowly, and each year the blossoms left far too quickly, the trees' flowers gone by early June. A hard rain or wind would knock them to the streets, and for a moment a carpet of pink made the streets lovely, and Sam knew it was not the Emerald City but the Pink City. The flowers moved her and made her feel sad in an inexplicably deep way. The speed of their cycle frightened her, made her want to scream stop, stop, stop. Hold on, this is going too fast. The coming and going weighed on her and almost made it too painful to enjoy.

Sam ran and then she walked. When she got close to her house, she could see that the front door was slightly ajar. She immediately pictured the young desperate woman from before. Sam hurried to the door and pushed it open. She stood at the threshold and beheld her home. Chairs by the table knocked over, drawers in the built-ins pulled open and left hanging like gaping mouths. Her bed with its expensive mattress pulled halfway off the frame. Everything appeared touched, handled, messed with. Why would someone fuck up her house? But of course it was simply a burglary, not some mysterious creepy crawling. What valuables did she even have to take? Her old MacBook, check, that was gone. And her phone charger. One half-empty stupidly extravagant bottle of single-malt scotch that she had spitefully taken from Matt, some food (cans of dolphin-safe tuna, organic peanut butter, bittersweet chocolate). She didn't have a TV. Her medicine cabinet: of course, that was the first thing they looked through, and, boy, that must have been disappointing. She glanced in the bathroom. The natural proges-terone cream and face cream had been pitched to the floor. She didn't have any drugs, certainly no opioids and not even a tablet of Ambien or Xanax, just CBD oil for sleep (didn't work), which they'd taken, and a bottle of Bayer aspirin, which they'd left.

Sam was proud that she had so few possessions, congratulat-ing herself, and then she remembered her small antique lacquered chinoiserie jewelry box and saw that it was gone. She took a deep breath. It didn't have a lot of valuable pieces. Sam had already given Ally her mother's diamond studs for her sixteenth birthday. The only things you could sell were a gold cocktail ring with an amethyst, an engraved tennis bracelet, and a very nice watch Sam had forgotten to wear today. She didn't care, really. But she did care about the little trinkets that Ally had given her for birthdays and Mother's Days over the years. Some silver rings and inexpensive earrings. Worth nothing to anyone but Sam. She started to cry, thinking about them. It was just stuff, silly sentimental things. Little Ally had picked them out, and they were a line to the past. That's all. Also lost in that box was her platinum wedding band, engraved with her wedding date. She had planned to give it to Ally, but who wants a ring from a failed marriage anyway. A memento of a broken promise—Ally would be infuriated by it. Now she didn't have to worry about what to do with it. It was in a pawnshop.

She put the house back in order. No real harm done. But she grew more and more upset as she noticed and righted all that had been touched. Someone (not the desperate young woman from before; that thought came again and she dismissed it again, unlikely, silly thought, as if everything that happened to her fit some kind of causal narrative rather than just being arbitrary), some person, had come in and ransacked all her things. Hungry and full of needs. And they'd worked fast so they wouldn't get caught. But Sam still felt a kind of hostility in it. Did they have to pull everything out of the drawers and dump it? Knock over the chairs, touch all her things? No, they didn't need to be so angry about it. And she felt an anger and resentment rise in her, and then a fear. She thought she should call the police, get locks installed.

It didn't take her long to clean up. She made a cup of coffee, sat by the window, and smoked one of her two herbal cigarettes of the day. Instead of regular cigarettes or vaping, she had settled on smoking quick-burning, hollow, non-nicotine herbal cigarettes that still gave you lung cancer but wouldn't get you addicted to nicotine. "Made with love and clarity in Portland, Oregon." They smelled good, and they gave her a way to punctuate her solitary days. They calmed her.

Her sense of violation didn't dispel quickly. Had someone cased her, cased her house? It had to be one of those vacant-faced people living on the street, the ones that frightened her at night. Her moving in had been noticed. That the house was no longer empty had been noticed. Her vulnerability had been noticed.

She looked around. She loved this house, she was house-proud, she had her bourgeois vanity. Even if her things were modest, she liked how it felt with everything in its place. But to like this particular place, to feel at home here, was to also be in this neighborhood and this city. She dismissed calling the police. Remember Dorothy Day. Shouldn't Sam get to the point where she shared what she had? Leave the doors open, possess nothing beyond what she needed? Anything extra should be given away, and she should live on the least she could manage. Sam wasn't there yet. She still would lock her door. But if someone really wanted in, it wouldn't take much. And no police.

"Hello?" her mother said. Her voice made Sam feel things when she was like this.

"Hi," Sam said, a croakiness in her throat.

"What's wrong?"

Sam definitely couldn't tell her mom about the break-in.

"Ally is still not talking to me. Or responding to me," Sam said, pouring all her emotion in that container of self-pity. Her voice squeezed through her longing for Ally; she began to sob and then pulled it back.

"Oh, honey, I know. I spoke to her a few days ago."

"What did she say?"

"She's sad about you leaving, but she tries to act tough, so it comes out as anger."

"Yeah," Sam said.

"But she loves you—that is, of course, why she is mad."

"Maybe. She doesn't want to be distracted from her GPA and her college-bound activities. Her YAD rankings."

"It's a lot of pressure, junior year."

"I know, I know," Sam said. "I'm an awful mother, wife. And daughter. But really, beyond that, I'm a terrible person."

"You're not at all." Her mother went through the evidence, which she could be counted on to do. It was silly for Sam to call her one partisan and ask that the case be made on her behalf. Yet it made Sam feel better. See how she still needed her? Didn't Lily see how needed Lily was, how she was the only person Sam let help her?

"I miss Ally so much," Sam said. "And I miss you."

"I miss you too. Why don't you come visit me," Lily said.

"Yes," Sam said. "I'll come this weekend."

"This weekend isn't good for me," Lily said.

"Why?"

"The weekend after, maybe. Let's talk tomorrow."

When she got off the phone, she lit her second cigarette and texted Ally.

Grandma said you spoke to her.

I think I am going to visit her next weekend if you want to come.

Nice. Use her mother to get to her daughter.

It was too hot to make a fire, and the liquor was gone. Sam would go to bed. She was putting the matches back in the built-in cupboard next to the mantel when she saw it. She sucked in her breath. A tile was missing from her fireplace. They had taken one of her hundred-year-old Moravian tiles. The green one on the lower right corner, which is why she hadn't noticed it until now. It was small, had come loose and needed to be remortared.

"No, no, no, no," she said out loud, kneeling, putting her finger in the crumbling dust. Why take a tile? To hurt her, no doubt, by hurting this old house. To take a piece of it for themselves like a trophy. Maybe chucked in the street somewhere.

She was an outsider, an interloper, a fake member of this community. Her comfort amid so much discomfort was a form of affront. It was not personal and it was insanely personal. It wasn't hostile but it also really was.

She should go to bed. At night, the lights inside the house made her visible to everyone outside the house. She turned off all the lights except the porch light. She felt invisible, she felt safe, and she lay down on her bed. She was so deeply tired, and right away a merciful, beautiful sleep came over her.

TWO

Ally

I

"Tell me everything," he said. "As you remember it."

So she did:

"I think the tension started around fourteen, like ninth grade. I remember on many mornings there was some version of the fight. As in, I come down the stairs in a rush, trying to make it to the bus on time, but also hardly awake. I shove every possible needed book into my backpack, so it pulls on my shoulder. All I want is a glass of juice. She will try to get me to eat some toast, which I will take a tiny bite of and leave the rest. Every morning she hears me thump down, and every morning her smile fades as she takes me in. She recovers the smile, but I know something is coming.

"'Good morning!'

"I nod, waiting, my head down, hair in my face.

"'Juice?'

"'I'll get it.' Just leave me be. Just one morning.

"'Are you going to brush your hair on the bus?'

"Here it comes. I nod. Gulp juice, avoid her gaze.

"'Honey,' she says, the lilt of disappointment in the word. As if she regrets having to point something out, and also it is tediously familiar to us both.

"'What?' I say, but it sounds more contemptuous than I mean it to. It all has to exist on a tone plane just beneath anger or it could set her off. Which I really can't handle right now. She looks at my chest—*yes, looks at my breasts*. I look down, and my sweater, a V-neck, has slipped a bit down and cleavage and bra top are visible. I pull it up.

"'Remember those camisoles I bought you? Then you don't have to worry about your sweater falling down and showing your bra.'

"I nod, not looking at her. 'It's fine, it will stay covered. See?'

"Her lips purse. More to come. I move toward the door to leave.

"'Do you have everything? Inhaler, glasses, phone?'

"'Yeah,' I say.

"She pulls out my inhaler, which was on the coffee table in the TV room. Trick question. I grab it. She smiles that 'what would you do without me' mom smile. I move to leave.

"'Have a good day, honey.'

"I nod. She hugs me, backpack and all. I hug back, frowning. I can't not hug her; she needs it.

"'See you later, Mom.'

"'Have fun!' But then she can't help herself: 'Brush your hair!'

"There are other versions of the fight. Like I remember shopping for clothes. That was always a joy."

"For example?"

"We are at Marshalls or wherever. She pulls from the rack some heinous smocky blouse, something more frumpy than demure, and says, 'What about this?' I shake my head no, with great vehemence, and she sighs and shakes her head as if there is no pleasing me. I then find a red tube top in size extra small, which I know is demented, but I can't help it when she provokes me. She's like, uh, no. But I have set the parameters with my extremes—I know what she caves in to will be much closer to what I want."

"But you dress pretty conservatively now."

"I do—I have to wear 'Western business attire' for YAD conferences. And I like the way those clothes make me feel, so I started dressing that way all the time. She doesn't know what to make of it, she doesn't comment on it—how can she—but I think it unnerves her. As much as the trashy clothes were counter to her, the business attire is also counter to her taste."

"Is it—or was it—always about clothes?" he asked.

"No. There is other stuff."

Ally's phone pinged. Around nine o'clock, every night, her mother sent a text. Ally always read it, she even left her read receipts on so her mother would know the message had been received, but she wouldn't text back. But five new texts? So far, her mother never texted more than once. It was a miracle of mother restraint to send only one text a night, and yet that was how it had gone for almost three months. Her mother had never missed a night (expected), and she had never sent more than one (unexpected). Maybe her mother had finally cracked and given in to her need to overdo everything when it came to Ally, loving Ally, bearing down on Ally. "Overbearing" was the word, and when she thought of it, she imagined a giant mother bear. Ally wondered for a second if "bear," as in "borne," had the same roots as "bear" the animal, maybe some old English word. Ally had taken five years of Latin, and one of her nerdy habits was to unwind words, to look up their histories. And one reason she needed to know about words was that she liked to stick new (well, new-to-her) words in her papers. Plus her vocab helped make her the top-ranked YAD student in her grade. She sometimes used a thesaurus, but it resulted in some embarrassing misuses of words, because a thesaurus pretended that words had synonyms but they didn't really. They all had different meanings if you dug into it, which she had started to. She even had an app on her phone that gave you word derivations and etymological breakdowns from like twenty dictionaries ("-logic"/"logos" she knew meant knowledge or study of, but "etumos" meaning "true" puzzled her). And another app gave her morpheme meanings and derivations. But she didn't open the app and look up "borne"/"bear." Instead she touched the green talk-bubble icon, and the lists of texts sprang open. She discovered that the number was five because she also had texts that were not from her mother. A bright flare opened—bloomed, really—in her belly when she saw the glowing blue indicator dot next to the letter N and then the name "Nina." Just this week, when he'd told her that he might text her, she had input "Nina" for Joe's name on her phone, just in case someone snooped. Which was why she also turned off her lock-screen text notifications except for that ping sound. Her father wouldn't snoop, she was almost certain. He lacked curiosity about other people; it never occurred to him that anyone else had anything going on beneath her surface. That was why he'd missed that Ally's mother was leaving him. Completely missed it. But Ally's mother would totally snoop. She had plenty of curiosity. And although her mother would feel bad about it, historically it seemed clear to Ally that her mother could talk herself into crossing a line when it came to all things Ally. However, her mother no longer got near her phone or her. That was a kind of miracle, one of so many amazing things that had come to pass this year: that Ally could shut her mother out for so long, and that Ally was alive, walking, existing, still entirely herself away from her mother. Wait, correction. More entirely herself. And just as amazing, now Joe, hers, someone no one would even guess at. Because Ally was the last person anyone would imagine doing this. Certainly, her father had no idea. Her teachers. The girls at school. She could keep it from all of them—that was another surprise. She was careful, and quite good, it turned out, at keeping secrets. She also knew that maybe she wasn't quite seeing it all through the way she should, she wasn't letting herself think about what would happen when it would finally come out. All she thought was that she wanted it to continue and therefore keeping it a secret was essential. Ally even changed her phone's passcode every week or so.

Back in ninth grade, her mother had tracked her phone with an app called Family Tracker. Nice idea/name. Her mother got notifications about what numbers Ally called and texted and at what time, even if the app didn't reveal the content. What trust. Plus Ally was the last person in her grade to get a smartphone. Why? Because her mother had raised her as an effing Amish, was why, insisting on only a rudimentary flip phone for emergencies, which Ally lost several times, maybe somewhat (but totally unconsciously) on purpose. Ally had to admit that she was less mesmerized by what her smartphone offered than some of the kids in her class. By her fourteenth birthday and the presentation of her own device, it was a letdown, or maybe by that time she already maintained herself without her phone being an essential part of that maintenance. It changed little about her daily life except her parents called or texted her constantly and she could listen to Spotify when she went for a run. She could do homework, prepare her YAD papers on her phone using Google Docs when she was on the bus or waiting in line somewhere. Also she could look up ideas and words the moment she thought of them, which she liked. As for contacting friends, she only had two she actually trusted. And Ally was so used to not being part of Snapchat that she just never signed up. She had heard how some of the kids were really stressed out about maintaining streaks. Two boys had a streak going for over 380 days. And breaking a streak was some big—whatever, it was really stupid. Not being involved was a badge of maturity. And the AMA apps— kids setting themselves up for anonymous comments. Just inviting cruelty: "What is the best/worst thing about me?" They seemed to be asking for it. At first Ally thought they were sadly overestimating the kindness of anon hordes. Then she figured it out: mean attention was still attention. So as much as she would not admit it, maybe her early deprivation was good in some way. She was glad she cared little for her device. Until she met Joe. Until she had Joe.

Joe.

When everything else pissed her off, she thought of him and she felt better. Just his name, in her head, was enough. Although she sometimes mouthed his name, almost whispered it, just to feel it in her body. A kind of mantra. Mantras, she thought, were like a hymn, a way of turning words into abstract vibrations of meaning. The word started with the meaning, zoomed out into your body (your mouth, your ears) and then returned to the meaning, but with your whole body involved now.

Joe.

• N Nina. The dot by the name, pregnant with unread texts. She made herself savor the feeling.

> • N Nina
> my sweet girl! I miss u . . .

Joe texting her was new. Usually they spoke on the phone. She would go for a run and stop in the park so they could talk with no one overhearing. Every day she did this. He didn't want to text. They had to be careful. She told him he was "Nina" and convinced him that it would be safe. In any case, the boundaries were breaking down; it had become impossible to resist crossing them for both of them.

Ally pressed the dot. Oh, the microsecond as it swiped to the left and sprang open.

The full text bubble filled the screen. And three bubbles below that. It was so exciting to get all these messages from him that she scanned them quickly and then forced herself to go slowly, read each one.

> my sweet girl! I miss u, what r u doing?

She almost trembled. She was worried that one day she would see a text from Joe and she wouldn't feel that blossoming inside her body. How did that work, could a feeling like that just go away one day? What a sad thing to notice—but she couldn't imagine it fading. She gave up trying to read slowly.

> can u send me a pic of yr beautiful face?

> or any pic of any part of u? a perfect pinkie, perhaps?

> (sorry, so flowery. yr fault.)

She knew what she was doing was dangerous, but it was also the most exciting thing that had ever happened to her. She had no idea that she could be this person, this adult. She had no idea that it was in her to be so bad, so reckless, so disobedient. It felt fantastic, it truly did, and she did not, as her mother would have had her believe, feel out of control or frightened. She felt utterly in control—her grades were perfect, but more than that, she had a new sense of herself. She looked in the mirror and could see joy radiating out of her. She felt alive to her future adult self. This glimpse gave her a confidence about what she knew. For example, virtually everything your parents tell you after the age of thirteen turns out to be false—if not a manipulation, then a distortion for some unstated higher purpose that they refuse to admit to. She wished the relevant and "wise" adults in her life just leveled with her, gave her a little room to decide what was good or dangerous. Besides, it wasn't like Joe wasn't taking a risk. She was almost seventeen and he was twenty-nine, so technically, it was statutory rape. But that word made her wince, not only because it didn't remotely describe her experience, but also because it derived from "rapere," which meant seizure of property. When women were considered property you could take. The truth was, again, the opposite. She was not anyone's property, and Joe was not taking anything from her but, rather, giving her everything.

Sex was another thing that was not at all what everyone said it was. It wasn't informed consent like in health class, a script of "can I" and "yes." It was a suicide pact, and equal danger and transgression on both sides was part of what made it exciting. They both needed jeopardy for the connection to be equal. On her side, she could get found out by her parents. She could get pregnant. And if she sent him photos, he would have them, could make some kind of revenge porn out of them. Because the texting was going to include photos, wasn't it? They both knew without saying that photos came with the texts. The thought of it, of the transgression, was part of the blooming feeling. The one thing everyone had drilled into her since fifth grade was not to send anyone naked photos, ever. Don't believe boys when they promise never to show them to anyone or that they will delete them. But—and in this she was romantic, really, even if it sounded otherwise—she would send him photos. What was the point of sex and love if you didn't trust the other person completely? If you were already gaming out the breakup and the "after" fallout, then you were just acting in bad faith.

She had read her Sartre, but she had also read her Kant, and she had read her Rawls. Or in any case, she had read their Wikipedia pages, which were quite extensive. She knew what bad faith was. What all the concerned adults advised was degrading, crude. Such as, if you do send a naked pic, never show your face with your body. Again, so cynical. They actually want you to disembody yourself, separate your identity from your body to "protect" you. Everything is doomed if you expect so little of the world. If you expect so little of other people. Besides, what are they protecting you from, even in the scenario that the snap finds its way out from his phone into the wider spheres of the internet? The humiliation (apparently profound and suicide-inducing) of having your body exposed. To be shown in a private act of desire. The message is clear: our "private" self must be a source of shame. And the photo will last forever, they warn. You can never scrub it once it is unleashed. Which used to terrify her. But she no longer felt that way, terrified. On the one hand, they say they want the culture to be "body positive," but when you get down to it, the concerned adults are very wary of your body. Ally will be glad that when she is old, images of her young self will still be there for anyone who bothers to put her name in a search bar and click on Images.

Most of what everyone said didn't really apply to her. She understood that now. Besides, Joe would not betray her, but even if he did, she would care more about what it meant about them than the actual fate of her digital images. So sending—the decision to send—photos was a fait accompli. Or at least a moot point. (Moot points were a go-to in her simulations—she understood that every proposition was arguable.)

The first time they met in private, in a hotel room, he was visiting Syracuse for business. Instead of staying downtown, he took a room at the Syracuse University Sheraton. That way it wasn't so hard to get her dad to drop her at the nearby campus library, Bird, which was open until midnight and you didn't need an ID or anything to get in. She explained that she was working on a research paper, which she pretty much always was, so that part wasn't a lie. Plus now she had her license, so everything was getting easier.

The fact that Joe was one of her CMs (Citizen Mentors), one of her father's friends actually, was not creepy. It was exciting. It was interesting. She got to know him through YAD, which arranged for promising young people to be mentored by community leaders and entrepreneurs (an etymologically disappointing word, it was simply derived from "entreprendre," meaning "undertake" but also, if you dug deeper, "take in hand," which made her laugh). Her father called it YAD like it rhymed with "cad," even as Ally corrected him, "It is WHY AY DEE, not YAD." "Then it should be punctuated like Y period A period D period," her mother said, not looking up from her book.

"Exactly," her father said, laughing. She hated when they bonded over making fun of things she took seriously. "What does Y-A-D stand for again?"

"Young American Dissidents," her mother said.

"Young American Disrupters," Ally said. "For god's sake!"

Her mother looked up at her and smiled. "Disrupters. Right. Break stuff and all that."

Ally sighed with weariness. "Innovators. They are not breaking things, but altering them from within. People with new ideas disrupting the world as they found it to change it for the better."

"And what are they disrupting, really?"

"The status quo," Ally said.

"Uh-huh. By dint of profit? By 'building' "—and here her mother made air quotes—"businesses?"

"Look, you need to get out of your eighties mentality. Not everything worthwhile is about destroying capitalism."

"But your mother is a Marxist, honey," her father said. Both her parents cracked up at that. Ally sighed loudly and walked toward the door of the kitchen.

"I know," her mother said, her voice low now because she was worried that Ally would leave in a huff. "I know you get a lot out of it. I just think the name is a bit much."

Ally stopped. All of her books and her backpack weighed her down, so her turning back toward her parents made her wobble unsteadily. She spoke over her shoulder, her eyes trained on her mother:

"Not only are you operating from some woefully outdated paradigm. But you live here, in this house, in this suburb, the way you do, and you want me to be a dissident?"

"Dis ain't your old-lady dissidence, Sam," her father said, laughing.

Ally groaned loudly, turned toward the swinging kitchen door and pressed her book-and-backpack-laden body into it.

"C'mon, he's joking," her mother said.

"I'm mad at you, not him," Ally said, now inexplicably furious.

Outside the kitchen, as if she couldn't hear, her mother's loud voice: "Naturally she's mad at me and not you."

"We really shouldn't pick on YAD, I mean Y-A-D. We shouldn't. It's a very impressive organization," he said.

"It's a cult," her mother said. Her stupid, unrepentant, big-mouthed mother. Could she never stop?

"C'mon," her father said.

"It is. It has its own jargon, for god's sake. Acronym-drunk Silicon Valley peen patois."

"Tech bro bashing commence now," he said.

"OVR—Optimal Virtue Ratios. Sharing Economics. Dynamic Evolution. Covert Scalability. Beta Blockchains. Internet of Backyard Things. SLA—Strategic Limited Accountability. Crowdsourced Actionable Intel—"

"Now you're just making things up," he said. "Platform-based Interrogations! Peer-to-Peer Haptics! Drone Epistemology!"

"Good one," her mother said.

Much laughing. They really thought they were clever.

"Seriously, though, it is culty. They make her work so much that she is sleep deprived, easily indoctrinated. Disrupters, *please*. It's a young strivers' club pretending to be something exciting and new so young people will sign on."

"Shhh," her father said. But her mother was in full blabber mode.

"Do you know I saw her reading Ayn Rand? Where do you think she got that?"

Joe had given her the Rand. She tried to like it. At least Rand was a woman. It struck Ally as odd but fascinating that so many libertarian heroes were women. The foundational texts were women heavy. Oddest was Rose Wilder Lane, Laura Ingalls Wilder's daughter. She had written an important libertarian text, and maybe even ghostwrote her mother's books (books that Ally's mother had read aloud to her, books they devoured one after the other, rushing toward each night's chapter like a secret pact between them). But Rose Wilder disappointed Ally. Her essays were not as good as Laura Ingalls Wilder's books, whoever wrote them. There was no life embedded in them, no—what was the word? Feeling? Bodies? Things? Just ideas and assertions.

"*The Fountainhead*. I never read it, but I remember this scene in the Gary Cooper movie."

And now she admits she never even read it.

"Roark, the architect as superman, gets a big commission for his modernist maverick building design—so new, so pure—and then, in this very subtle complication, they say yes, you can build it, *but* you have to put this reproduction of the Parthenon all around the facade and totally compromise your superior vision—"

"I'm glad she's reading it. Curiosity about the world is a good thing. You have to trust her to figure things out."

Sure, that will be the day. Ally put her earbuds in.

One day Ally would tell her mom about Joe, and it would astonish her. Ally stared down at her message bubbles, her glowing, miraculous phone. Mom has no idea how far I am from her. She knew her mother imagined she would confide all her boy stuff to her, they would be like girls at a slumber party. Mom wanted that so badly. But it was very hard to give it to her or even to have enough room to admit that Ally kind of wanted that too. Just not yet; this was so completely hers, so exquisite in its compartment, in its isolation from the rest of her life.

As secret as she was about Joe, her YAD activities were very much entwined with her Joe activities. YAD used the word "enterprise" instead of "business." Each rubric of the class involved studying with a disrupter, of which Joe was one. Some Citizen Mentors were designated as RLDs, Real Life Disrupters, people who operated within the business world but also remade it. Undertook an innovation of how people think of something at some fundamental level. (Undertaking made sense in this context, how "enterprise" came from "prehendere.") It was about foundational questioning and imagination. It asks why can't we find a way to make money and make something that moves the ball forward for the better. Everyone wins. Take the environment, for example. When she mentioned her nightmare about rising sea levels, about living in a waterlogged, forever-flooded future, with she herself sitting on a roof waiting to be rescued as the filthy water rose and rose until she woke up sweaty and damp, Joe told her that entrepreneurs will find ways to mitigate the effects of climate change. There is so much money to be made that the best minds will be on it as long as no one hems them in. The hive mind, the genius of economic incentive combined with the power at stake, will unleash the brilliance of GDE (Goal-Driven Enterprise). There will be a Bill Gates of climate Armageddon. You know it, Ally. The capacity is right around the corner, he said, and maybe it was true. Real Life Disrupters looked for the bigger cultural, even social, impacts. And real financial viability. An essential element of RLDs was that they succeeded—yes, they made money, because that was a clear measure of success, and it meant that it was sustainable—and as a consequence of the successful enterprise, the landscape of the status quo was permanently altered, broken and then remade.

Break Things *and* Make Things was Joe's update of that notorious edict.

Joe was a developer who worked on renovating and repurposing existing structures "with preservationist sensitivity." As he explained in his presentation to her YAD class, he was expert at marshaling the available tax-abatement and exemption programs as well as historical property and economic-development grants at the city, county, and state levels. Although he was based in New York City, he had put together a deal for the historic but ruined James Hotel downtown. It had been built in 1915, was once grand, but fell into low years with a 1970s cheapo update, then became a sad nightclub, then a failed restaurant, until it was finally shuttered five years ago, another abandoned building downtown. Through Joe's intervention, it became a Hilton property, with all the contemporary corporate standards that name suggested, but it was nonetheless brought back to its former glory with a tasteful and accurate restoration. Even her mother admitted it was glorious. Unlike so many building renovations, she said, this one has a real sensibility, a relation to history. Before Joe was appointed as her CM, Ally had met him through her parents. Ally's father was one of Joe's lawyers, and so all three of them went to the hotel's opening. The lobby had been restored with all of its original fixtures, huge gilt chandeliers with many small exposed bulbs, like the lights at Grand Central in New York City. Also intact were the original Stickley wood cages for the front desk check-in, including wood mailboxes for each guest room. Naturally her mother had an orgasm when she heard the name "Stickley." "The coup de grâce," Joe said, "is over here." Ally noticed that he looked unexpectedly young and cute, and she also registered that she actually found a guy in a suit sexy. He gestured to a large mural covering one whole wall.

"It used to be a mirrored wall when this place was badly updated in high 'modern' style. Then it was a restaurant, and they kept it that way."

"Because who doesn't want to watch themselves eat, right?" her father said.

"Right! Luckily, with most of these changes, they didn't bother tearing stuff out, they just covered things. I tell you, it was a big surprise to discover this mural when we removed the mirror. It was painted in the 1930s."

"It's beautiful. I love that WPA style," her mother said.

"Like Diego Rivera," Ally said.

"Yes, exactly. That's very impressive," Joe said, smiling at her. His attention was like a drug.

"My mother steeped me in all the standard lefty icons," Ally said, and Joe laughed. "The icons of iconoclasm." He laughed again, looked at her, clearly en-fucking-chanted with her. Which was crazy, but she could feel it, knew it, even though she had no experience whatsoever in these kinds of moments. She had read books and seen movies, but still, the feeling was unmistakable, like a damn airlift to adulthood and all its promised possibility. She had a sense then that her own taciturn, miserable teendom was about to open on something much, much more suited to her. And so it had.

The funny part was that the mural, which her mother described as beautiful, was only beautiful at first glance, or if you looked at it in an ambient, roundabout way. The colors were earthy brushed browns and soft, warm golds. The figures in the composition were pleasing. Crowded but bountiful. The technique too, the hatched rays of sun, the lines and shapes. But the subject, a history of Syracuse, was Podunk for sure. It was treated in a kind of medieval primitive put-everyone-in-time-all-in-the-same-room way, with varying planes of perspective applied, depending on the story being illustrated. Here were some unfortunate Iroquois, assigned to the margin, of course. And here were some canal-digging immigrants next to a white-sashed suffragette by some other loud-faced women. Behind them, the early spires of Syracuse University. And, rather prominently foregrounded, a Black man in shackles (!) with some white men towering over him with concerned faces. Ally said nothing about it at the time, but later she was not surprised when guests objected to the shackled figure. So controversial that the hotel had to post an informational plaque next to the mural. This was Ally's suggestion to Joe, and he took it gratefully. It explained that the depiction was of the "Jerry Rescue," a historic incident in which Syracuse abolitionists defied the Fugitive Slave Act. Locals used the city's centrality and its commerce lines (the railroad, the canals, the wagons) to spirit escaped enslaved people to Canada.

Such activism required money, you know. They were disrupters, like Joe. But the mural was still a problem because the image made the enslaved person—Jerry—look too passive and the white men looked more like owners than liberators. The solution Hilton ultimately decided on was to hang a small curtain over the controversial image. Was it a failure of the viewer or of the painter? Ally wasn't sure.

Meeting Joe in New York was a huge escalation of what they were doing. Because things intensify, don't they? Nothing stayed where it was. And she knew she could pull this off too. There was a summer YAD conference in the city. Of course, it was highly chaperoned. But there was some free time. After bed check, she snuck out. Annie, her roommate, did not know everything (like who Joe was exactly, or that he was someone known to all of them through YAD), but what she did know she would not tell anyone. It would be their secret.

She told her mom nothing; she told Annie some things. Well, not at first. At first it was Joe and Ally only. Later she hinted to Annie that she had an older boyfriend and that they had sex. But no one would know about the photos. He would have her photos, she would have his age: a perfect détente. "Détente" was another word she had learned, but in history, not YAD. It technically meant relaxation, security. But only via the tension of "mutually assured destruction." What a concept! When she sends him her first naked pic, she will make a joke about it, that he now had something on her, so they were taking equal risks. Feminism—liberation—to Ally meant figuring out how to make the power and the risk equal.

She pressed the camera button. She sent him a photo of her pinkie, as requested. But pressed between her pinkie and her next finger was Ally's pink, puckered nipple.

THREE

Sam

Watch the mothers: blotchy in stretched-out yoga pants, faded, bloated versions of their lithe, vivid daughters. What happened to them, Sam wondered. Weight creep (since the pregnancies, since the divorce); perimenopause; thrombotic, spidered blood vessels (too much chardonnay); patches of keratosis; a general slackening. Ugh, the duration made ruins of every beauty, even these spoiled suburban moms. But even worse? Watch the other mothers: gleaming and brutally taut in boots and skinny jeans, picking up their blotchy, bloated daughters, lumpen versions of their mothers.

Either kind of mother—any kind of mother—was awful.

Sam was lurking at the suburban Y, where Ally took tennis lessons. Sam drove all the way out there to lift weights, but she also hoped for a glimpse of Ally. Lessons got out at six. The mothers steadily streamed in to collect their daughters, which did not help Sam's emotional state. Sam ruthlessly scrutinized the women and girls, guessing who belonged to whom. It was not hard to pair them off, which made her feel a closing in her throat, a welling in the corners of her eyes. She could cry or scream for virtually any reason these days. She ignored herself, but she felt removed from these women, different in her fasted, adrenalized, unmade-up state, with her spiky, razor-cut hair making conspicuous the lines across her forehead and at the corners of her eyes. The mothers and daughters (some had two daughters, even, the greedy pigs) were quickly off to their evenings together, doing what families with teens do. What was that again? It was what—two and a half months ago, but it felt like another life. Driving. (Can I drive, Mom?) Going to Wegmans. Eating/not eating dinner. (Don't diet/restrict. But *you* do it.)

Checking their phones. (Laughter. What? Nothing. Or she takes pity and shows you the meme.) That was all: a series of ordinary, unconscious life details. Not trivial even if it seemed that way. Tender feelings for those moments, my god. Why was so much noticed only in the breach, in the loss, by the regret-filled longing for what was left behind? The mothers and the daughters left together and they slept under the same roof without even realizing how lucky they were.

No sign of Ally. She had vanished. Sam looked at her phone: the green square with the white talk bubble had no numbers on it to indicate unread texts. She pressed it anyway. She scrolled through the texts she had sent Ally over the past ten weeks and saw all the blue bubbles stacked on her side, nothing on the left, no gray bubbles from Ally. One response, that would be nice. Mustn't ask for it, must not be needful of her attention or response. It never, ever worked to show them your need. Not that she knew anything about the lives of other mothers and daughters. But of this she was fairly certain: it never worked for her to show Ally her need.

Not hearing from you is killing me.
Can you please just respond?

r u trying 2 make me feel sorry 4 u?

Well, yes, and so?

No, that wouldn't work.

Sam pushed the phone into her gym bag and stopped creeping on those poor women and their children. So what if the moms had some cult shade of hipster nail polish that matched their skin tone so they appeared to have mannequin hands? So what if they had blond highlights, a cool ash or a warm honey that perfectly complemented their complexions? Because all of them were with their daughters, weren't they? Because clearly Sam's mothering had been a disaster—and the shame of that returned to her now. Sam hadn't handled things the way she wished she had. Their estrangement seemed to have happened so fast. But it began a long time ago, she knew, when the beauty Sam had always seen in Ally became visible to the world in a new and potent way. It first struck her when Ally was newly fourteen.

Ally had pounded down the stairs, in a rush to get a ride to the mall, where she could hang out with her friends. It was the first time with no parental supervision, just twenty bucks for food at the food court with all the other teenagers. She burst into the kitchen, where Sam sat. Ally wore a little kilt that hit mid-thigh and a little sweater with a V-neck that revealed the peach-white curves of her upper breasts. A pendant hung between them—a puffy red enamel heart dangling from a gold chain. A vintage necklace Sam had bought, and she got a little familiar jolt of pleasure whenever Ally wore something she had given her. Pathetic, really. But there it was, and so Sam started with a compliment: "Oh, you are wearing the heart necklace!"

Shortly before Ally had gotten her period, her body had changed dramatically. From her childish androgyny emerged long, elegant legs, a tiny waist, and high, small breasts that required a bra. Her skin never had a blemish. And no weird adolescent awkward nose, just a luminous, poreless doll face, still round and babyish, but attached to this new body. What had been childish became suddenly nubile, suggestive, sexual. This combination terrified Sam.

"Honey, I can see your bra with that sweater," Sam said.

Ally sighed. "No you can't." She pulled on the shoulders of her sweater so that the V covered more. "And stop looking at my chest!"

What could Sam say to that, really? "You need to put on a cami or a tank top under that sweater if you want to wear it to the mall."

"Are you kidding?"

"Ally, the tight sweater and the booty skirt send a message to the world that you are . . . looking for attention," Sam said. "To your body," she added and then regretted the addition.

"Then the world is perverted. How is that my fault? Should I be ashamed of my body?"

"No, of course not," Sam said.

"Then why should I cover up?" And it was a fair point. Why should she accommodate the leering of men? Why was it her problem and not theirs? Could Sam tell Ally that Ally had not landed on her outfit choices in a vacuum? That how she thought she ought to look, that the skirt and that low-cut sweater had been thrust on her from cultural corners that commodified misogyny into mall-rat aesthetics? Sam could not.

Sam tried out another tack, though it did sound undeniably retrograde as it fell from her mouth. "In an ideal world, you wouldn't have to. But we don't live in an ideal world, and you don't realize how stressful it feels to have men hit on you." Sam sighed. Ally frowned at her, her arms folded in front of her chest.

Sam tried again, although more talking seldom led to a good outcome with Ally. Sam couldn't stop herself from believing that everything could be talked out. "Remember I said either the top or the bottom can be revealing but not both? Remember? But the combination of the booty skirt with the tight, low-cut sweater . . . will attract not just the attention of boys your age but men your dad's age, and it isn't always easy to handle."

"Eww. Just stop, okay? I'll change my sweater because the world is full of pedos, I guess." She stomped upstairs. "Why don't you just buy me a burqa?" she shouted from the second floor. And: "We're going to be late now!" Also: "It isn't a *booty* skirt. That isn't even a thing."

Sam had hated this whole exchange. That she felt the need to cover her daughter up. Because Ally didn't yet understand how unsafe the world was for her. But mothers must operate from realpolitik, not ideology. Just as when Ally goes to college, Sam will tell her daughter not to get drunk at a frat party and to have a buddy system. And if that makes it seem like the potential victim needs to adjust her behavior instead of the boys, so be it. The system that makes sexual predators and encourages grown men to leer at fourteen-year-old girls should change. But Sam had no control over frat boys looking for the drunkest girl in the room. Sam had no control over grown-ass men at the mall. Sam only had control over her daughter. A mother cannot take chances with her daughter. Mothers cannot afford to be sentimental about how the world should be. (Sam tried not to think about her memories of going to the movies with her friends when she was Ally's age and how, after her mother dropped her off, she put on eyeliner and removed a bulky sweater that had covered up a tight bodysuit that both held and revealed the shape and details of her braless young breasts.)

Ally came back downstairs wearing a totally different shirt, a ruffled sleeveless white blouse that was not low-cut but was actually see-through. You could see her bra. Fuck it. Sam said nothing and drove Ally to the mall, dropping her in front of the multiplex entrance where her friends were waiting. Then Sam drove to the back of the mall, parked, and surreptitiously headed over to the multiplex side, where she proceeded to discreetly follow Ally and her friends around. Yes, she did. For hours she tracked them, staying far enough back that she was not seen. She pretended to be a person absorbed in her phone, but even then she had suburban female invisibility, and no one noticed the fifty-ish white lady lurking about the kiosks, pillars, and fountains. She glimpsed Ally laughing, unaccosted. Only looking at Ally from a distance, estranged, did she see how not a child she was. She had an ease, too, on her own, with people her age. It felt terrible, wrong, to spy on her daughter like this. But she made no move to stop. She didn't know what else to do.

Sam walked back to the free-weight section of the gym. She had given up on spotting Ally, but she still intended to work out. Loading on the weight, pushing herself up hard.

She had made a lot of stupid errors. The upsetting thing was that her instincts were all wrong, obviously—look how it had turned out. Yet if she had to do it all over, she might do it the same way. No, not all of it. Some of it was plain wrong in retrospect.

The times she tracked her daughter via Find My Friends on her phone. She discovered her daughter's passwords. She lurked and stalked and checked various social media accounts, her email, her friend lists. She had finally stopped, turned off the phone tracker, resisted clicking on Ally's Google account when it came up below hers on her email sign-in. It felt creepy. But the terror of not checking, especially when Ally started driving, got to her, and then she would panic, weaken, and go in. (It was easy to fall back; her laptop "remembered" the passwords—one almost accidental click away with a pre-filled sign-in button—and Ally was careless in those days about her accounts. Or maybe the correct word was not "careless" but "carefree," a form of innocence she had lost by now.) How to resist after reading some article about a girl hounded by bullies on social media? The stupid parents didn't know anything until after she killed herself. ("We had no idea she had followers and that they had piled on.") The kid was an influencer on Instagram but couldn't take the pressure of likes/not likes/comments. Troll-bullied or something. This other one had a YouTube channel her parents knew nothing about. The message was clear. Kids have whole secret (not that secret) lives online. Some have accounts where they post benign things for their parents to monitor, and then they have secret accounts, under a pseudonym, where the real action happens. It was Sam's job to discover and monitor these things. But even when she tried, she was too out of the tech/social media loop to be effective. She swore it off until she got worried and couldn't resist again.

Sam could deadlift two hundred pounds now. One of her power-lifts. (Deadlift! Powerlift! Such dopey terms. "Dude, what is your deadlift?") Powerlifts were something she had a genetic gift for. Her trainer, Nico, had downloaded her raw data from 23andMe to come up with her fitness plan. A miracle that her body was getting stronger, in some way improving, at this late date. She was breathless, sweating. Why was weight lifting so satisfying? Maybe because you got to rest so often and still be "working out." That methodical, necessary, pregnant rest between sets.

The last time Sam got weak and checked up on Ally's online life was two days ago. Ally had turned off the Find My Friends connection to her phone. And changed all her passwords, it seemed. She had cut Sam off.

(Still.)

Sam grunted through a very slow rep. TUT, Nico's voice in her head. Time Under Tension.

(At least.)

Sam breathed in at the top and exhaled as she controlled the return. LUL: Lengthening Under Load. Slow concentric and eccentric contractions.

(Ally hadn't blocked her.)

Sam paused, rested, waited, as her heart worked to catch up.

Sweaty but now in the zone, Sam moved to landmine squats. The satisfying clank of adding plates to a barbell. Her muscles responded and got stronger, but it all still felt like a performance, a weight-lifting cosplay for her own amusement. She laughed at herself as she grunted through the set. Or did she do it to please Nico?

Sam had started training with him a year earlier. Someone had told her about this miracle worker. He had devotees like a cult leader. It turned out that people, especially at certain points in their lives, just loved—craved—being told exactly what to do. At the time, the feeling that she had lost her tether had just begun, and she still suspected that it was something to be solved on the plane of the body: exercise or diet or perhaps some renewing treatment that walked up to plastic surgery but technically didn't apply. Microdermabrasion or pulsed laser treatments. (Anything outpatient was still somehow a spa thing and not some woefully vain capitulation, not some hopeless and pathetic bid for lost youthfulness.) Some of these processes had some plausible use besides vanity. They remediated sun damage or some such. The argument—although it wasn't thought out as much as it was a contagion among the women she knew—seemed to point to sex, sex appeal, as the counter against midlife depression or confusion. Sam resisted the beauty treatments and the high-tech improvements. Sex wouldn't solve much, she knew, as she and Matt had always had satisfying sex, frequent sex. But the training registered something curious in her. (It was Alicia, of course. Alicia, a fellow mother Sam's age with shockingly cut arms, had told her about Nico.) Nico was twenty-five and in top shape. He was constantly on a cut, or else he was on a bulk. But he always looked the same to her: young, perfect, ridiculous. And he talked constantly about body science and cutting-edge workout theories. As she trained with him (their interactions so bodily intimate and yet almost entirely shallow), Sam developed a fascination for these bro-science types, not the roidy bodybuilders, but the "natural" performance athletes like Nico. When she drove to her boring daily errands or just drove, she began listening to hard-core fitness podcasts in which one bro interviewed another ("Walk me through your bulk protocol"— everyone was always "walking you through" something on these podcasts). She learned about slow regression, pyramid sets, flipping truck tires, Body by Science, (Navy) SEALFIT™ Kokoro Camp, kinesiology tape, Wim Hof (and warrior) breathing, OODA loop (Observe, Orient, Decide, Act), sledgehammers, log PT (physical training that involves carrying, lifting, and balancing a heavy log), rope climbs, wall ball throws, the benefits of hyper-oxygenating or hypo-oxygenating while exercising, kettlebells, AMRAPS (as many rounds as possible), reverse pyramid sets, slow-twitch versus fast-twitch muscle fibers. Was it possible that inhabiting a human body was this complicated, she asked Nico at one point, more or less joking. But humor was lost on him.

"It is if you want to reach your highest potential, if you want to make real gains." What did she want? Did she want gains? Who didn't want gains over subtractions? Quantifiable, trackable, tape-measure gains. There were the podcasts and then the YouTube videos. And Nico in real life, the in-the-flesh embodiment of a fully cultivated male body.

Never before had she cared about these things, but here she was. Her middle-aged fascination with these young, hyperfit men was a mystery to her. It was not sexual, not at all, almost the opposite. She gawked at them and their robust narcissism. Wondrous beings who felt no shame in exhibiting their vain pursuit of perfection. In fact, they bragged about it. They weren't self-absorbed; they were optimizing. Not just looking better, they insisted, but improving life span. Not just life span but health span, which meant you looked and felt good, you became and remained a paragon human specimen. You attended the unquestioned goal of getting ever stronger, lowering body fat, building lean muscle mass. The daily hours in the gym, the measuring of dietary macros. Tabulating blood sugar and ketones and heart rate. They considered themselves biohackers, pushing their bodies into whatever shapes they wanted. Fitter, Stronger, Better. Better look and better performance.

But, she wondered, better performance of what? Strength for what? Enhanced life span to do what? The rigor and discipline she got. The community, sure, the endorphin release, definitely. (Endorphins were a form of endogenous morphine; they did make you feel a kind of body bliss.) But the precious treatment of your own life span, the obsessive yet superficial self-betterment, the fetishy focus on the body, the relentless and desperate pursuit of constant improvement? And although it might seem that strengthening meant no longer weakening and that pursuing "gains" stopped or even reversed the decline we all experienced, this couldn't be true. Your body went in one direction, didn't it? It wound up and then slowly wound down. Her wacked periods were a clear sign of the direction her body was taking. Maybe for men it felt like less of an overt direction? But beyond the futility of body gains, what amazed her was their persistent insistence on boosting the self when the world—and this country, in particular—was in disgraceful shambles. The progressing, ever-widening gulf of disparity in every sphere. And were we not also on the verge of an environmental apocalypse? People seemed more fixated than ever on notions of "self-tend, self-care, self." In the current context, wasn't naked pursuit of health obscene? The self-contemplation down to the microbiomic makeup of your alimentary system, yet such contemplation was divorced from any reflection.

This seemed, now more than ever, the most American of myopias, this unapologetic—boastful, even—attention to the surface self. It sort of made sense, though. A retreat to the local. The hyperlocal and controllable: your heart, your lungs, your flesh.

Fecal transplants, stem-cell injections, increased mitochondrial sensitivity. "One set to failure," Nico said. Isn't that what we are all doing, one set to failure, she joked, but he just smiled and lifted his glorious, chiseled, unwavering chin at the barbell. Let's go, Sam.

She did her reps. She needed the wave of endorphins that came with intense exertion.

After weight lifting, she walked to the shower area, which was open. She heard laughing. A woman was showering with her adult daughter, who had Down syndrome or something like it. The mother poured water on the daughter's round belly from a little bucket, and the daughter laughed and hugged her. They were naked and joyful, and Sam didn't want to make them self-conscious, but she found herself mesmerized. They had old-looking bodies (daughter in her late forties, mother in her late sixties), and Sam had never seen naked old bodies in a state of play. They didn't notice Sam; they were busy. The mother washed her daughter with a soapy washcloth. Sam showered, not watching them but hearing them. The daughter bellowed when her mother rinsed her. Sam glanced at them and then down at her own old body as she washed.

There is a lie in young fit bodies. There is something human—touching—in the older body, in its honest relationship to decay and time. Seeing the two women's bodies, Sam felt a form of enchantment. To look, to behold, to abide age gave her an almost narcotic clarity; she could, for this moment, as long as it lasted, see and face what life really was. It was as if people mostly live in a state of terror about what is to come, what is happening to their bodies. It wasn't just terror; it was shame. You had to hide the shame of your body's age and your body's fragility from others and from yourself. This state of terror and shame made us desperate, cruel, occasionally savage. But here was human love, joy, innocence. The mother wrapped her daughter in a towel and used a second towel to dry her daughter's long hair. The daughter moaned again. The mother caught Sam glancing at them, and smiled at her, as if to say, I know you get it, I know you see us. And Sam had a constriction in her throat as she recognized how familiar their gestures were to her; there was a time she had experienced this particular kind of body intimacy. She didn't feel envy, exactly, but a wistfulness, a futile longing. When Ally was little, she let Sam wash her, dry her. Ally squealed with joy, and no one was self-conscious, everything was easy. Sam wrapped her clean child in a huge cotton towel, and then she hugged Ally close, as if they were one body. What she was witnessing wasn't as perfect as that (the child body was not complicated, not weighted with mortality or decay), but it was close. This mother got to have that body love, that pure mothering closeness, for the rest of her life. What would sixty years of that be like! Of course what lurked beyond this tableau was also what gave it its poignancy. What becomes of the daughter when the mother dies? Or what of the mother when the daughter dies? Sam knew that raising a child like this one had many challenges, and she recognized that her own loneliness colored how idyllic it seemed as she gazed at the two of them.

Yes. That's what this emotion is, Sam thought. Loneliness.

In the sauna afterward (heat "stress" also improved health markers; it was good, homeostatic stress, Nico insisted, but Sam just did it because the heat felt soothing to her soon-to-be-sore muscles), she thumbed through a sweated-upon, ancient *People* magazine. There was an article about the old lady who had again been arrested for sneaking onto a flight without a ticket. The tone of the article was condescending, amused: "Run, Grandma, Run!" was the headline. Marilyn Hartman, the "Serial Stowaway," was up to her old tricks.

Marilyn's story had long obsessed Sam, since she'd first read about the woman a few years earlier: a sixty-something wacky old lady had snuck onto a plane to Hawaii. And was apprehended only when she landed. She had been given a warning, but she kept sneaking onto planes. What got to Sam was not what got to other people. News reporters treated it as a joke story—kooky grandma foils the authorities. But as Marilyn repeated her transgressions with dutiful, obsessive regularity, some articles took on a different tone. It wasn't a funny story; it was a sad story about mental illness and poverty. She was an object of pity. She had a thought disorder. All of which was probably true. But Sam felt drawn to her for still other reasons. One was her photo—her mug shot—in which she smiled meekly, as if she were apologetic for making you look at her. Sam believed that this woman—Marilyn—went unnoticed because no one wanted to notice her. She was a testament to the inconsequence of old ladies. It was such a strange confluence of privilege (no jail for you) and dismissal (because you are innocuous, really). This was insulting—as if she were prima facie a harmless creature. A judge finally admonished her and diagnosed the reason for her recidivism. "I think you're addicted to the attention," the judge said before releasing her. Sam resented the condescension and the dismissal. The refusal to allow Marilyn any substance, any potency.

Sam had set up a Google alert about Marilyn, who confounded everyone by continuing her stowaway tricks, and yet she was not jailed or jailed for long. Partly they kept releasing her because she was up to nothing—her intent was simply to ride the plane or hang out in the airport. (The perversity of it impressed Sam—her purposeless travel and wanting/needing to be in airports and on planes.) But partly she evaded jail because people read her as benign. And in the trough of the inoffensive, she was protected. Paradoxically, that protection both advantaged and effaced her. To be seen, a woman like Marilyn would have to really push it. Be angry. Get hugely, impressively muscular or fat. Be loud and obnoxious. Dangerous. Or maybe it was possible to embrace your invisibility and do something with it. Turn it into a covert power. Do something good.

Sweat started to drip off Sam. Her eyes blurred. The last article she had read about Marilyn had described how she'd been banned from Heathrow Airport. But despite that, she not only stayed at the airport, she made it past security and onto several planes. She was relentless, and no one cared. She operated on a stealth bandwidth; she hardly existed.

Something else about the article unnerved Sam. In her current state, what was the difference between the Serial Stowaway and her? Was it simply money?

Oh god. Sam sweated, but along with the sweat, she was also starting to cry. Out of self-pity, really? Moved to tears by her own insecurity, her fears, her precious vulnerability? She was sickened by this sentiment for self. So weak. But! What if she didn't have Matt's money, what would she do or be? She couldn't even get a job as a waitress or as a temp or in retail. She was too old. And it wasn't about being too proud. She wasn't that proud. She would work in a diner or be an aide at a school. Drive a bus, work at the DMV or the post office. She would do those jobs, but even those were unlikely at her age. She could be one of the people who check receipts at

Walmart, the greeters. Walmart hired old people. What would her life be like if that were her job? Who would she be? And still, part of her wanted to see, wanted to know. Seeing the stowaway, the old-lady hobo, it made her curious. Subtract everything and see what was left.

One reason she had stayed in her suburban life for so long also became one reason she had left, another "real" reason: money. She was terrified of how much she needed the money she had. When she was young, being poor was no big deal. She was elastic and even a little scrappy in her twenties. But as she approached and then entered middle age, that changed. She had left Matt, but she kept accepting money from Matt. (And there were always excuses for taking more money. She needed money for a laptop to replace the stolen one, for example.) She was so lucky, so grateful, so wedded to her money. She was dipping her toe into doing without in a totally controlled and safe (cowardly) way: How much do I really need? How little can I get by on? Can I be Dorothy Day with an allowance from an ex? And even if you renounce wealth, does that make you a different kind of poor? Genuine renouncing, not her faux, *Sullivan's Travels* bullshit. (That was the name of the movie. She did remember it.) If she just lived on the money she made and got a second job and even food stamps, would it be the same as someone who struggled that way all their life? She knew for certain that it would not be the same.

Not only did she take money from Matt ("Our money," he kept saying, "Okay, our money," she agreed), but in the second month after she left, she had begun sleeping with him again. But not sleeping, of course, as he didn't spend the night. Just having sex with Matt.

He was due at noon. A nooner on a hot August day. Especially hot for two bodies in her narrow bed. She refused to get an air conditioner. (Not in that beautiful casement window. Also climate change/global extinction. Oh that, he'd said. Another letterpress, elegant flyer card had been tucked into her door frame. WAKE UP: NTE. And this time she had realized what the letters stood for: Near-Term Extinction.)

This would be the fourth time they'd done this. It was becoming a regular thing they did. The first time he came over on his lunch hour on some pretext of signing a paper or bringing her mail. Okay, maybe it wasn't a pretext, he clearly didn't plan or hope for anything. But she could tell by his face that he had wanted to see her. To look at her in person. That particular expression, the one in which he didn't smile and his eyes were open and steady and trained on her, in which he actually saw her, not some replicated, familiar "Sam" he had seen already, that expression gave her an erotic charge. And reminded her of their intensity when they first met in the '90s.

He walked next to her at a NARAL march. He didn't have a sign in his hand, but she did (Sharpie on a flap of flattened cardboard, "women against women against women"), and he told her it was funny. Sam liked him right away. He looked preppy in a button-down shirt, flat-front khakis, and a brown leather belt. Not like the men she usually saw at women's marches. No Jamaican beanie on blond dreads. No buttons about Earth First! or Sandinistas. Okay, he was very handsome. He was beautiful. Should you trust or not trust a man who goes to a reproductive rights march by himself? Should you trust or not trust a beautiful man? It actually didn't begin with her sign. Matthew and Sam began when she caught him looking at her.

The security was very tight; riot-gear police lined the streets, keeping them corralled and disengaged from the city. Inoculated protest was how it felt to her, sort of pointless. She made herself march anyway. Two months earlier, she had attended a protest against the Gulf War. She was stuck behind some "Peace and Liberty Party" activists and their preprinted signs. They were vaguely culty, dishonest, one notch up from the Lyndon LaRouche idiots. She hated protests for this reason, but what else could she do? She didn't want war, or to be complicit with the sickening bellicosity and patriotism of Bush. In the name of, and so on. But even if she knew the reasons she should be there, in the local specifics the marches were awkward and not doing much. So she was glad to let this man walk beside her. Chants were being hurled and repeated, but they were in some odd zone where two sets of chants could be heard, and the rhythms were competing with each other. A person to her left was going with the group ahead, but a person next to her was going with the group chanting from behind. Matthew looked over at her in the midst of it, and they started laughing. Then he noticed her joke sign and suggested they leave the march when it reached Central Park and people pooled and huddled for the speakers. (One harbinger of what would work between them— Matt finding Sam funny, and Sam loving getting a laugh out of Matt.)

"We won't be able to see or hear anything," he said. "Want to get warm somewhere, get a drink?" It was a bright day, but it was bitterly cold.

"Yeah," she said, and she followed him past the police line, across Fifth Avenue, and onto Madison, a world of business, of men and women in suits, much more adult-seeming than the two of them were, protesting and not-working at midday. She pressed the cardboard in half and shoved it into the slot of a garbage bin. He put a hand lightly on the middle of her back and guided her to a basement restaurant. Lunch was finishing, and only a few people were in the dining room. They sat at a little table against the wall. Probably the space had been there forever, if not necessarily in this incarnation. It had that old New York vibe, a quaint devotion to commerce that she found oddly comforting after the march.

"I like seeing businesspeople doing business," she said. Matthew smiled at her but raised his eyebrows. "It means that not everyone is concerned. Not everyone is as spooked as I am. Life is just going on. Nothing to panic about."

He nodded, considering but unconvinced.

"What I mean is that no one is hysterical. No one here is thinking about Saddam Hussein or the unborn fetuses."

"Because they're thinking about money," he said.

"Yeah, that's right. There's something reassuring in that. The adults are still making money. The world isn't ending."

"Or, the world is ending and someone will be figuring out how to make money off it until it ends. Until the very last second." (He was smart. He had leftist political views. He thought she was funny.)

She smiled, nodded. She took a sip of whiskey. Without asking, he had ordered one for her and one for him. The sip warmed and braced her. She was braced and he was beautiful. He liked her, and his attention made her happy. Everything was yet to come, the air electric with possibility. They hadn't even kissed, yet. Such moments were a glorious, unambiguous good, weren't they?

"I wonder," Sam said, "if seeing a man by himself at a march for women's reproductive rights makes him more trustworthy or more suspect than meeting a man on the subway or at a show or in a bar."

"Good question," he said. He sipped his whiskey. "And now because of me, you have left the march, you are drinking whiskey in the afternoon, and you are praising commerce as a stabilizing cultural force."

"It might even get worse from here," she said, touching his arm, surprising herself. He smiled; then the smile gradually faded. He took another sip of whiskey, looked into the glass for a moment, and then looked into her eyes. She didn't look away, and she could feel the heat between them. He leaned in toward her, and she closed her eyes and waited. A soft kiss: his lips pressed against hers. Once, then again. He pulled back, and when she opened her eyes, he was still looking at her. He took her hand and raised it toward his face. He turned her hand over, so that the inside of her wrist was exposed. He lowered his head, closed his eyes, and very gently, very slowly, pressed his lips to her wrist. She felt a quiver of pleasure that radiated from his kiss to her entire body. She trusted him, she realized, and it felt major already, undeniably. She wanted to go back to his apartment or back to her apartment right away. She was falling for him, now, in this moment. She wanted to leap into this new portal of her life.

She took him to her place, because he had a roommate and she didn't. She had a very cheap illegal sublet on Jane Street near Eighth Avenue. She pointed out the Corner Bistro, right next to the door of her building. "They have a great jukebox there," she said. She already planned to take him there, to listen to John Coltrane with him, to eat bar food and talk into the night.

He was slow and assured and attentive in bed. He was focused on her orgasms, which was new for her.

"I have never had anything like this," he said.

"Me either," she said. Meant to be.

Years later, after Ally was born and their connection gradually eroded, Sam would discover that even such attentive sex could become routine, ordinary, just bodies doing their thing in space while your heart still felt lonely. But that very first afternoon, on her bed under her vintage rose satin duvet, they were all there, all in, nothing short of joyful.

This new version of them. Sweat on his back. He smelled good. He felt muscular, strong, familiar. But also strange: him, in her nun bed, in this house, dislocated from their suburban life. It was true that their orgasms were particularly intense. The same old gestures and habits were somehow different. He was on the floor, on his knees, hunched toward her. She sat on the side of the bed, her legs apart, her hips pulled back. He leaned in and flicked his tongue on her—he knew the spot she liked; he put a finger (fingers) inside her and pressed from the inside of her toward his tongue on the outside. This, with the awkward position of her hips, was almost excruciating. A sensation of indirection and direction, an almost feeling that denied a peaking, that elongated her climax, that made her stop everything in her head and her body but those tiny points of pressure until she came with a thunderous, body-shaking relief. Yes, the sex comprised familiar gestures, but scrambled and reconstituted.

She caught her breath, looked at him. He smiled.

"This," she said, with a slight wave of her hand at him.

"Let's not worry about what it is. Let's just see," he said. He sat up. It was too hot for two people in the tiny bed. She got up with the sheet around her. Reached into her purse and pulled out a cigarette. He laughed. She shrugged.

"I will smoke by the window," she said. He watched her crank open the leaded window. She sat in a chair, partly covered by the sheet, and she smoked.

"You look like a girl in a French New Wave film," he said.

She laughed because she was hardly a girl; she was a hard, old woman. When will she catch up to herself?

"What's so funny?"

"Nothing," she said and exhaled. He watched her.

"I like that new hair," he said. Sam brushed her hand through her short hair. It was bristly but soft, fun to touch.

"What about my new body?" She had grown harder since she had left him.

"I like your new body, I like your old body. I like all your bodies."

"Good answer," she said.

They fucked one more time before he went back to work.

It's a thing. Don't worry about what it is.

The next day he called her. "You should get central air," he said. "I'll call Isaac's and get it installed."

"No," she said.

"It won't hurt or change your house. It will just use the heat registers to circulate the cool air."

"I just told you I don't want it," she said, her voice rising, the heat rising. God, it was hot in her house. Or was it a hot flash? Never mind. She didn't have time for this!

"I'll pay for it if—"

"I don't fucking want AC. If you don't like it, you don't have to come here."

"Okay, okay," he said. "Calm down, Sam."

She hated being told to calm down. She moved her phone away from her ear and wiped a trickle of sweat off the side of her face. She switched ears.

"Just. Listen," Sam said. "We can continue to see each other, but I don't want any more support in the form of money or unsolicited advice, okay?"

There was a long pause.

"All right," he said. "Sure."

She hung up. His concession aggravated her. Or maybe it was

that he hesitated before he conceded. She sat sweating, steaming, refusing to get AC even if it might help her sleep better. Perverse. But what she sometimes felt was beyond anger. It was a visceral and volcanic rage that came from some urgent, undeniable place. It could not be reasoned with.

One of Laci's friends, Gina, surprised Sam with a visit to Clara Loomis House. She handed her a photocopied and stapled booklet. It existed in real life, in a tangible, messy form; it wasn't a PDF, endlessly reproducible. It wore the signs of being copied, the photos abstract contrasts and the type obliterated or cut off at some of the edges. The title page: "Heresiarchs," by Xero Zine Collective of Central New York (i.e., Gina).

"Heresiarchs are like arch-heretics. *Her*-e-tics. *Her*-esi-archs. Get it?" Gina said.

Uh, yeah.

"'Heretic' and 'heresiarch' both have 'her' in them," Gina said.

"Yes," Sam said. "I noticed that."

"I put your girl Clara in it. I thought you could carry it in the shop here."

Inside the booklet were bios of women. The photos were not much, but Gina also had drawings, which were clearer and kind of striking. Each page also had a thick block of expository text telling the story of the particular woman's heresy. Sam flipped through it, stopping on Elizabeth Cady Stanton, Mary Ann Shadd Cary, Rosa Parks, Rachel Carson, Mary Daly. Sam nodded.

"Here is what I wanted you to see. What do these women have in common?" Gina asked.

Sam shook her head, smiled.

"When they commit the so-called heresies, they are of a certain age. Middle-aged. Midpoint, mezzogiorno, menopausers, post-period, ya know?"

"I still have periods," Sam said.

"You're close enough."

Sam shrugged.

"Besides, you give off major menopostal energy. Get it? That's 'postal' and 'meno—'"

"I fucking get it."

"People used to call it the change of life. The Change," Gina said.

"How old are you, anyway?"

"Twenty-two."

Sam nodded. "Menopause, you know," Sam said, "has the word 'men' in it." Two can play at this game.

"Exactly!" Gina said. "You get it. I know you do."

"You know, I think a better term for it is 'post-use.'"

Gina's eyes bugged. "That's terrible—"

Sam smiled. She was being ironic, sort of, which apparently was not in Gina's bandwidth.

Gina pressed on: "You know what I think we should call it? 'Suprafertilis.' Beyond fertility. Transcending it, surpassing it."

"I don't think that's going to catch on."

After she left, Sam stacked the zines in the More Information kiosk by the door. Everyone figured Sam was going through some kind of midlife meltdown. Sam decided that she preferred the term "climacteric." The female climacteric, a critical, profound, protean stage in life. She was not menopostal. She was experiencing her climacteric. Okay, but also: she had some postal moments, actually some moments so angry she had scared herself.

That was yet another real reason she had to change her life: her fucking rage. She had always been an emotional person, quick to laugh or cry or scream. This was of a different order. There had been a progression of notable "rage events" that disturbed her, particularly as they continued to escalate. We live in angry times, sure. But what she felt was in a special category.

11

The first time she noticed something, some alteration in her self-arrangement, her disposition (let's call it that), happened last year, after she began lifting weights with Nico. She was working out on her own at the Downtown YMCA in the weight room. This was in the basement, and a real no-frills space, open late into the evening. It had barbells, dumbbells, weight-plate machines, boxing equipment. No Nautilus or ellipticals or anything like that. And it seemed exclusively male. That evening there were three men, all in their twenties or thirties, and Sam. She started by putting two forty-five-pound weights on the leg press sled. One of the young guys—an ugly, paunchy, pockmarked bro—watched her as she lugged another two weights over to the bar, shoved one on each side and clamped them securely, just as she had seen her trainer do. The ugly man continued to watch her. Sam didn't look up. She didn't want to see his amusement, his condescension. She felt a little heat on her neck. Great, she had to be watched, just what she wanted, a goddamned gawker. She decided to ignore him. She lowered herself under the weight, put her feet against the plate, and readied herself to push up so she could release the safety lever.

"Hey—"

She knew he would say something, she just fucking knew it.

"Are you sure you want that much weight?"

What happened then was almost a dissociative state. She was animated by a force within that, unleashed, gathered momentum. Later she would joke to Matt, to her friend Emily, to Ally, and even to her doctor, about how she had gotten a little ragey. But only on the phone to her mother would she admit the truth: how what she'd felt was strange because it was irresistible.

"So I said, 'I know what I'm doing,' but the voice I said it in was not my usual voice, you know?"

"How?" Lily said.

"It was deeper, and it had a real warning in it, like back the fuck up."

"Good," Lily said.

"No," Sam said. "I then went on. I said, 'Why are you talking to me? Because I'm a woman, you think I need your help.' My voice was loud, a kind of snarl in it. The other men looked at me, then looked away. I was breaching some protocol. But I knew I was right, he was wrong. I spat my words: 'Because I'm a woman, you think I don't know what I am doing. Just leave me the fuck alone. If I need your help, I will ask for it.'"

"Oh, Sam," her mother said. Then she said, "Good for you."

"I was unnerved then, and embarrassed, and now doubting the weight I had put on the bar. So I just left, didn't put the weights back like you are supposed to. I was like, fuck this. But I was shaking."

Lily sighed. "You were in the right."

"You know what I realized?"

"What?"

"It wasn't that the thought, my objection to his presumption, was new to me. I realized I have had these feelings my whole life. It's just that in the past I would have thought it instead of spoken it. If I had said anything, I would have couched it in gratitude, I would have—"

"You would have thanked him for his concern, laughed it off."

It was true. Sam was a big laugher. And she knew men found her laugh bright and appealing.

"Yep. I would have vouchsafed his male ego, before gently refusing his help. Worse, I would be flirty or jokey or humble."

"I know it well," her mother said. "But swallowing and accommodating also takes a toll."

This Sam knew was true. But the outsized rage, the body quaver of it, that took a piece out of you as well. The post-rage moment was not good. The sense that proportion was becoming out of reach. And the disorienting feeling that you couldn't recognize yourself. Like an out-of-body experience, a possession of sorts.

The next incident occurred on a plane a few months later. She was flying to LA to see her friend Emily when it happened. Boarding in ridiculous microcategories. All of the them, her fellow passengers, fighting for space. She was there first, her appropriately sized carry-on bag fit easily in the bin space above her seat. She felt relief that she had overcome a stressor (will I get space, will I be okay), but then some latecomer, some late boarder with a giant rolling suitcase (well above, she noted, the size limit for a carry-on) came down the aisle. He lifted his big roller and tried to cram it into the space over her seat. Her space, her seat. It didn't fit. He was holding up the flow. He no doubt felt pressure, the crowd of anxious passengers building behind him. He tried his suitcase wheels in, wheels out. Then sideways, and she could see him pushing things around up there. She stared at his hoodie-clad midsection. He feels entitled to all the space he wants, doesn't he? He just needs more than everyone else. Then she watched as he pulled her bag partly out—he touched her bag, her appropriately and previously situated, modest bag. She inhaled, pushed out an "Uh," in a warning, I-see-you huff, which he ignored, and then she watched him shove—ram, really—her bag into the corner to make room for his suitcase.

"Watch my bag!" she finally screeched. "It has my laptop, please don't crush it!" Her face was hot. She was the only one speaking. People did this boarding and bag storing while grunting, not looking at one another. The misery of forced adherence to unpleasant procedure radiated off everyone, but no one spoke. He reached up on his toes and gave his suitcase one more shove. His bag was in, he was free to sit. She got up suddenly, gave his hoodie—not his face—a glare. "My bag," she said, defeated already. She stood in front of him, peered into the bin. She saw her bag squished in the corner, trapped by the tension of his bag against hers. She pushed at his bag—*see how it feels*—but no give. Through her bag's fabric, she could feel that her laptop was jammed under the tension of his hard-wheeled suitcase pressing on her property, no doubt compromising her laptop's structural integrity. But the hoodie guy had moved on, sat down in a seat. The crowd was now behind her, milling with anxious, impatient energy. "My bag needs room too!" she huffed to no one, really, as she pushed it until her laptop fell a bit within the fabric, at least loosened from the bin pressure. She was indignant. She was entitled to her ticket's 1.2 cubic feet of airplane space. She sat back down, feeling a blotchiness rise on her cheeks and then settle, making her hot. No one else had uttered a complaint, or even a sound.

She was right, righteous. Her bag was small. She had followed the rules, which were clearly delineated in the carry-on sizing measure at the gate. True, she did have the advantage of being first. Guarding her advantage felt awful, her sorry purchase on getting ahead, getting in. She knew she protected these small things jealously, ridiculously, but she could not help it. She wanted to scream. She was right, but the post-snarl feeling was shameful, humiliating. She had become this snarly, awful person. A person who snapped at fellow passengers if they dared to touch her property in the overhead bin. What was worse was that afterward, she compensated by acting super friendly to everyone: flight attendant, fellow seatmate, even tried to catch the eye of hoodie guy to smile at him. She forced her unctuous smiles and nods, pretended sanity, stability, calm. She fooled no one. "Thank you so much!" she said to the attendant when he gave her a club soda with a mildewed lemon wedge.

She knew how she looked: bitchy, old, bitter. Unfit for the pressures of the world. She seemed that way because she was that way. Unfit, unforgiving. Inflexible. How had she come to be like this? So impatient, so touchy? ("Touchy" was the exact right word for how she was, how she felt. Do not touch me or my shit.)

But even that wasn't the worst of it; she had to admit that lately there were spaces where the unleashing of the snarl brought no shame, even approached what she might describe as bouts of genuine pleasure. When she was driving, for example.

When she was in her car, in her closed, private but windowed space, when she drove, she kept up a steady stream of invective, of curses, hurled at other drivers. At a four-way stop, she waited her turn but others didn't. Some people would barely slow as they approached a stop sign, forcing her to stop abruptly to accommodate their purloined right of way. "Goddamn you!" she shouted. "You fucking asshole," she spat and worse. All the curses flew out of her mouth and didn't stop. At the intersection of 690 and I-81, in an insane bit of highway engineering (designed to sabotage the very idea of merging, it seemed), the on-ramp lane merged quickly into the right slow lane and disappeared. One must merge or crash. And yet the driver alongside of her refused to yield, and she almost ran out of merge lane. "Are you fucking kidding me?" she bellowed, honking. She swerved, and finally got into the lane. "You have to yield, you selfish motherfucker!" Her body was hot, and she felt the special toxic energy of rage spill into her blood. She twitched with it, her heart beating faster. Her sympathetic nervous system jacked her body into a synaptic frenzy. Cortisol, blood pressure, adrenaline: she felt the rush of it wave through her. And there was nothing like shame in her, anywhere.

They started happening all the time, these private moments of road rage. A sign warned of a lane closing ahead. Two lanes must merge into one. The cars from each lane were meant to take turns. The zipper merge—they showed you movies about it in driver's ed. And yet, a dude (invariably—almost certainly—a man) decided to zip up the shoulder and cut the line. He drove until he passed all the cars and then nosed into the merge. She even yelled through her window, "Zipper merge, you line-cutting piece of shit!" Another time: "You must be so important, so much more important than everyone else!" These men—once she had one try to merge in front of her after flagrant line cutting. He wouldn't even make eye contact. He just presumed she would be bullied into letting him in. "No fucking way," she said, keeping the nose of her car right on the back bumper of the car in front of her. "No way do you get in front of me after you cheated!" Civilization depended on it, her resistance to these cutters.

Then one snowy, shitty January day, she truly crossed a line. She went to park her car in a full lot and she saw another car (a truck, actually, a giant, gleaming truck) parked on the line between two spaces. This filled her with a profound and pathetic rage. It wasn't a mistake, this person had deliberately parked on top of a line and took up two spaces. Probably so that no one would ding his paint job. So no one would get their car doors anywhere near his. So hey, fuck everyone else. She slowed her car, stared in astonishment at the arrogance. Or maybe he just hadn't bothered to check the lines, which was also selfish and entitled. And now others must drive around and around, looking for a space. She should have swallowed her rage, let it go. That was what normal people did. Normal, functional people. Instead, she stopped her car. She got out and moved toward his truck. She had her key in her hand. She thought, You asshole, you awful asshole, and she held the key out— just an inch or two by her hip as she walked the length of his truck. She allowed—she pressed—the key into the side of the inappropriately parked vehicle. She felt it dig in and scrape as she walked. At the time she was unconcerned that this was serious vandalism, an actual crime. Instead, she felt a rush of pleasure and a wonderful relief. The relief of justice finally done. She thought, I am a parking vigilante! *And she laughed out loud.* She didn't even look around to see if she'd been seen. She imagined him discovering the scratch, imagined his impotent anger. For a moment, it delighted her; it filled her with light.

But. What if he was walking toward his truck right now? A person with a truck like this could shoot her; keying was the kind of thing people got beat up for. She rushed to get back into her car. He's lucky I didn't ram him, she thought. And she threw the car into gear and hurried off to park far, far away. She was glad, but now she was no longer satisfied. She was angry still. More angry. Her action multiplied and squared her rage, which made no sense, how no satisfaction lasted. She had parked, it was over, whatever it was. She knew she had no right to be angry, no reason. But this was the time for this feeling of no reason. Rage was in the air, stupid, impulsive. The age of no-reason.

Boundaries were dissolving. She could do things not for the sake of mere transgression or aggression, but because of a certain porosity, a flimsy sense of her self-limits, maybe. For example, if there was a line for the women's room (always), why not just use the men's room? She felt impulse, and then the barest repression of impulse.

The keying, though, that was the line, a clear indicator. She confessed that to no one—not even her mother, her defender. Sam could not behave any longer. You put it all in motion, and then you watched as your life fell apart.

"I need to postpone your visit." Her mother called while Matt was getting dressed. Sam put her finger to her mouth to shush him, but she planned to tell her mother that she was "seeing" Matt again when she visited her. (She knew her mother would approve, which both irritated and pleased Sam.)

"Postpone again? I haven't seen you in so long. Why?"

"I just have some appointments I needed to book, and this week doesn't work any longer."

Sam said nothing. Lily kept putting her off. "Okay, of course. I'll come next weekend instead."

"Ally might come next weekend."

"Really?" Sam's voice caught.

"I know it's hard. She's driving herself."

"It's good, I want her to see you."

"I love you, sweetheart. Please don't worry."

"I love you too."

"Let's talk after I see Ally."

They hung up.

"Is Lily okay?" Matt asked. He was very fond of Sam's mother, and she of him. And then, before she could respond, Sam started to cry. "Oh no, Sam."

"She's fine," Sam finally said, but that was a lie. Lily was not fine. "I just miss her." Matt sat next to her and rubbed her back.

"I know," he said. "I knew it."

Matt thought he had figured it all out, figured her out. But his sympathy just felt like another demand on her.

"You should go," she said.

"Okay," he said.

Matt's first guess had been wrong. The catalyst for leaving him wasn't the election. Honestly, the world had felt broken and unjust her entire life. This was just a very crude example. An appalling and crude example. It was not the election. It wasn't even the house, she realized. But she had to admit that Matt's last guess was closer. Of all the reasons, of all the things making her lose her mind, if it were any one thing, it had to be Lily, her mother.

On a clear cold day back in February, she had gone for an overnight visit with Lily. Her mother lived by herself near a rural hamlet in the Mohawk Valley, one hour and forty-five minutes east of Syracuse. Ten years ago, after Sam's father had died, Lily sold their apartment in the city and bought this pretty little house in the country.

Sam loved her mother's place. It was an eccentric, rustic hippie modernist dwelling built in the seventies by a talented carpenter weirdo. It was small, one story, made of glass and reclaimed wood, angled into a hill with a view of the farm-quilted valley. It had a wall of double-paned windows facing south for passive solar heat, and the kitchen and living area were one open room. The centerpiece was a large enamel wood-burning stove. It truly was cozy, with the winter miracle of light and warmth, probably because of the radiant heat under the concrete, rug-covered floors. Her mother lived modestly, but the rugs were extravagant. Other than the rugs, there were bookshelves on the non-windowed walls, and a painting by one of her mother's ex-boyfriends. (Her mother was one of those women whose old boyfriends continued to love for their entire lives.) The couch was an old, heavy sectional. The kitchen was functional, with a big gas stove and a large vintage fruitwood table, which doubled as a desk. It was the perfect house to live in on your own. Sam felt its serenity, how you would wake up and feel okay there. In the summer, the house was surrounded by a garden that Lily tended with devotion. She had raised beds for vegetables; she had flowers that bloomed in succession all season long. She was no hermit, though. She saw friends in town; she drove a small SUV. She had a television, a nearby library, and a strong internet connection. She was alone, but not lonely. ("Besides, I have Raisin for company." Raisin was her inexplicably named nine-year-old German shepherd, a serious dog with a propensity for thoughtfully resting his chin on your knee. Sam admitted that Raisin was adorable and hypercompanionable, like an advertisement for dog love. He even cocked his head and listened when her mother spoke.) It was exactly what Lily wanted. And really, she seemed happier than she had in the city, although Sam wished she were closer to Syracuse.

Every month or so, Sam came to visit and stayed overnight. The house notably had no guest room (draw your own conclusions), but one part of the sectional couch converted to a comfortable bed. When she used to visit with Ally, they would camp out on the sectional and have a slumber party. When Ally was very young and her mother still lived in the city, they would all climb into bed with Lily. The three of them, whispering in the dark, giggling. Sam would get very goofy in these moments. Spending time with her mother and her daughter. Sometimes she would feel so happy she would do funny dances for them, perform scenes from movies, do pratfalls. Sam had a bad voice, Sam was a bad dancer, but she liked being foolish. She had an inner clown. She often broke into made-up songs for her daughter's amusement. And a few adults: her mother, and Matt when he was with Ally. This was Sam's secret weapon, goofiness, which was a form of trust, really. She remembered how it felt to get Ally to exclaim, "You are so silly, Mama!" All of them laughing.

One of the last nights they spent together in her parents' city apartment, Ally, Lily, and Sam were all sleeping in her mother's king bed. This made six-year-old Ally giddy rather than sleepy. They were "reading," but Sam and Ally kept whispering, and then Ally would ask a ridiculous question ("Grandma, why do cats always land on their feet?") and Lily would barely look up from her book, shaking her head in exaggerated exasperation, which made Sam and Ally erupt into volcanic laughter. Finally they all quieted down. Sam got up to go to the bathroom, and on the way back she began to reenact a commercial that had popped into her head from her childhood. It was for bubble bath.

Apropos of nothing, she sang the stupid, stupid jingle, burned into her childhood brain forever:

"I can bring home the bacon," Sam sang, vamping around the bedroom with an imaginary briefcase, which she threw.

"Fry it up in a pan," she sang, sexily frying something with one hand, the other on a jutty hip.

Lily was laughing, and this made Ally hysterical.

"And never, never, never let you forget that you're a man, cause I'm a woooo-man, Enjoli."

Then Sam stopped, laughing, and fell on the bed, breathless.

"What on earth made you think of that?" Lily said.

"Do you remember it?"

"Yes, oh yes," her mother said.

"What an effed-up commercial. Appealing to the modern working woman."

"What was it?" Ally said. So Sam found the commercial on YouTube, and they watched it. It was exactly as she remembered, as silly as she remembered.

It was the greatest thing, being with them in the bed, making them both laugh. She remembered the moment so well, and part of what made it memorable was how easy it was. A natural ease and enjoyment they all had with one another. At the time, the pleasure of their togetherness, their love, felt endless. She longed to go back to that moment, to relive it but, really, to stay in it forever.

Now everything rushed forward so fast she could hardly keep up. She didn't want what lay ahead, the future, for the first time in her life. She wanted that moment, and all the ordinary moments before and after it. She could conjure how the days surrounding that sleepover went, the simple routine of that time in their lives. All of it felt better than now.

It was in the weeks preceding her February visit that Lily had begun her odd distance toward Sam, putting her off when Sam tried to make a plan. Her mother used to visit them too—to see one of Ally's concerts or soccer games. And holidays, of course. But Lily had a bad knee, and the long drive was becoming too much for her. For the previous six months, Sam had come to her. But the last two times Sam had said she wanted to come, her mother had some excuse. Usually a doctor's appointment.

"What's wrong?"

"Nothing, routine, at a certain age there is a routine of tests and visits."

Then Lily couldn't have a visit because she had her book group. Or she had her local resistance meeting, which was pretty much the same group as the book club. Also, Lily was too tired for a visit right now.

"You would tell me if something was wrong, wouldn't you?"

"Yes, I would. I'm just tired. Please don't worry."

Sam believed that if she brought up her fears to people, spoke them aloud, the fears would lose their valence, their hold over her. Or maybe it was more selfish than that. She wanted her mother to reassure her, tell her everything would be fine, when of course nothing would be fine and there was no reassurance to be had. Her beautiful mother was almost eighty.

Finally, Lily had agreed to a visit. Sam arrived in the late afternoon. She took a hot bath in her mother's extra-large tub while her mother made them a thick soup with vegetables from her garden she had frozen from the summer and some "fantastic sausages" she'd gotten from the farmers' market. Sam smelled the garlic and spices, closed her eyes, and leaned back against the porcelain. She

wished she could have brought Ally, but Ally had so much school-
work. Next time.

They ate dinner, and Sam caught Lily up on all things Ally. Sam
also told her amusing, slightly mean stories about people who vis-
ited Clara Loomis House and more than slightly mean descriptions
of the women in the local resistance meeting Sam had attended.
They rehashed takes on the inauguration, the Women's March,
stuff they had already discussed by phone. They were both tired
and went to bed early. The morning was always the time for them
to really talk, the time they relaxed. Maybe it was because all the
chatter and updates had been burned through the night before.
Or maybe it was something about sleeping in the same house that
made Sam relax like nothing else.

Sam woke to the smell of the coffee her mother had already
made. She gazed sleepily at her mother sitting at the table and tak-
ing a sip from her mug. Beyond her mother was the valley and the
horizon. Clouds hung low, horizontal and strewn, the dawn pinch-
ing their edges pink and gold.

Lily was not looking at the view or at Sam. She was writing in a
notebook. She had written two books: one of personal essays and
one novel. She claimed to be working on a third book, a collection
of stories, but it had been fifteen years since her last book, so who
knew? Her mother looked highly focused, and Sam hesitated to
interrupt her. Sam closed her eyes and huddled in the warmth of
the blanket. The blanket smelled like her mother's lavender laun-
dry soap. Raisin slept at Sam's feet.

Sam couldn't fall back asleep, but she stayed quiet and continued
to watch her mother. Lily looked frail, her face troubled. But she
was thinking and writing. After a few minutes of this, she looked
over at Sam and smiled.

"Good morning! Did I wake you, sweetheart?"

"No," Sam said. "I get up super early these days." She sat up on
the couch, pulled on the ugly but warm Acorn slipper socks and
the thick flannel robe her mother kept at her house just for her.
She went over to the wood-burning stove and warmed her hands.

Her mother handed her a cup of strong black coffee. It was the best moment of the day, of any day. The coffee, the warmth and smell of the stove, the tending from Lily. Sam tried not to taint her pleasure with morbid thoughts, but they were always at the edge of her mind these days. It was as if she had a low drumming under her at all times. It supplied an elegiac backbeat to nearly every joy. Was this what it meant to get older? That the little time left would never be carefree? Would morbidity increase with each year?

(Once she had asked her mother about how she conceived of the future now that she was in her late seventies.

"You mean how do I think about the future when I probably don't have much of one?"

"No," Sam said, but that was what she meant.

"Honestly, I don't think about it," Lily had said.

Sam had hoped for some wisdom, but maybe that was wisdom.)

Her mother's illness, whatever disease or malady it was that she withheld from Sam, did not seem real until later, after Sam had left her mother and was driving home. Sometimes, in the middle of discussions, Sam found a fleeting refuge. It was out of the rush to fill the air with language, to ask and to speak and to listen. It was not just that the words could get Sam what she wanted if she kept using them. She believed that if she asked the right question, there was hope for connection or a transaction of some kind. What is wrong? Followed by the answer, even the shitty dodge of "I don't want to talk about it" was still something, a point made and understood between them. They were alive and together in the talk; it buzzed the air and it was the primary messy stuff of life. And it would supply language to memory, give it an extra reality shaped and defined by words.

But in the car, during the long drive home on the tedious interstate, even if she listened to the radio or a podcast, and especially if she listened to music, Sam found the space for her thoughts beyond her own noise. It wasn't that she needed the world to be silent; it was that she needed her own silence. The quiet was a matter of her not speaking and grabbing at her mother with questions and statements and pleadings. When Sam was not listening or speaking, she could think. Not ruminate—that belonged to the middle of the night, full of her masticated hysterics. This thinking was something soberer and further-reaching, often sparked not by a reflection of her own fears, but by being in the world and not trying to get or do anything except a mundane task, like driving across the state.

She was listening to a health podcast she subscribed to. Someone talking about genes. Epigenetics, which seemed to mean how you can shape gene expression, a sort of self-help dressed up as "hacking your genetics" so you too can avoid these diseases. And "snips," whatever defect that was, related to Alzheimer's, Parkinson's, cancer, heart disease, diabetes. As if taking choline and getting deep sleep would overcome your genetic destiny. The discussion turned to how the interviewee, a PhD of some kind who also deadlifted three times her body weight in the gym, suggested one should grow broccoli sprouts so one could consume high-potency sulforaphane, which was going to shut off some flawed gene signal. What a thing to think: your body was just in need of some tweak, some little actionable intervention, and it would be perfect, whole, untainted with error or flaw. All such desire was, of course, about erasing our destiny, fixing the fatal flaw contained in the code, escaping the glitch that would lead to our demise. Overwriting your code. Reprogramming. But maybe the code was perfect, built (if not designed) to destruct in its own unique and unforeseen way, as much in our control as Atropos cutting your mortal thread with her scissors, no matter how many sprouts and pure encapsulated supplements you left as offerings at her feet.

Her mother was sick.

Her mother would die, if not right away, then soon. Sam had tried to make herself think about it. She felt she should come to terms with it (and "come to terms" was funny, and wrong, as if you had some negotiating to do, as if *terms* could be worked out: *here are my terms on how I will let my mom—*), but it was impossible, because the fact of her mother's end didn't feel real to Sam. When she was with her, talking to her, arguing with her, watching her pour coffee into her white mug and then add a tab of sweetener and then stir it with a spoon, she wondered, how could this not go on forever? The ordinary details of her mother and of their relationship felt immutable and endless as the earth itself, because Lily had always been in Sam's world. But the signs were there, always, that time was running out and that the stasis was an illusion. Her mother's hands—the very hand that stirred the coffee was now thin and knuckled and ugly. Her once-perfect skin mottled, her veins exposed, her body clearly stiffer, less able. But how can we notice such things when they happen so slowly, so gradually? And why should we? We are designed to not notice, to accept and stay with the moment. If Sam grabbed her mother's hands and wept over them, what difference would it make except to ruin one of the comfortable times left, one of the easy times in which her mother would tell a story about Raisin or they would talk about the garden or, probably their favorite subject, the details of Ally's maturing, as Ally was the embodiment of their connection, but not merely that. Ally was genetics plus magic. She took their stuff, whatever random bits of genetic code ("snips" the woman on the podcast said, which were actually, it was explained, "SNPs," which stood for "single-nucleotide polymorphisms") she inherited and whatever bits of behavior she witnessed and learned from, and Ally became someone neither Sam nor Lily had ever known before—a candescent, radiant new being, always as startling to them as a newborn, even as they attended every aspect of her emerging mature personhood. Thank god for Ally.

"I told her I would give her the money for her YAD trip this summer," her mother had mentioned over breakfast.

"That's very generous of you." At this point the visit had been like all the others. Sam sat at the table across from her mother. There were berries that Lily had grown last summer and frozen, and she served them with homemade vanilla scones.

Everything was perfect. But then Lily put down her cup and Sam knew. Sam knew before Lily even spoke.

"I need to tell you about something, and I need you to listen and not overreact," Lily said.

"Okay, what?" Sam said, her voice already too loud and urgent. "What?"

"There's a thing that happens when you get to my age. You become aware, whether you want to or not, that this is your last chapter. This"—Lily gestured around the room and toward the window—"this is your last place, the last place you will live. Only recently did it dawn on me all the things I will never do: I will never have an apartment in Rome. I will never have another lover. I will never radically change my life again."

"How do you know that? People live a lot longer than eighty these days."

Lily looked down and smiled. Nodded.

"The older you get, these considerations get smaller and closer, until one day you realize you won't see another summer, and then finally, I suppose, another morning."

"Ma, what are you talking about?"

"My doctor noticed something, and it seems I'm not well."

"What do you mean, 'something'? What exactly is wrong?"

"Listen to me, Sam. I don't want to talk about it. I don't want you looking up stuff on the internet or searching for clinics or experimental trials."

"On my god. You have cancer, what kind? Where? What is the prognosis?" Sam could feel the tears coming. Pathetic, but it just happened. She wiped her eyes and pointed at the scone on her mother's plate. "You shouldn't eat sugar, Ma!"

"This is what I mean. I don't want advice or help."

"You have to let me help. I have to talk to your doctor."

"No, I don't want help. That is exactly what I don't want."

Sam was sobbing now, getting angry but still trying to convince her mother of something.

"If it's serious, you need help. You can't do this by yourself. Whatever you need, I will do it. I'll move here and help you," Sam said.

"Sam," her mother said calmly.

"What?"

"Move here and I will kill you."

Sam laughed, but also continued to cry. She looked at her mother through her tears. Sam shook her head, shocked at her mother's resistance. Sam leaned over and put her head on the table, weary. Then put her hands over her head as if the ceiling might fall on it.

"I will not be a reason for you to upend your life." Lily put her hand on Sam's hand, turned it over, pressed it. Sam looked up at her.

"Want to help me? I need you to be strong. Your falling apart makes things worse."

Sam sat up, took a deep breath, collected herself.

"But why can't you tell me? I can help you with whatever it is on your terms. I need to make sure you get what you need."

"I don't want that, don't you see? I want things to be normal. I want you to call me and tell me about your life. I want to hear about Ally, and I want to talk politics. I want to garden and walk my dog. I want my life as it is and as it has been, until I die."

Sam nodded, her eyes sore and red and swollen. Her mother smiled at her.

"Thank you," she said.

Sam took another deep breath and sighed. She felt a heavy calm descend, something that felt chemical rather than emotional, the tears releasing or refusing to reuptake a neurotransmitter deep in her brain.

"I promise you that I'll fill you in once I've made my decisions. My plans."

Her mother clutched her mug and gazed at Sam with a stoic, placid expression. Not happy, but in control of her feelings. "I know this is hard." She had clearly thought this through and allowed Sam to visit only when she had it all worked out. "But you need to prepare yourself for what comes next, Sammy."

"No," Sam whispered. "No. You can't just give in."

"I am not giving in. I'm being honest with myself, with you.

It's no secret that this is how it goes. What did you think would happen?"

Sam wanted to throw something across the room, smash something. She was not prepared! Not now, not yet.

"But I still need you," Sam said.

"I know, and I am still here," Lily said.

In the car, with the podcast woman droning on about adaptogens, she parsed her mother's words, looking for clues. She should have asked how long. Her mother was stubborn. Sam conceded that her own stubbornness was just as intractable. What was worse was that Sam felt so childish and selfish. Her mother was sick, and, Sam realized, she expected her mother to comfort her about it. Really, Sam was pathetic. Useless. No wonder her mother wouldn't involve her. She couldn't handle it.

When Sam arrived back at her family's house in the suburb, both Matt and Ally were out. Both of them had texted that they wouldn't make it home in time for dinner. Matt, whatever. But Ally—Sam wanted to see Ally, just behold her was all. Ally was supposed to be the buttress against losing her mother, the counter. Sam sat at her kitchen table and ate some water crackers with slices of salty hard cheese and sipped on a glass of red wine. Her dinner.

She just needed to be in the same room with Ally. Sam had fucked it all up. She had stupidly timed her motherhood so that Ally would be leaving for college right when Sam lost her mother. Sam gasped at that sudden, naked thought. She was losing, was in the process of losing, her mother. She cried again, and she did not like the feeling of drinking wine while crying. Even for her, even all alone, especially all alone, it created a distracting performance of self-pity. Pull it together. She couldn't think about Lily, not yet. Sam needed to do something, but at that point it wasn't clear what. There were, however, some things she didn't do.

Sam did not tell Matt that her mother was ill. She did not tell

Ally either. When Sam called her mother the next day, she did not bring it up.

Several weeks later, she found the house. The broken, needy house on Highland. The house buy was an act of instinct. What Sam wanted was not a safe house or an escape or even a sanctuary but, rather, a place to be alone, to do some time, to change herself. Whatever she was—the sum total of fifty-three years on the earth in this body—was insufficient to what would come next. She clearly had to change.

The only certainty she felt was that she had done everything wrong. Her accommodations to the future were insufficient. Foolish, shallow, meaningless.

Alone now in her new house, she coped by smoking a cigarette. Sam was bereft, bereaved. Ahead of time. Pre-bereaved. She should explain her mother's illness to Ally. Then Ally would understand why Sam had to upend her life, why Sam was so unhappy. But she didn't want Ally to know about Lily. Ally was so close to Lily; Sam wanted to protect her from this terrible grief. Ally needed to leave, not be bound to her mother and grandmother. Even in her loneliness, Sam tried to figure out what she could do for Ally.

She sent her daily text. Nothing still. Would this chill go on forever?

Sam knew that her love for Ally distorted her view of her. Sam was always shocked when the world didn't fall at Ally's feet. Sometimes Sam wondered—if Ally were another person's daughter, would I even like her? But she couldn't actually imagine that. It was impossible for her brain to have perspective on her girl; it was like not being able to smell your own breath. The ferocity of Sam's attachment was what made Sam feel like herself.

From the moment Ally was born, pushed out of Sam's body (nothing could be more common than motherhood and yet nothing about it could ever be banal), Ally became Sam's sun, Sam's primary concern. She felt a directedness and a purpose and a meaning she had never experienced before. Another way of putting it: it was the least fake feeling she had ever had, the most earnest. Did all mothers feel this way? Did fathers feel this way? No, yes, doesn't matter. On some level, it was Ally and then there was every other human on the earth.

At first it was physical. The need to hold and feed and comfort. That was the best part of being a mother, answering that need. It was so simple and complete. Sure, there were times Sam longed for sleep, times she felt positively enslaved, but all it took was the head on her chest, the hand clutching at her, Sam's own hand supporting the plump, perfect back. Touching her was like taking a drug. The back, the foot, the leg, the little arm; the lips, the ears, the toes, the perfect tiny nose. The thighs, the dimpled knees, the lines of fat at the wrists, the tapered, padded fingers with the tiny oval of a nail. Look at her. The eyes, well, they were the same always, the same today. Large, heavy lidded, dark brown, wide-set, extravagantly lashed. What a beauty she was and is. Even at the height of her adolescent awkwardness, Sam had found her profoundly, significantly beautiful. Was it "true"? Did others see her the way Sam did? It didn't matter. What mattered was that Sam had felt this abiding love for sixteen years, and it was the best thing she had ever felt or would ever feel. And the twinge came every day when she remembered that Ally wasn't talking to her because of what Sam had done. Sam had left. The twinge was there when she texted her each night. Her pretend-cheerful unanswered texts. Even estranged, this love was the most real thing Sam felt, the feeling that gave the lie to all the other things people called love. She was immoderate, overwrought, many stupid things. But she was constant, and it took no effort at all. Maybe that was the thing about love and constancy. When you really felt it, there wasn't any going back. It wasn't maintained or cultivated, like a rare flower. It didn't need work. It was or it wasn't.

Did Lily feel this way about her? Of course. Yet her mother was pushing Sam back, avoiding her.

And did Ally feel about Sam what Sam felt about her own mother? A skyward, air-sucking entirety? As if her mother were not a person, but a part of her life-support system. A person whose existence enabled yours. A totalizing—and therefore not quite visible—force. Sam didn't feel any more purpose toward Lily than she did the sun or the earth itself. So when she had walked into Lily's house and seen, at once, that her mother was hunched, small, fragile—dying, really—she had put it as far out of her mind and heart as she could. She'd gulped down a glass of wine and tried to not notice anything. No cruel inventory of Lily's wrinkles, her forgetfulness, her blurring features. The beauty she had always possessed was there, but it was blurring, melting . . . leaving.

After she had texted Ally, Sam sat alone at her table and ate wedges of apple and some salted almonds. Then she moved to her window and smoked another herbal cigarette.

For the past few weeks, Sam worked extra days because she needed more hours and she had agreed to update all the displays. Sam had invited Laci and MH to meet her at Loomis House and maybe go out for a drink or a bite after. She was closing up when Laci walked in with a young woman Sam had not seen before. The young woman looked around Loomis House with pursed, skeptical lips.

"Is MH coming?" Sam asked. MH had not returned her text.

"I don't think so," Laci said.

"Oh," Sam said.

Laci and the girl exchanged a look.

"This is Tugg," Laci said. "This is Sam. She works here."

Tugg opened her eyes super wide and put her hands to her face, emulating the Screaming in Fear emoji.

"Oh for god's sake," Sam said, but she was over defending Clara's life. Recently someone had edited the Clara Loomis Wikipedia page and added a "Eugenics Controversy" section, verified and footnoted. Sam couldn't bring herself to even read it. And today, when she did the spiel about Loomis's sickly favorite daughter, someone said she had read on Wikipedia that Clara's oldest daughter was actually the child of John Humphrey Noyes, the spiritual leader of the Oneida Community and that "we really need to address the whole sex cult/abuse issue."

Sam wanted to show MH her new project. She was making a curios cabinet. A cabinet of Syracuse curiosities, the way people used to collect and display in the nineteenth century. She was having a letterpress pamphlet printed too, facts about historical Syracuse that she had compiled. Something to give people beyond Clara's life, her compromised life. A context for her life.

"Where is MH?" Sam asked. "Have you talked to her?"

"I haven't," Laci said.

"MH is canceled," Tugg said.

Laci shook her head. "We are not canceling her. More like deplatforming her," she said. "Too much power and influence, and she abused it. She is being contained, so she can't do any more harm."

"What? What happened? What did she do?" Sam said.

"There's a petition on Medium," Laci said.

Sam's phone pinged.

"I just AirDropped you the link," said Tugg.

Sam looked down at her phone and tapped. She scrolled and read. "It doesn't say what she did."

"Believe women," Tugg said.

"But MH is a woman too," Sam said.

Tugg scowled at her.

"Believe victims. Multiple men came forward too," Laci said.

Sam looked at her watch and locked the curio cabinet. She gestured them toward the door as she shut the lights. They waited for her outside.

Laci told her it was bad, but she couldn't reveal the details. Just take her word for it. Take the victims' word for it.

"Who are the victims?" Sam asked. "How many are there?"

"I'm not at liberty to say," Laci said.

Who was "at liberty"? Sam believed them, of course, but what if their idea of a firing offense was different from her idea of one?

"She's my friend. I can't cut her off without knowing what she did."

"Let me make it simple for you. She is an error message. She is malware. Do not open the attachment. Delete. Put in trash. Empty trash," Tugg said. "And sign the petition."

"Yes," Laci said. "Sign the petition."

"Then signal boost the petition," Tugg said.

"How can I condemn what I don't know," Sam said.

"Look, you have to trust that we have heard it and it is predatory. We don't want to traumatize the victims any more by making them speak, making them targets," Laci said.

Sam nodded. Speaking up did make people targets. Sam knew this was true. Accused people lashed out in manipulative ways. But MH?

"Who is 'we'? And what happens if I don't sign it? I mean, what is the petition for, exactly?" Sam said.

"So we know who is on what side. Where you stand. It is not okay to be on the sidelines, talking of complexity and hem-hawing. This is Gen X bullshit," Laci said.

Laci was approximately the same age as Sam. So also "Gen X," for what it was worth, which wasn't much.

"There is nothing miraculous about making things more complicated," Laci said. "Overly complicated. You think it makes you virtuous, honest, compassionate. But it just makes you weak and unable to take a stand."

"No," Sam said. Or not just that, but she didn't say it aloud.

"Maybe all your nuances, your 'on the other hand's, are just a way of letting yourself off the hook."

"But—I have to talk to MH first."

Laci shook her head.

"Don't be fooled by her charisma. MH is full of shit. Do you know she has a house on the lake in Skaneateles?"

"Really?"

"Yeah, the hobo with the five-hundred-dollar motorcycle boots. Don't pretend you haven't noticed. All of it is lies."

"But you're close friends. You introduced her to me."

Laci nodded. "Which shows you, doesn't it, how fucked up this is."

"Let me think about the petition."

Laci frowned at her.

Sam sighed. She glanced at Tugg, who was swiping and tapping her screen. "I'm sorry," Sam said. "I have to go home. I hardly slept last night. I'm wrecked."

"All right," Laci said. "I'll talk to you tomorrow."

"Okay, yeah."

When Sam got in her car, she texted MH.

Is it true?

Three moving "typing" dots for almost a minute. Then:

Nah.
No.

Sam didn't know what *it* was, even if it seemed that MH knew.
All she knew was that MH was guilty of something, and everyone
was shunning her. When she got home, she decided to investigate.
She reread the petition, looked at the signees. Then she signed into
Facebook for the first time in months. Twitter too. Laci/Earl had
posted links to the Medium petition. There were lots of cryptic
comments, some defending MH but most condemning. No specif-
ics. (As Sam dug in, she saw that even as she had done what Laci and
MH said to do and gone "off-book, off-grid," as she had opted out
and unplugged, Laci and MH had never stopped posting and com-
menting and tweeting.) MH's last statement was from a day ago,
a cross-posted tweet/status update/Instagram share: "I'm turning
this down for a while. DM me if you want to talk IRL." Right next
to her crucified Saint Wilgefortis profile picture. Comments on
her Facebook wall had been disabled.

Sam was not surprised when neither MH nor Laci showed up at
open mic at the Smiley Face the next night. But she decided to go
through with it anyway.

She would discharge some of her anxieties. Inner life would spill
out and become outer life. Almost a public confession, it would be
out of her body and into the air.

"I promise you—after you stand up at that place, after you
endure their contempt, you will still be there, standing. You will
feel invincible," MH had claimed. But that turned out not to be
true. It was a disaster.

"I am bad at being a person sometimes," Sam whispered, gripping the microphone with both hands. Her eyes were closed, and her mouth was nearly kissing the mic. Titters, barely, from the sparse audience. A bright surge of electricity rose up her body. Her shoulders twitched; she focused. Sam opened her eyes and looked out. "I am," she said, almost angry. She looked out at the eleven p.m. yawning open-mic crowd. A chain stand-up joint in a mall in Central New York. What did she expect? "But I guess no one cares about being a bad person," she said. "Okay. I'm a bad mother. Yeah, you should be good at that, you shouldn't fuck that up." One single nervous giggle from a woman to her left. She didn't care. She didn't want them to laugh. They wanted comedy, and she was way past wanting to give people what they wanted.

"I don't mean bad like neglect, no, the opposite really. And I don't mean abuse, but that's a tricky word, right? I mean we can find someone's behavior abusive, and that person might not see it that way, or it might not have *seemed* that way at the time, you know?" Now there was no laughter, even some head shaking. "It's complicated. We don't know, actually, or we don't want to know." Good, she thought. Good. "Maybe I am a bad mother." An audible groan. "I am a bad mother. I am. Isn't repetition a bitch? It's so boring, like give us something: a joke. Or if not a joke, a story. If not a joke or a story, some self-deprecating comment and/or a charmingly apologetic admission, amirite?" A male voice, barely audible, to her right. Hard to see with the light in her face. She turned, shielded her eyes from the spot, and peered down at her heckler. "What's that?" she said to the young man drinking what was clearly not his first beer.

"Boring!" he yelled. "Shut up."

"I'm boring you?"

He nodded, grinning. Gave her the finger.

"Well, you bore me," she said. "Everything about you." Not a witty comeback, but charm was not on the agenda tonight. Now there were boos, and lots of them. There were hardly any people there, and yet the boos were loud. It was an easy sound to make, it vibrated from deep in the throat, and it made a few people sound like a lot. The booing made the back of her neck tingle, gave her another little surge of energy.

She hadn't planned this direction, but she had tried not to plan anything. Yet she had something in mind that she wanted to get to. The kicker: she would let them titter about "bad" mothering, and then they would expect some kooky sweet story, something faux confessional about being too good of a mother, a sort of ultra-humblebrag about CARING TOO MUCH. And the story they were expecting would make it clear that she was not a bad mother at all; it would be clear that she was actually THE BEST MOTHER EVER, or at least a very bumbly-but-well-meaning nincompoop of a mother, someone harmless and nonthreatening. And she would string them along, because that light self-loathing was so reassuring coming from a middle-aged woman. But instead Sam smiled and said, "Yeah, about my relationship to my daughter, Ally. It wasn't exactly neglect or abuse, but try telling that to Child Protective Services, right?" And she said it in the tone of a joke, but they did not laugh, and the room started to feel very uncomfortable. That was what she was shooting for: discomfort, uneasiness, a sense that this was veering somewhere skin-crawly. But when she actually said these words, when they spilled out, it was all wrong. There was a pause, and for a moment, Sam stood silent in the spotlight. Then anger and yelling all over her, at her. Her face turned red. More boos. She said nothing, just glared back at the audience and the lights.

Then the boos, legion and angry, turned into instructions, audience wishes hurled at her. Shut up, go home, fuck off.

"Shut up, dumb bitch."

Laughter. Then.

"Go home, ugly old cunt."

There it was. So easily surfaced, all that hate for her. It wasn't only what she said or didn't say but who she was while she said it. Anger was easy, easy, easy to get. Easy to find. It was the dullest thing ever, the default of every moment these days. She had blown it.

People scowled at her as she turned to walk off. There was something in that scowling, she had to admit. Getting it was too easy, but at least she was visible. She felt a weird high from the face-to-face of it, the human, emoji-free faces, the raw in-real-life moment of it. But right as she reached the edge of the stage, the door to her escape, Sam looked back at the audience. And there she was. Ally. She had come. Ally had actually been reading her texts, even if she didn't respond. Sam stopped, suppressing her urge to stage-dive toward her daughter, to throw herself at Ally's feet. Sam smiled, waved at her, but also instantly saw herself through Ally's eyes. Sam was foolish, her monologue embarrassing. Poor Ally had to listen to her mother talk about her, say her name, drag her into Sam's own weird need for humiliation. Sam felt herself flush hot. What have I done. Ally stared back. Her perfect oval of a face brought an instant wave of love from Sam, but Ally's mouth was a hard, tense line. Ally shook her head, shook Sam off, looked down and got up to leave. Sam shouted, "Ally! Wait!" but Ally disappeared. Sam wanted to cry. All of her bravado, all of her juicy defiance, undone and replaced with this shame. (And beyond the shame was the shock: Ally looked so old, so like an adult. And next to the shock, the familiar concerns rushed in: Ally probably had fake ID but didn't get carded. Ally acted, carried herself, like an adult, but she was only sixteen—so young, so insanely young that Ally had no idea how young she was or what that word actually meant.)

After she got home, Sam paced her living room, smoking. (Her two-a-day habit was now more like five.) Good luck sleeping tonight. Adrenaline and various other stress and counterregulatory hormones from the performance and its aftermath fired through her body still. Shaky, a little nauseous, she ground down on how she'd managed to blow her chance for reconciliation.

Impulsively, improbably, Sam called Ally. Straight to voicemail with no ring. Then she sent two desperate texts:

Where did you go?

I'm so sorry—please talk to me, Ally, please

Sam knew she must have finally fallen asleep because she woke with a jerk at three a.m. She pulled on her clothes, drank a coffee, and glanced at her phone. Nothing, of course. She was blocked. She left her phone on her table (she refused to take that instrument of pain with her) and went out into the street for a walk. The late August night air was already chilly, already inching toward the fall. She walked past the cemetery and kept going toward Park Street. The streetlights gave her bright splashes of visibility, and when she came to a block with few lights, her skin pricked slightly with fear, but then she just walked a little faster. No one was out, not even the pale opioid ghosts.

When she reached Park Street, she saw lights flashing. She turned right and looked in the direction of the lights. Halfway down the block, she saw a police cruiser, the source of the flashing. And two figures, a woman and a man, guns drawn, rushed toward a streetlight, and someone shouted, "Get down, get down!"

Sam stopped where she was, looked where they looked.

"Stop! Don't move!"

Sam saw a smaller figure move from shadow into the light holding a plastic soda bottle. He looked in the direction of the shouts. She could see his face in the light, confused, terrified. He wheeled abruptly to his left. Sam heard *crack,* echo, then *crack, crack,* echo. The wheeling figure yelped and dropped to the pavement, spilling his liter of soda. His leg bent oddly. The two cops rushed to him with guns still out and pointing at him. Then they bent over his body. Sam could see his face clearly as he lay there. He was a teenager, a boy with a boy's face. He was not moving.

One of the cops called into his radio, "Shots fired. Subject down. Alert Medical." The female cop holstered her gun and then seemed to put her ear to the boy's chest. The two cops' faces were in shadows, but the uniforms were clearly identifiable. The female cop stood up and shook her head at the male cop. Sam could see her face now, red, breathing heavily.

"Why did you fire?" he said, his voice loud and shaken.

She looked back down. "He was charging us; he had a weapon."

He directed his flashlight around the boy. It lighted on something, the spilled soda. He kept flashing, looking for something that lay next to the body on the ground. (It was a body, Sam knew this somehow, could see that he didn't move, the boy. And that's called a body.) The cop shook his head. Sam carefully moved a step back, putting herself out of the light as she watched, but they didn't notice her. She could hear distant sirens.

She turned back toward the corner, away from them, and stepped quietly into the darkness of the unlit street. No one had seen her, but she had seen them. And then she ran as fast as she could down Highland.

It was bound to happen. She had inserted herself, she had willed herself into this world. (Into *the* world.) She had bought the house in this direly poor neighborhood. She roamed at three a.m., when only bad things happened. She in her restless, hypervigilant state.

When she was well out of sight, she stopped running. She sat down on the curb, and she tried to breathe. Her heart was loud and fast in her body: the pumping, she could feel and hear it. She was alive. The boy was no longer alive.

They must be thinking about it now. What they did, just as she was thinking about what she saw. Her body was shaking. She felt ill. She will throw up soon, but she had nothing in her stomach. Her gut ached and churned. It was so cold, she felt cold. A wind had picked up, and it blew little drops of rain against her. She shivered and stood up. Cold from her lips to her fingertips, cold pushing up through the soles of her sneakers and whistling through the seams of her jeans, the same jeans she had worn every day for the past week. They were stretched from use, and they felt baggy, as if the cold lurked in the spaces between her thighs and the fabric.

The cold penetrated when the wind whipped across the cemetery park, then barely retreated until the next awful gust. But the wind focused her, and she needed to focus. (Reflexively, she thought about the fall, how late in August it was, how betrayed she was by the sudden drop in temperature.) She could go inside, get warm, make some coffee. She could even sit back down on the curb, hug her knees, make a cocoon of warmth. Instead she continued to stand and shiver.

My God!

A boy is dead. A boy is dead. A boy is dead.

FOUR

Ally

It was Joe's idea that she should go to the horrendous comedy club to see her ridiculous mother. He couldn't go with Ally, of course, but he thought it would be a way for her to repair things. Her grandma had also told her to forgive her mother. Even her father had told her that the breakup was his fault. So when her mother texted her the night of the open mic, Ally decided to show up. She sat in the back, drank a Coke, and ate some disgusting rubbery "Caprese" salad to make the minimum. She endured several terrible stand-up performances before her mother came on.

Ally barely recognized her: thin, old, her hair spiky short. She smiled, but there was something twitchy in her face, as if she were animated by an odd and destructive force that at the same time pleased her. Her mother didn't see her. Ally was in the back, in shadows, and the stage lights made it hard for her mother to see. She held her hand to her forehead and squinted out. Ally felt a little sorry for her; she looked weirdly fragile despite her muscles. Her silly mother, making a fool of herself. It was almost funny, just how much the audience hated her, but mostly it was the cringefest Ally had expected. Then her mother ranted about being a bad mother and brought up Child Protective Services and Ally by name. Ally was stunned. How could her mother drag her in as if everything were a big joke? As if that time, that scrutiny, was not horrible and traumatic and totally not anyone's fucking business.

"She has no sense of limit, no restraint. My personal life. MY personal life. And to bring up that incident. She has no shame."

"What happened? Tell me."

Joe wanted to hear, and why shouldn't Ally tell him.

"I was fifteen. I had fainted during a test at school. It was the first quarter of tenth grade, and I was obsessed with getting perfect grades. I knew it was nuts, but I was secretly proud of how driven I was. It was a way to be—I'm still like that. It's who I am. But I had overdone it with an all-nighter. I drank some cold coffee left over in the pot from the morning. I mixed it with almond milk and a ton of sugar and decided to power through. By the time I had to go to school, I started to feel a little strange. I didn't say anything to anyone—AP World History was first period, that's all I had to hold it together for. Mom didn't notice I was off, but I'm pretty good at hiding. She could see I was studying my notes. Already I was sweating.

"The test had some multiple choice and an essay question. The information was all there, in my head. I just needed to calm down and execute. But I felt clammy, light-headed. Nauseous too. My heartbeat sped up. I knew it wasn't an asthma attack—I've had those. I got up to splash water on my face or just to do something besides vomit. And down I went: I blacked out. I just managed to put my hands out and cushion my trip to the floor of the room. Turned out I had suffered a vasovagal syncope. 'Vaso'—that's blood. 'Vagal'—that's your stomach, your vagus nerve. And 'syncope.' That means a blackout: 'syn' is 'together'—and 'cope' is 'koptein,' to cut out. So basically I had a stress-induced body fail. But no one knew that. I could have had a brain tumor or a heart arrhythmia. So they called my parents and sent me to the ER.

"I was in the back seat, looking sick as hell. My dad was driving, and my mom was doing her primary job, flipping out. When we got to the ER, I threw up in the parking lot. They made us wait for an hour, which spun my parents out, but especially Mom. And then when we did get a room, we waited another hour. At this point, I felt so exhausted that I could barely stay awake, and my parents didn't know if that was bad or not. Should they keep me awake until I was checked for concussions and so on? There were no nurses or aides that could answer our questions.

"Finally, I was seen by someone. He looked at my eyes with a penlight, and I could tell he thought I was on drugs or something. Let's just say he lacked a great bedside manner. Maybe because my mother kept talking, insisting that I was healthy and such a thing had never happened before.

"He ignored Mom, and then he said he wanted blood tests and a CT scan to see what was going on. My parents nodded.

"After he left, my mom whispered to us. 'Did you see that he is an NP? All this time, and we don't get to see a doctor?'

"'It's fine, Sam. NPs have more clinical experience than doctors.'

"'What about diagnostic skills? Isn't that what doctors are for? Why does a perfectly healthy teenager pass out?'

"This was where things got weird, got wrong. I finally confessed to my parents that I didn't sleep at all the night before and maybe I drank a gallon of iced coffee. Also I fake-ate breakfast, so maybe I hadn't eaten anything but coffee since the night before. But the good news was that I probably didn't have a tumor, and I fell on my hands and didn't hit my head. I was hoping this would calm them down, and also maybe we could just go home so I could sleep. But Mom has a way of making everything worse. A need, a need to make everything worse. And things beyond my control—our control—were in motion.

"So Mom went to his counter where he was putting orders into his computer. She doesn't think I saw what happened, but I could see and hear it all.

"She told him about all my recent X-rays. My wrist was sprained at soccer two weeks earlier. 'In fact, we came here then,' she said. Four months ago I had a skating crash and twisted an ankle. And over the previous winter I had had a concussion. All of these times I had X-rays. In addition, there was the orthodontist, and the new three-hundred-and-sixty machine at the dentist, the panoramic radiograph machine—boy, she hated that thing. 'Her teeth are fine,' she said, but then she caved, which is maybe why she was so wound up about this one. She told the NP she didn't want me to have another bout of radiation exposure. No scan.

"He finally looked up at her and frowned. He said nothing, just went back to his computer and his typing. He pretended she wasn't talking.

"'Excuse me,' she said. And her voice was loud. I knew she was upset. 'But do you really think it's necessary for her to get a brain scan? She says she didn't hit her head.'

"He stopped typing and looked back up at her with a sigh.

"'Yes, it is necessary. She blacked out.'

"'But she told me she blacked out after she sank to the ground. She remembers not hitting her head.'

"Again he said nothing. Just tapping into the computer.

"'I don't want her to have another exposure.'

"'She needs the scan—that is my professional judgment and it is the standard of care.' He was, to be fair, not giving Mom much here. But he couldn't be bothered with assuaging her fears. You could tell he hated her. His expression was, well, contemptuous. You know if it had been my dad, it would have been handled differently by this dick. He had sized her up; she was shrill, controlling, noncompliant."

"You sound like you're on her side," Joe said.

"Up to a point. But then she escalated things, raised her voice, and absolutely insisted that I not get a scan. That in her judgment as a mother, it was not needed.

"I could see them squaring off. He grew quieter, she grew louder. She told him that in fact I had stayed up all night and drunk a bunch of coffee. He looked at her and click, clicked into his computer. She saw his face, and then she mentioned it wasn't any kind of a problem; I simply got carried away. I was an honors student. Why did she have to keep talking? What difference does it make if I'm an honors student?

"So now he thinks I was lying about everything because I didn't tell him the full story. That we are all lying. Things are quiet, but there is like a clip to his tone, a kind of adversarial feel to his treatment from here on out.

"They didn't give me the CT. But the next thing I know, I was alone in a room with a social worker, getting interrogated about my lifestyle, from drug use to sex. Lol. Once all the blood tests came in, we were finally allowed to go home. He glared at my mother as we left. And yeah, she smiled right at him as she walked out with her arm around me, like 'I told you so, I win.'

"Nightmare but it was over, right? Wrong.

"The next day, two people show up at our house from Child Protective Services. Turns out anyone can anonymously sic them on you. The charge? Denying medical care to a minor. Hah! My mother laughed out loud at this, but then she let them into our living room. She went to her desk and pulled out a file of my medical records.

"'No care, huh? Here.' And out came all my papers from the ER visits and the doctor visits for asthma, glasses, dermatologist, pediatrician. With all the ER stuff, I worried for a moment that they might flip the charges to Munchausen syndrome by proxy or something.

"'Here's the thing,' Mom said in a calm voice. 'The nurse-practitioner who called this in is a power-mad asshole. He didn't like being questioned by a pain-in-the-ass loud woman like me. He was a condescending prick, and he should be fired for misusing government resources.'

"So whatever, she had escalated things and I suffered. In the investigation that followed I had to convince one social worker after another that all was fine. She had to be questioned. Dad had to be questioned. 'It is a process,' Dad said. 'We just have to let it run its course. I'll write a letter of complaint to the hospital. But this is the law. So we submit to whatever the process entails.' And no one—even Mom—could be indignant about any of it: they had so much power to ruin your life. Full compliance or they could even show up at school and question me. Can you imagine? The whole experience was traumatizing."

"Overreach," Joe said, shaking his head.

"That's not the point. As Dad said, it's rigorous for a reason. To uncover hidden abuse or neglect. Of course, they closed the case after the required investigation. But it would be on some super-secret record for ten years in case another incident happened. We all agreed to never breathe a word of it to anyone—Mom swore me to secrecy. But then there she was, onstage at Destiny mall, telling a bunch of hateful bros about it."

"I'm sorry, Ally."

"I am just collateral damage to her self-immolation."

"But I don't think she meant to upset you."

"Immolate is exactly what she has done to her life." She read from her phone: "'To sacrifice.' The Latin root word 'immolatus' means 'to sprinkle with sacrificial meal.'"

Joe didn't just give her serious gifts, like books he thought she should read. He bought her romantic expensive gifts, like jewelry, candles, lingerie, and perfume. This was fun, receiving the grosgrain ribbon–tied shopping bags with the tissue. Then reaching in and finding a little box or a little fabric bag. Opening it up and seeing what Joe imagined she would like. It wasn't about buying her or spoiling her because she didn't expect or ask for it. But she saw it as a tribute to her, a proof of how much he thought about her when he wasn't with her.

She liked how Joe watched her when she opened a gift. She liked putting on soft things that smelled good. Like fine black stockings and silk tap pants. And how much it turned them both on to see Ally anointed with and then stripped of these trappings. It was like pretending to be someone else, which was fun, because she didn't know yet who she wanted to be. Am I the sort of woman who enjoys lingerie? If I am, what does that mean? It could be cool to be buttoned up and conservative on the outside and sort of wild and kinky on the inside. But that is just capitulating to the most obvious and reductive commodification of sexual arousal, her mother would probably say. Maybe, but how would she know if she didn't try it out for herself? And what if it aroused her?

"I like corrupting you," he said, pouring her a glass of pink champagne. She smiled, took a sip. It looked sweet but it smelled like bread. By the third sip, she liked the way it tingled the back of her tongue and seemed to warm her from the inside. And kissing between sips was heaven. He gave her another box. "More?" she said. He laughed. "Open it." It was a sleek purple-and-white oblong device that fit into her hand. A fancy vibrator that charged via USB. She covered her mouth. He laughed and laughed.

"We don't have to use it. It's kind of a joke. Are you upset with me?"

"No!" Ally said. She was dying to try it. "But we have to charge it."

"I already did that," he said.

"I guess you were pretty confident I would go for it."

"You are adventurous," he said. "Plus champagne."

They played with it, and to her shock, she discovered that he or she could just hold the smooth silicone tip against her clitoris and an orgasm would come super fast, and then another, even if she didn't urge it on or focus herself. Even if she resisted it.

"What do you think?" he asked, after four of them in a row.

"It feels good, but I also feel like I fucked a robot."

He nodded. "Just something to add to the repertoire."

"Sex via technology. Is this what they mean by the Internet of Things?"

He laughed and kissed her.

Later she thought, do we have a repertoire? An index or inventory of things they did? Did that mean he was already bored—she'd heard about this, how things tended to go over time—or did he know that they would run out of things to do if they didn't keep adding new ones? She sent him a pic of her in the lingerie he had bought. She regretted it, because it didn't feel thrilling. It felt a little panicked, actually. And maybe the truth was that she was a little bored herself with sending pictures.

He loved it, though. He sent a bunch of heart emojis and a heart-eyed emoji face.

Joe was in town for a whole week. He was cutting the ribbon on his new project, "The Cope," an old convent he had transformed into unique high-end apartments and a co-working space. Ally would attend the ribbon cutting but not as his date, of course. "You'll be my date, but we must be discreet. You come as part of the public. As my YAD mentee, it makes sense for you to attend."

"Right," she said.

"We just can't hold hands and make out," he said. She laughed. "We'll meet at my hotel room later and celebrate."

Ally would have to make up some story for her dad, but honestly, he barely noticed. He always figured she had vocal practice or studying or simulations. Or soccer. Which she did, actually. She was taking a precollege summer course, and she had a shit ton of homework she had to do tonight too, so her time with Joe would set her back a bit. Still, she was proud of him, excited to see him and be with him as he showcased another of his development transformations.

The ribbon cutting was preceded by a tour of the apartments for VIPs and the press. They followed him through the arched door-way of the former convent dormitory.

"The building was designed by Archimedes Russell in 1896 for the Sisters of St. Francis. The exterior has barely been touched except for repointed brick and replacing the roof."

Joe led the group down the hall to the apartments. "Notice the oak wainscoting. Some of it is original to the halls, some of it is repurposed boiserie from the chapel."

It was a rich deep oak, and it looked great in the high-ceilinged hall. Joe had amazing taste, and he had saved this extraordinary building.

He ushered everyone into one of the apartments.

"Here is our top-end apartment: a two-bedroom with a full eat-in kitchen, terrace, and city view."

It was true there was a city view. Floor-to-ceiling multipaned windows were original to the building, with the wood muntins refinished to a rich glow. Joe showed them the black kitchen cabinets with the gray granite countertops and the subway tile backsplashes. The appliances were stainless steel.

Ally walked over and inspected the "open plan" kitchen with the stools at the counter. She could easily picture the kind of guy who would rent this place. And it was for a guy, of course. A single guy. Someone, she thought, with one of those expensive gaming chairs.

Joe pointed out the exposed brick wall, the exposed ductwork, the exposed support beams, and the distressed hardwood floors.

Ally thought, again, of the guy who would rent this place and what he would find cool and beautiful about exposed ductwork. Did it really go with the elegant convent building? It wasn't a factory warehouse. Yet here were those bulbs in cages—what did they call them?

"Note the Edison bulbs. And the bedroom features reclaimed wood sliding barn doors, a gorgeous contrast with the industrial gray walls."

Edison bulbs! And barn doors? But she pushed it from her mind; the windows were beautiful, and if it weren't for Joe they would be unused, dusty, falling apart.

They followed Joe to the three-story-tall chapel. Here, thank god, things were pretty untouched. The oak pews, the organ, the vaulted ceilings. Ever since she was a kid, she had loved going into churches. They were never religious, her family, but her mother told her that churches were the most beautiful buildings in any place you visited. "And you can sit in peace, for free." They would go in for a moment of quiet. A place where people still spoke in hushed voices and felt embarrassed to text.

She remembered a trip to Montreal with her mother when she was ten. It was a mother-daughter weekend, with a hotel room and a rooftop pool. Her mother let her swim in the pool after dinner, at ten p.m. Her mother watched her do tricks, underwater somersaults and flip dives. The next day they walked through the old part of the city. It was hot and crowded. Her mother pulled her into a tiny stone church that sat right on the harbor. Ally didn't remember the name, but her mother told her it had been built by Jesuits in the seventeenth century. They sat on a pew. It was cool and dark inside. Light was filtered through stained-glass rose windows. Her mother pointed out that the hanging lights over the pews were all in the shapes of ships. "This is where you would come to pray before you set out to sea. Just like in *Moby-Dick*," she whispered. They had listened to parts of *Moby-Dick* on their drives last summer. And then they had watched the old movie version. "Can you imagine?" Ally looked at the dangling little ship-shaped lights, and she could imagine.

Joe was explaining all the support he had gathered from the state and federal historic preservation programs, the Regional Economic Development Council initiative, and a county revitalization grant. Ally knew he'd gotten a twelve-year tax break for rehabbing an existing structure. He'd also gotten a recording tax break—whatever that was—and a waiver on sales tax for construction materials.

But he had saved this building, hadn't he? And wasn't that worth the taxpayers' money? Her eyes grew used to the dark chapel, and she could really see the detail in the huge stained-glass window to her right. It showed a woman in a nun's habit, with her hands on some downtrodden people. The rays of the sun were behind her. Words beneath her read, "Mother to the Sick and the Poor." Ally knew who it was. Marianne Cope, who had been named a saint not long ago. She'd been one of the sisters in this convent. She had volunteered to work at a leper colony when no one else would take care of the infectious sick or their orphaned, unwanted children.

Joe finished talking and took questions from the press.

Ally worked on a draft of her college essay. She tried to write about her YAD growth, her sense of empowerment through . . . ugh, so phony and boring already. Instead she wrote this:

WHY I AM NOT A LIBERTARIAN
by Ally Raymond

At first, some of it made sense. But not totally, the way some people look pretty if you kind of squint at them. But then you really look and, uh, not so much.

My mentor gave me a book, *The Fountainhead,* which I only read part of because it is long and pretty badly written—highly didactic and super hacky. I also read some essays my mentor directed me to. And I did some research on my own.

Let's start with that word, "libertarian." Which appears nowhere in Ayn Rand, btw. From the root "liberty," which ultimately leads to "liber" and "libertas": free, unrestricted, absent of restraint. Who doesn't want to be free? So does a libertarian identify with his need to be free, like a vegetarian identifies with his need to not eat animals? One is not a person who values freedom among other ideals. One is a person who puts his freedom above all other concerns. Further definitions of "liber": unbridled, unchecked, licentious.

So libertarians, they describe themselves as believing in ultimate equality without condescending "nanny-state" interference; they extol an unfettered marketplace where all can compete fairly. And by fair, they draw a careful distinction.

Equality of opportunity, not equality of outcome. But let's look at how that plays out in the real world.

A libertarian might see a homeless person with a sign asking for money and say something like "Don't give him money—he'll just spend it on beer." And you might be thinking, so what? Wouldn't you want a beer if you had to sleep under a fucking highway overpass? Maybe you don't want to say all of that. If you press the libertarian to elaborate further, he will tell you that he believes the person is homeless because he made "poor choices." We shouldn't be responsible for the consequences of other people's poor choices. So my question is, how much are our choices shaped by things we didn't choose? *But I didn't say that.*

A libertarian might also take federal, state, and county tax breaks in shitty desperate cities that will do anything for development. But how is that the unfettered marketplace? Isn't that the same as taking government handouts, just handouts for already rich developers? *I never said this either.*

And what about all the things people need to do collectively, like fire departments and utilities and the post office and schools? What about the rapidly unfolding climate cataclysm? Maybe the market has a role, but what if people's interests are at odds with profits? How can that be resolved except through collective values and, well, constraints? Even if you think the market can solve climate change with private entrepreneurship—via semi-publicly funded privately owned 5G, the Fourth Industrial Revolution, AI, nanotech, data hubs, "additive" manufacturing, and edge computing, etc.—then why isn't it happening yet? *I didn't ask this question, but I thought of versions of it many times.*

Also, protection of private property requires police and prisons and copyrights. So libertarians like rules in some cases. Maybe they are not for total liberty, but for protecting their own liberty at the expense of others'. *Nope, didn't once suggest this idea.*

Finally, is it really a net good to take beautiful old buildings (old schools, libraries, religious buildings) and, by dint of, I don't know, say 4.6 million dollars in tax breaks, turn them into tacky condos and co-work spaces for tech bros? Shouldn't we all have access to these buildings even if we don't have the public will to build like that anymore, or especially, maybe? Is it a little problematic to turn spaces dedicated to people like Saint Marianne Cope into private spaces? And furthermore, what about mixing in design clichés, like barn doors, on buildings designed for elegant respite, not gaming chairs and Tabata gym sessions? *Okay, now I am scaring myself, because I sound like my mom, lol.*

Still, one can see that the publicly funded rehab of beautiful old buildings for private profit is an interesting way to regard Joe and his philosophy. There is something fake in the apartments, in how they are not really well made. The key is to appear well made. It is a prosthesis for actually making something beautiful. "Pro" means "add" or "in," and "thesis" is from "tithenai," meaning put down/place in place of something missing. So he uses high-key cliché touches to signal something classy, like subway tile and granite slabs and reclaimed gray-tinted hardwood in place of actual historically relevant and thoughtful renovation. But my point is that could apply to—could be a metaphor for—a lot of what Joe does in his life.

Ally stopped writing and stared at her laptop. She realized that this was not really a college essay. Or what had begun as her college essay had morphed into a harsh breakup letter to Joe. Yet when she thought of him, his body with his soapy smell and the way he kissed her neck and her ears—she shook off the thought, buried it. Thus she discovered, and could not undiscover, that you could want someone—really want them—even though you no longer liked or respected them.

FIVE

Sam

As soon as she got home, she found her phone and called the one person she knew would be awake. MH.

"What should I do now? Not call the police, right?" Sam said, feeling as if she had already blown it, that she should have reported it by now.

"You should go to the Citizen Review Board and file a complaint. Do you have video?"

"No."

"Why not?"

"I didn't bring my phone. I was taking a phone-free walk." She could hear MH sigh.

"You should write down exactly what you remember, times, location, what you heard, everything."

"Right, right. Okay."

"You can call the district attorney's office. The ACLU. And you can call Syracuse Streets."

"Good, yes." Sam opened her laptop, and it woke up. The page she'd been on when she'd last opened it—"Best Sleep Apps 2017." A trivial concern from her previous, innocent life. Not innocent, maybe. Ignorant.

"But, Sam?"

"What?"

"Nothing will come of it."

"How so?"

"Here's how it goes. You will tell who you tell. You have no video evidence, just your word. But you are credible, and you are white, so there is that. The CRB will investigate. There will be a simultaneous Office of Professional Standards investigation. It will get sent to Fitzpatrick, the county DA. Then what?"

"What?" Sam said.

"Nothing happens to the cops. They always have cause, they are allowed to make mistakes, to misjudge, to escalate. Everyone else is not allowed to make mistakes or misjudge or escalate."

"This was a kid, a boy. Unarmed. Not holding anything but what was clearly a soda bottle."

"You know, you could do nothing, just let it go. Because reporting it does no good, and you might even make yourself a target. The police, the union, and the district attorney's office all take care of each other—"

"I have to tell what I saw."

"Yeah. I figured you would say that. I gotta go," MH said. "We'll talk in person soon. I'll call you when I get back to town."

Where was she? Sam didn't really care anymore.

She typed it all out in a Word file. But the exact details were hard. It had happened so fast. She was sure she saw the woman shoot him, but really her eyes were on the boy. She heard the shots and saw the boy fall. His back was facing them as they shouted and then he spun around and then turned again. Then he fell. She heard the pops and then saw him fall. She saw the man stand over him, heard him ask her why she fired. Sam was far away—how far exactly? She had left the scene. She didn't have a video. She was suspicious too. Why had she been out at three a.m. in that neighborhood? She could imagine being cross-examined. They would make her out to be a sleep-deprived crazy woman.

When she was done writing, she filled out the eight-page complaint form on the CRB website. When she hit the Submit by Email button, nothing happened. She tried again and again. She would have to submit it in person when city hall opened, at eight o'clock. Now what? It was too early to call anyone. She looked at Syracuse.com. Already there was a story up about the shooting.

NORTHSIDE SHOOTING

Posted August 31, 2017 5:00 a.m.

by William Conner | wconner@syracuse.com

SYRACUSE—A man was shot in an officer-related shooting in the 200 block of Park Street shortly after 3:00 this morning. As of 5:00 a.m. today, the area was blocked off by police crime tape. A uniformed police officer discharged at least one round from her weapon, Syracuse police said. The man died at the scene and was declared dead at St. Joseph's Hospital at 3:45 a.m. He was not identified by the police.

She should wait to talk to a lawyer or the district attorney or the Citizen Review Board, but instead she emailed the reporter and told him she was a witness. He immediately called her.

"The reason I contacted you is that your story is wrong. It wasn't a man that was shot. It was a boy. He looked fourteen, fifteen." Then, when he asked, she told him exactly what she remembered seeing: nothing more, nothing less.

By seven a.m., the story was the same but amended with this:

A witness to the shooting spoke to Syracuse.com: "A female police officer shouted, 'Stop!' and then when the boy turned around, she shot the boy three times. He clearly was not armed. He had a soda bottle in one hand. The soda spilled into the street. After he fell, they called for help on their radio. Then the female officer stood by while the male officer bent over him. I heard him ask her, 'Why did you fire?' And she replied, 'He was charging us, he had a weapon.'" The police did not respond to reporter inquiries.

The full story was public now. She waited for what would happen next.

After she filed her report with the Citizen Review Board, after she spoke to an ACLU lawyer, after the police interviewed her, after she talked to an alarmed Matt and told him she was okay, she went home and collapsed into a deep sleep.

She woke in the dark middle of the night. She felt the panic before the thoughts came and shaped it: what she'd seen, what she'd heard. She let herself see the moment again: the panic in the voice, the shots. The boy bleeding out, the cops fumbling. The "Why did you fire?"

Heat and sweat; she couldn't breathe and threw off her blanket. The air was cold, but she burned inside.

Sam did not check the time or pick up her phone. She knew it was two or three. Four is an early morning; one is a late night. Two or three are only for violence and prayer. Desperate hours. She swung her legs over the side of the bed and sat up. She felt the floorboards under her bare feet. The house throbbed against her. She heard the wind in the trees outside. The city was out there. She was in the house and the house was in the city. The city was in the world.

This was why you came here. You came here to witness, to see the world and then to act and make it better. To re-form it. She was fake poor, *Sullivan's Travels*, slumming-it "poor." But now she understood her obligation. The obligation of history, of her wealth, of her position. Even recasting her losses as gifts emerged with new purpose: the night waking drove her out to the street; her invisibility made her seem as innocuous as the pavement. She was a secret creature, a cryptogon. Her loneliness, with its grotesque emotions, outsized in the suburbs, here made her feel the pain—the weight—of what she saw. What was the extra-life for? You woke because it was not the time for gentle sleep. You sought the world with clarity, and it turned out it had been here all along, waiting for you to see it.

She was in the house. The house was in the city. The city was in the world. The world was history. This was why she bought this house in this place.

Sam opened her laptop and read an article that had just been posted about the dead boy. He now had a name, Aadil Mapunda (his friends called him Adi). Adi Mapunda. Here was his picture from ninth grade (fourteen, his expression, his baby face, even younger than Ally). He looked ready for the world, open, one of those awkward adolescent toothy smiles, the face floating in the school-photo blue of no space, no time. But he was a boy in time, and when Sam looked at it, she tried to connect that face with his face in the light the moment before he fell. And here was a photo of his mother, Imani Mapunda, in a gold print head scarf next to her son at his eighth-grade graduation.

(His mother. The boy's mother. Aadil's mother, Imani.)

She looked very young and lovely, but even then, her face did not have an open smile like his. The feature focused on the irony and tragedy of their story. They were Bantu from Somalia. He had been born in the Dagahaley refugee camp in Kenya. Aadil had a brother, but he had died before Aadil was born (so this was the second child she has lost). He and his mother lived in the camp until he was six. Then—in a great stroke of fortune—they were granted asylum and emigrated to the United States. Catholic Charities found them a small apartment. Her son was enrolled in the large, run-down, but cheerful primary school full of children from all over the world. And many Somali people. He learned quickly, and by the time he got to middle school, he excelled at sports and his studies. The article described how the mother learned English and then began working as an aide in a nursing home.

Sam thought of her father, and the young aides who had taken care of him in the end, when he'd spent a year in Withrow Center. The women who would let him joke and wink at them so that he would let them shave, feed, and, finally, change him. All the indignities and intimacies of a dying body, yet they managed it with a quiet, practical kindness.

Mapunda was a rising sophomore at Henninger High School. He had made the honor roll, had many friends and even a girlfriend. He became American in ways his mother would not. He dressed American, he listened to American music. He was American; he understood America in a way she never could. Aadil was the bridge. Everything had gone so well, a story of progression and a fulfilled hope for true refuge. (But there is no true refuge for anyone, not really.) They must have felt so lucky—to have escaped a war zone and made it safely to America. The article noted what a particularly cruel turn of fate it was to have violent death come here, in the place you thought was safe.

Fate, huh?

Sam wanted to go see the mother. Imani Mapunda. Why? To do and say what? Hold her, talk to her, comfort her? Give her money? Or tell her what she had seen? Who would that help?

She could imagine losing Ally, had imagined losing Ally many times, and she knew it would be unbearable. It would make everything Sam had done her entire life feel meaningless and wrong. It would be one thing if your adult child died before you, it would devastate you, but at least they'd had a life. To lose someone so young would change your life, make it a broken, cursed life. Parents who lost children were her Mid fears in the flesh. And here was this woman, not only losing a second child but losing a child to violence—to murder, just call it that. Her son shot and dying in the street with only his killers to keep him company. If she spoke to her, told her what she'd seen, Sam would sob and lose control. Besides, she had nothing of comfort to report to Aadil's mother. It was a terrible death—a lonely shitty pointless death.

Contacting her would give Sam something (what, exactly? a purpose, a place, for what she had seen), but at what cost to this woman? Just back the fuck up. Monstrous, to think she had a purpose here. Was the boy who'd been killed a part of her purpose? Her penance? Was Aadil Mapunda not a human with his own purpose, all dashed and spilled on the concrete in a matter of seconds. And what about the two police officers. Was he a fulfillment of their purpose, their crossing over into the realm of killers? The officers, the woman (apparently a twenty-two-year-old rookie) and the man, the police officers. Don't, for god's sake, think about them. Don't think about yourself. For the sake of decency.

So instead Sam wrote a letter to Aadil's mother, and she asked the ACLU lawyer to give it to her. She wrote that she would testify at the trial, and if there was also a civil suit, she would of course testify for that too. Sam wrote that she was so sorry for what had happened, and she wished her peace. She wrote her address, email, and phone number on the letter in case the woman wanted anything more from her. She wrote "Please feel free to contact me" as a PS. But then she rewrote it without the PS. Wasn't it implied? And putting it explicitly in writing made it a sort of pressure, she thought.

Using all the remaining funds in her checking account, she made an anonymous donation to the GoFundMe someone had set up for his funeral and other expenses.

The only thing left for Sam to do was to keep reporting what she'd seen, which would do very little for this mother or her son. (Are you still a mother once your child dies? Or did you used to be a mother?)

She wanted to hear Ally's voice, to see her, touch her and know that she was okay. But of course she was okay. Ally was protected, Ally would never be shot in the street. What a luxury, what an advantage, that the world believed in her child's innocence. Or, maybe, the right way to think about it was that it was not a luxury at all, but the basic thing every person should have. Which was not the case, not now, not in this moment.

Sam's struggles with sleep worsened despite everything she did: the light-blocking face mask, meditation breathing, melatonin, not eating or drinking before bed. And yet here she was in the Mid, wide awake and without even a hot flash to blame. Her careful calibrations of body and mind led her to one thing: the face of Aadil as he lay dying on the street. It had been two nights, and it had replaced all her other Mid ruminations and fears. The way it came to her was so odd, like a movie: she could see the details of his face, not the blur of the moment the way it had seemed to happen. Was it possible that her brain, under stress, had been hyperrecording, taking in more details than she'd realized? She thought then of the statement she had turned in to the Citizen Review Board. It seemed stingy to her, insufficient. Why did she think of it in the language of an accounting ledger, double entry, with lines of liabilities being offset with what? Equities? No. Her statement was anorexic, anemic, bloodless.

She got up, looked at her phone. Since she'd been blocked, there was no point in texting Ally, and the phone had considerably less allure for her now. MH had texted and wanted to meet her so they could talk. Soon she would text with a safe location and a time. MH wrote that she was dopamine fasting and checked her phone only once per day. Whatever.

The MH stuff bothered Sam, but it was a kind of referred pain at this point. A place her pain was expressed, but it wasn't the real source of the pain. It was a dislocation and barely a distraction.

She made coffee, sat at her table, and pressed a button on her sleeping laptop. Syracuse.com was already open on her browser. She scrolled down. Another article about the shooting. But this article had tacked in a predictable direction. The chief of police had released a statement: Mapunda had been drinking at a party earlier in the evening, and he'd had a vape pen with marijuana residue on his person when he died. The chief hinted at the possibility that he'd been out at three a.m. to buy weed (of course they couldn't comment on the shooting, and yet they had revealed this detail). The police union president spoke to the press: "I feel confident the investigation will show that the officer acted reasonably and responsibly." However, he couldn't answer questions about an ongoing investigation. They had to wait for the ballistics test results, the forensic report, the gathering of all the evidence.

Sam did not read the comments. She knew—because the ACLU lawyer had told her—that Aadil had been at his girlfriend's after the party and had fallen asleep. When he woke up, he walked home, drinking a soda, and was suspect because he was a Black teenager on the street at three a.m. For this, he was dangerous and a threat. For this, he was shot. No, she did not care to read the comments. Pot in a vape? So what? Even if he'd been out looking for weed, what difference could that possibly make?

The ACLU lawyer had told her that because it was a police-involved fatality with an unarmed victim, it would be investigated by the state's attorney general, not the county. She also explained to Sam that her eyewitness testimony was important but easily impeachable. She'd been half a block away. It was nighttime— could she really hear what they said? Okay, but even without what she had heard, another unarmed Black person had been killed by police officers. They had not acted "reasonably and responsibly." She had seen it.

MH was guilty of something, that Sam knew, but of what?

Meet me at 2 at the State Fair.
In front of the Grange building.

Sam arrived at the fair early and walked around. It figured this
was MH's idea, like going to the comedy open-mic night, another
of MH's field trips or safaris into the true and awful American soul.
Gawk at the gorging and so on. It was Labor Day, the last weekend
of the fair, and it teemed with people even though it was unsea-
sonably cold and rainy. People trudged around in damp shorts and
tank tops, ignoring the weather.

The last time Sam had been to the fair was the summer before
Ally started ninth grade. It was hot and crowded as she watched
Ally and her friends go on the most nauseating rides on the mid-
way. She remembered waiting on lines to eat a series of more and
more preposterously unhealthy foods, from fried Oreos to melt-
ing, triple-loaded sundaes to fried hamburgers stuffed with mac
and cheese, bunned with pancakes instead of bread, and then
dipped into maple syrup (which she ate only one bite of). Never-
theless, Sam had always loved the fair, mostly because of the beau-
tiful buildings of the fairgrounds, constructed in the early part of
the century, with their celebration of agriculture and industry—
a WPA-like focus on work and workers. Each building was a cel-
ebration of production: the Center of Progress Building, the Dairy
Products Building, the Horticulture Building, the Art and Home
Center, and the Grange Building. The structures inside were
simply warehouses to stage expos, but the entryways had mosaic

detailing and grand arches made of cast stone, iron, and painted wood. Interiors had industrial lights, but were also lit by decorative ornate windows, giving them a palace-like feel, or like the entrance to a foreign grand bazaar. When Ally was young, they had loved the fair traditions: the giant butter sculpture that changed each year, the five-cent cup of milk, the talent contests, and especially the rows of perfectly kept and combed animals, looking pampered and bored. Sam kind of loved the people too, the exhibitors with their 4-H old-fashioned Americana everything, and even the everyday fairgoers, around whom Sam felt she could muster a semi-tender feeling for the ordinary American. Here they were in XXL cargo shorts and T-shirts that had sports teams or corny jokes or MOR bands on them. Baseball hats and grandma in her "Rascal" wheelchair, little kids holding cotton candy that stained their mouths blue or pink, mom and dad getting quietly drunk off beer in giant plastic cups as they walked and ate things in the hot sun. Sam remembered thinking that these were the real people, the working class, the unpretentious majority, the non-elite who didn't read *The New York Times* or buy wild salmon or pay for SAT tutors. Sam had prided herself on being non-snobby, on enjoying the handsome copper-haired Highland cows and the delicate white Japanese bantam chickens that the odd farm kids showed her.

But all that had changed, hadn't it? Here she was at the fair in 2017, this awful year, after all she had seen and heard. Everything read differently to her now. The working class of Syracuse (and the surrounding blue-collar suburbs and especially the rural counties beyond the suburbs) were the ones who'd voted for him. Well, the white ones, anyway. The crowds seemed more sinister to her, just blithely stuffing their faces, wearing their crudeness as some kind of emblem of authenticity, just like their fat president. She watched a scruffy guy walk by drinking a beer; she just knew he had a "Repeal the SAFE Act/NRA" sticker on his Jeep. She knew he didn't vote for Hillary Clinton. He walked with his arm around his girlfriend, a tiny, haggard chick who looked at her phone while drinking a wine slushie. She didn't vote for Hillary Clinton either, not even in the privacy of the voting booth. Of course not. Maybe Sam now saw what had always been there, and it seemed much darker than she remembered. The whole place was an obscene, smelly, cheap display of willful, unapologetic American stupidity and cruelty. Sam passed a Camaro with the opening lines of the Constitution airbrushed on it, along with some soaring bald eagles. And there was this year's butter sculpture: two cops with holstered guns helping a kid milk a cow. A sign said the fair had a law enforcement theme this year. She passed a pull-up bar at the recruiting station for the Marines. And a mallet-striker, where you could whack the platform and a puck would shoot up a tower and stop at "Manly" or "Wimpy," etc. There were cops and soldiers everywhere. Had it always been like this? There were even some hybrid police-soldiers: three burly men in camo pants, holsters and guns, sunglasses, high-and-tight hair, and Army-green shirts that read "STATE POLICE." Plus everyone deferring to—parting for—the cop-soldiers. They had authority, they had uniforms, they had power.

(Watch the cops. Watch the boy, Aadil. Watch the pavement.)

Was part of the problem that law enforcement attracted sadists and racists? Or did being a cop turn people into sadists and racists? Was it in them, in everyone, waiting to come out?

A fucking cop butter sculpture?

She saw MH before MH saw her. She had her usual swagger, but it impressed Sam more than usual: MH, the unrepentant emissary from the land of the unloved. (No longer loved, anyway.) There she was, lean and muscled in a black T-shirt and jeans, her expensive motorcycle boots artfully turned down at the cuff of her jeans. Jeans, Sam realized, that were extraordinary, the kind of jeans that cost three hundred dollars. (How could Sam even know that? You can just tell.) Her crew cut was also an NYC job, probably obtained at some manscaping salon in Brooklyn. Everything about her looked contrived, expensive, not legit.

"Thanks for meeting me out here," MH said.

Sam smiled, nodded. "It's a strange place to meet for a private talk."

"No one we know will be here, I assure you. It's ground zero for the gunned-to-the-hilt, aggrieved white working class of upstate New York."

They walked. To be accurate, the fair wasn't entirely white. Some Black and Brown attendees walked among them. But Sam did spot a number of MAGA hats and some seriously aggro T-shirts for sale in the kiosks. They said things like "TRUMP 2020 THE SEQUEL: Make Liberals Cry Again," "LGBT (Liberty, Guns, Beer, Trump)," "Stand for the Flag and Kneel for the Cross"; one had an image of the American flag made out of rifles; and, of course, there were a number of "Hey Snowflake" shirts, including one that said, "I did not put my life on the line for My Country to have some SNOWFLAKE tell me how to LIVE IT!" (Which was super wordy for a damn T-shirt.) Some shirts made no sense to Sam but were alarming nonetheless, like "#notmetoo" over the image of a gun? Or "I stand for the anthem because I stand for something," with rifles for the letter "I"? Totally nonsensical, just shit-splattered hostility for its own sake. These T-shirts hung right alongside the Jack Daniel's, Fortnite, *Star Wars,* and mystical wolf-moon painting shirts. As if it were all normal.

MH ordered gator meat on a stick and two beers. They sat on a sticky bench under an awning. Wind blew and the edges of the oilcloth clamped to the tables kept blowing up. Raindrops leaked in with each gust of wind. It was cold and miserable. MH offered her a bite of the tough alligator meat.

"It needs a sauce or something," MH said, chewing.

"It's the concept of eating a gator, I guess, that they're going for rather than an actual culinary treat."

"Stunt food," MH said.

Sam nodded. She wanted to leave.

"So what did you want to discuss?" MH said and then winked at her.

"It's not funny. What did you do?"

MH took another bite of gator and chewed for a while, thinking.

"It isn't a complicated question, but I can't seem to get an answer from anyone," Sam said.

"Isn't it, though? What did I do to piss off so many people?"

"Last time I looked at the petition, it was over a hundred signatures."

"Denouncing me," MH said.

"Yes. I have been asked—told—to denounce you."

"But you haven't yet. Why not?"

"I know you, and I know you're a good person," Sam said, but the words already sounded naïve in her mouth. MH even laughed. "Are the accusations true? I don't even know what the accusations are. What did you do?"

MH looked to the side and then spoke.

"I don't want to deny or discuss. People are mad at me, and I accept that. I have crossed lines—I like to push people's buttons, provoke people. I think my reading of things was different from how others read them."

"So you made mistakes, is that what you're saying?"

"Less-than-innocent mistakes, I would say. Anyway, it is liberating, if you want to know the truth. You are judged, found wanting, but then on the other side of it, you are still you. You survived."

Sam shook her head. MH just called herself a survivor! What if you did something awful, or if someone told you that you hurt them. Maybe you discovered that something you thought was okay was not okay. And instead of remorse or making amends or changing, you were just like, *yeah, that's me.*

MH swiped at something on her wrist. It wasn't a continuous glucose monitor measuring her blood sugar in real time. Sam had seen that, it was a disk stuck on the back of her arm. This was some kind of microchip, actually visible just under the delicate skin of her inner wrist.

"What the fuck is that?"

"I can't discuss it. It's out of a private biohack subreddit—grinder, meat-morphing stuff. What I can tell you is that I am beta-testing a nanochip implant that measures cortisol and epinephrine. And this conversation is stimulating a biphasic stress response—the whole thing is really tanking my equilibrium. Oxidizing my organs. Way beyond any hormetic benefit, I might add."

"Is it true that you have a house on the lake in Skaneateles?"

MH started laughing. "I've disappointed you, is that it? You, the sanctimonious gentrifier with your fixer-upper house, your expensive mattress, and your husband slash boyfriend slash sugar daddy?"

Sam was ready to leave. "You are disappointing. But I have bigger concerns at the moment."

"So what happened with your report to the CRB?"

"Nothing yet. They are investigating. OPS is investigating. And the state attorney general's office is investigating."

"I told you that nothing—"

"I'm not interested in hearing your 'I told you so,' actually. I have to do what I am doing, and I have to do more."

"It will only make you a problem. A target."

Sam wanted MH to stop talking. "Look, I have to go."

"Is that it?"

"Yeah. I know you aren't a predator or a monster. But I do think you are full of shit."

MH nodded, half-smiling with pursed lips. She got up.

"Goodbye, Sam," she said. She held up her fingers in a peace sign.

"Goodbye," Sam said, getting up. "Thanks for trying to help me. I appreciate all of that." MH nodded and Sam turned and started to walk away.

"Sam!" MH came up behind her and touched her arm.

Sam spun around.

"How do you know I'm not a predator?" MH said. "How can you be so sure that you know who anyone is?"

Sam didn't hate, but intensely disliked MH in that moment.

"Your problem," MH said, "is that you think you can redeem

yourself from all your shit, all this shit. And by saving yourself, you think you're saving the world. Or maybe it's the other way around. Either way, none of it matters."

Sam folded her arms and frowned. "What about all your ideas, your political actions and groups? Why do any of that if you care so little for the world?"

They were both getting wet in the now heavier rain, but they stood there. Sam continued (why not just say it all). "I know you're the one printing up the little letterpress flyers. Who else would have the time or the resources or even the inclination to do that? Why bother with the flyers if you don't care?"

"Care? That the catastrophe that was human civilization is dribbling out? Why would I care about us? The planet will change and go on without us. What makes us so precious? Why can't we face our extinction? My notes were so we can face—even accept—our future. We are not as crucial as we think. We were a blip, a mistake, a failure."

"I don't agree."

MH shrugged and sort of waved Sam away with her hand. Then she turned and walked off into the crowd.

I don't agree. Standing there, at the fair in the rain, despite everything, Sam did care about the humans, the coming extinction. The idea that the world—the human world—would cease to exist came at her in a new way that seemed real and tragic. It was at these fairgrounds and in her house and everywhere around them still. The promise and life in all the buildings and paintings and books. The photos and the films, the music and the letters. Handwritten, saved, tied with ribbons. The jokes, the plays, the dances. The child's drawing folded and tucked into a wallet, yellow with age. The churches built, the stories told, the meals prepared, the gravestones attended, all the little and big rituals. Poignant, tragic even, but not ridiculous. Beautiful in their totality. Weren't they? Maybe we were going extinct, but did that make it all a failure, all meaningless? No, it did not.

Here was another thing. The MAGA hats were being sold, but

she had seen no MAGA hats on actual people here. Yes, the horrible aggro T-shirts hung in the kiosks (someone making money off the mood in the land), but few were on bodies. Mostly, Sam guessed, they didn't vote. Mostly they watched sports, ate crap, got drunk, worked on their diabetes, didn't follow the news very much. She had seen one jackass in a pro-gun shirt, but mostly just clueless, careless people, same as always. Ignorant if not innocent, same as she was. And continued to be, in her own self-justifying way.

The rain had let up to a summer shower. People were streaming into the fair. Sam walked to the exit near the parking lots. Just getting out of here would take an hour. But she didn't feel angry about it. Just weary.

As Sam rounded a corner and came into view of the entrance kiosks, Ally walked into the fairgrounds. Sam stopped where she was. Her Ally, standing there in leggings and an oversized T-shirt.

Ally hadn't spotted her. For a second, Sam thought she was alone, but then she saw. Ally was with a man. An older man. They were fifty yards away, but Sam could see that they were holding hands and studying a map. They didn't look up. Sam stared at Ally's face, astounded by how beautiful and foreign she looked. Even more so than that angry flash of her in the comedy club. Sam fell into her old blindness problem (could she ever really see Ally, see her the way the world did?), but it had been so long since Sam had actually looked at her that even as she felt all her love and longing for Ally come flooding in, she barely knew this nearly adult woman. A nearly adult woman with a fully adult boyfriend.

Wait. Sam knew this man. He was Joe Moreno, the developer. Matt's client.

They laughed about something, and then Ally leaned in and kissed him, lips pressed against lips. Sam flickered over revulsion about his age, about Ally and sex, about Ally's secrets and safety, the clear inappropriateness of the power difference between them. Not long ago, Sam would have had a freak-out, a stop-the-presses meltdown. But today she couldn't muster any outrage about this sighting.

They were about to look up, about to see her. Sam ducked out of their view.

Something had left her. It wasn't that she didn't care or worry anymore—she did. But she had many things she cared about, worried about. Ally would be okay. She would weather this asshole, this whole experience. Ally had everything she needed to land safely.

She waited until they were well past her. She walked toward the exit gate. There was one other thing: Ally looked happy.

Ally had every right to her privacy. Ally should block her, really. By rights. If intentions mattered, Sam had done her best. But what if your best was not all that good? Sam had done much worse than shame her daughter for her body. Much worse than secretly follow her around Destiny mall, spying on her beloved child (a child she held in such esteem, yet she couldn't let her make her own mistakes, couldn't let her feel growing pains). She had done worse than stalk Ally online, read Ally's emails and texts, use a parenting tracker to see where she was, turn on notifications so she would get a banner alert for when Ally moved from one place to another. All of that was rudimentary.

Her mothering had really gone off the rails when she'd argued with the emergency room nurse-practitioner and wouldn't back off. Which led to the Child Protective Services debacle. It was embarrassing what she had brought down on Ally, and then for Sam to use it for fodder in her performance, to treat it as if it were a joke, was even worse. It wasn't funny or even not-funny in a provocative way. All of Sam's good intentions mixed with her intense needs and her lack of restraint. Sam was a force of chaos in her daughter's life.

The CPS investigation had been painful for all of them, but especially for Ally.

They both had to go down to the CPS offices to be interviewed. The investigators separated Sam and Ally and questioned them about everything multiple times. Sam knew it was just part of the protocol. But poor Ally—at fifteen, inhabiting the world as your body changed was confusing enough without weird questions from strangers looking for issues. They were cleared, of course, but it was hard not to feel as if you were guilty of something. Then as they were leaving, a social worker handed Ally a package. In the car on the way home, Ally opened it. Inside was a teddy bear, some chocolates, and a quilt. Someone had hand-stitched the quilt and donated it, thinking it would comfort an abused or neglected child. Ally looked at it, and then she began to sniff. She covered her face. Ally never cried.

"What's wrong, honey?"

Ally shook her head. "Nothing." No tears, but her voice cracked.

"What?"

"It's just that I'm so lucky, aren't I?" she said. She looked at the blanket. "Can you imagine what some kids must go through? And can you imagine some sweet woman sewing blankets to comfort some kid she will never see?"

It wasn't funny, any of it.

As she waited in the line of cars exiting the fair, she looked at the Syracuse Streets Instagram page. There would be a protest against the police killing tomorrow at one p.m. in front of the Public Safety Building. She wondered if the boy's mother would be there. She messaged the group:

> I was a witness to the shooting. I will attend the protest tomorrow.
> I can even speak if you want.

No one messaged her back. (Sam had intended to go to more of the weekly Syracuse Streets meetings after the one she attended at the Luthern church. She managed just two.) Instead, the ACLU lawyer, Amina, called her. Yes, come speak at the protest. She would pick Sam up.

The knock on the door startled her. Sam barely registered that Amina was beautiful and looked hardly older than Ally. Sam could feel her heart working hard in her chest and her breath getting shallow. When they got to the crowd gathering in front of the Public Safety Building, she looked down at herself. How would she seem to this crowd? Her hands shook a bit when she held them out. She did not want to stand up in front of people (not stand up in front of strangers again, not after the awful night at the Smiley Face, and not about something so important). She had no idea what she would say. She had to do it because maybe it could help somehow, and even if it didn't, speaking was what made you a witness instead of a spectator.

The crowd of maybe two hundred was chanting, "Whose streets? Our streets!" and then "No justice, no peace."

There were many speakers. Amina told her she should talk for about two minutes. Some teenagers stood behind Amina in matching T-shirts with Aadil's face in black and white and the words "Justice for Adi" across the bottom.

"What do I say?"

"Just tell them what you saw and heard," she said, smiling.

Words were meager. What had she seen? The experience resisted language. Maybe she did make things too complicated, too cloudy with self-doubt, with self. Finding the right words was impossible, finding the perfect words a vanity. Flawed, stumbling speech was her offering to the truth.

"My name is Samantha Raymond." Her voice sounded odd, creaky and loud. "I was walking in my neighborhood when I saw Officer Amy Wayne shoot Aadil Mapunda. I saw her shoot him. I heard three shots. So did the other officer. We both saw it and heard it. Aadil Mapunda held a bottle of soda; it did not look anything like a weapon. I heard the other officer ask, 'Why did you fire?' I heard him. I saw her. I heard and I saw. Aadil Mapunda was killed because of who he was, not for anything he did." Sam stepped back and tripped, stumbling as she handed the mic to Amina.

The crowd chanted Aadil's name. "Say his name, Aadil Mapunda." Then they recited a litany of names, a catalog of murders. Aadil Mapunda was one of them now.

Sam stood in the crowd while other people spoke.

When the protest was over, she still felt the pulse of the crowd, an extra energy that discharged as she walked up the hill to her house. Her counterregulatory hormones had jacked through her and then bottomed out. Spent, she sat at her table and wished she had done better.

If only she had shown up sooner to the scene of the crime. Maybe she could have shouted and stopped it somehow instead of just standing there watching. If only she had brought her phone and filmed it. If only she had gone to more meetings, more protests. Sam was so tired, but her body kept going anyway. A jumpy, erratic energy as if she were combusting the wrong kind of fuel.

That night, Sam didn't bother trying to go to sleep. She sipped some salted broth and headed into the miserable night streets. For blocks, she saw no one except a stray dog trotting the other way under the streetlights. What was she doing? Night patrol. Looking to see what could be seen.

At the corner of Lodi, she saw a man from behind. He was near the sagging vestibule of a dark, abandoned house. A year ago, she would have stopped, turned, and hurried back the other way, frightened. But tonight she continued to walk right by him. She kept her eyes fixed on his back as she went by, her steps sure. He jerked his body out of view while looking over his shoulder at her. It was then she realized that he was in rough shape, probably living on the street. And he was taking a piss in that corner. She made an audible intake of air and hurried on, trying not to see anything. He scowled when she passed and moved farther behind the vestibule.

Then he leaned his head back out, shouting at her. "Do you have a problem, bitch?"

She shook her head, she reddened, she sped up her steps. Foolish to lurk and scour in the middle of the night. Foolish anytime. She rushed back to the house. Breathless and cold, she made a fire. She was too tired to eat. It had been so long since she'd slept. Did she lock the door? She should lock the door before she drifted off.

Here was what happened to her, although Sam would soon forget many of the details: She sat sleepily by the fire. She kept seeing things in the corner of her eye, but nothing was there. She figured she was just uneasy after days of barely any sleep. A little light-headed. Her heart rate slightly elevated, the way it sometimes was before one of her heat flares. Then she heard a noise behind her. She turned just as she felt a blow—a wickedly hard, blunt hit to the back of her head. She imagined a two-by-four or a blackjack—the thing hitting her heavy and inanimate. A weapon. She could not see who hit her.

It occurred to her, as she lay there, that the police officer had hit her, the woman or the man or both. That it was MH. Or maybe the guy she'd seen pissing. The people who nodded out in the park, one of the street ghosts, the pale opioid zombies. She had it all wrong. She was not invisible. They were the invisible ones. She drifted off and then came to on the floor.

Sam opened her eyes. She tried to lift her head, but too heavy. Pain. She felt the back of her skull where the pain was coming from. Wet.

Her phone was in her pocket. She pulled it up to her face, touched the screen, tapped the word "emergency" and then 911. Before she spoke, she fell back to sleep. This she had no memory of either.

SIX

Ally

When Joe said he would be in town over Labor Day weekend, Ally realized that she wanted to take him to the State Fair. She had always imagined that when she was older and had a boyfriend, they would have a laugh together at the corny stuff at the fair. Besides, she was a little sick of hotel rooms and hiding. When they were in New York, they got to eat out in restaurants, go to museums, walk in the park hand in hand. But since then it had been texts, phone calls, and furtive meetings in Syracuse in which she snuck into his hotel room.

She liked hotel rooms, and she liked it when they had sex and then had room service. But it made her realize how limited they were. They had gone this far and now were stuck there. He'd said that it had to remain a secret affair even after she turned seventeen. She tried not to think about it, but the hotel reminded her of it just the same. They lay in the king bed. She had told her dad that she had another practice. (He was so unsuspecting of her, so oblivious to it all, so fucking clueless, that she didn't even have to tell him anything. She could have just said, Gotta go, taken her car and left. He would still be like, Bye, honey!) Joe and Ally fooled around and then ordered breakfast. Even in the hotel he was paranoid about being seen with her; she had to meet him in the room and hide in the bathroom when the room service was delivered.

"Have you ever been to the State Fair?" she said and took a sip of French-press coffee. It didn't taste as good as she thought it should.

"Nope," he said.

"Maybe we should go today," she said. "Instead of being cooped up here."

"C'mon, Ally, you know we can't take any chances of being seen."

"No one I know goes to the fair anymore except if there's a band they want to see, which there never is because it's usually sad music for old people, like Herman's Hermits with only one Hermit," she said. He laughed. "The fair is for kids and parents. Plus no one I know will go on Labor Day weekend. Too crowded."

"Sounds great."

"But it'd be so fun to see the exhibits together. I can show you everything. Instead of you showing me everything all the time, you know?" She looked at him, suddenly bent on the fair. "Please?"

"Okay," he said.

"Really?"

"If it makes you happy. You make me reckless, I guess." He kissed her.

They drove in his black Audi. Ally hated to admit being impressed by a car, but as Joe shifted and accelerated, the car took corners and gripped the road like you were on a ride. It had black leather seats and a burl wood dashboard. It was exciting to be driven in it. It really was.

They walked from the parking lot to the fairgrounds, which required using a pedestrian overpass. She could see how this exposure made him nervous. He kept looking around as they walked. But it was cloudy and a little rainy, which made them feel less exposed. By the time they walked through the gate, he seemed more comfortable. He even let her hold his hand.

They ducked under the cover of a kiosk and studied the map. Then Ally looked up and saw her mother walking toward them. Her heart started going so fast she could hear it in her head. Her mother hadn't spotted her yet. If she moved Joe behind the kiosk, her mother wouldn't see them and all would continue as it had been. But instead, Ally looked intently at the map. She put an arm around Joe and leaned into him.

"Let's stay here a minute and see if the rain stops." She knew— could feel it on her skin—that her mother now saw them. Out of the tiniest corner of her vision, she could see her mother stop and look their way. She turned to Joe and kissed him. She waited for the fallout, the blowup, the meltdown.

She waited. But minutes went by, and nothing. Finally she looked in the direction of her mother and saw that she was gone. How was it possible? Her mother had seen them. Seen her with Joe, who was not only a man, but a much older man. And not only a much older man, but someone her mother knew as a colleague to her husband (ex-husband). Yet she did and said nothing.

"Ready to go check out some long-haired rabbits?" Joe said.

"Yes, yes, I am," Ally said.

They saw the animals, looked at the winners of the county art fairs, and even shared a giant sundae, despite how Joe was usually against consuming sugar of any kind. It was the oddest thing, the run-in with her mother. Not only did it surprise Ally that her mother had let her be, but Ally had also discovered that on some level, she wanted to get caught. She wanted things to blow up. Was that true?

When she got home, her father told her that her mother had witnessed a shooting.

"What? When?"

"A few days ago, in the middle of the night. It was bad—a cop shot some poor kid. An unarmed kid."

"Jesus, is she freaked out?" Ally said.

"Of course, Ally. Anyone would be, and she's always way more everything than anyone else. Did she say anything to you?"

"No," she said.

"Maybe you could check in with her? I know a call or a text from you would help."

"Yeah, okay," Ally said. She was a little ashamed that she had blocked her mother, but she also didn't feel like starting up some big text thing with her.

The next day, Ally drove to her grandmother's house for a visit. At Joe's suggestion, she listened to Mark Frosh on the Joe Rogan podcast. Frosh was a billionaire philosopher guru who was made famous by a viral tweetstorm about how to make money and retire by forty. Not make money, "acquire wealth." It inspired the FIRE movement (Financial Independence, Retire Early). The whole idea of FIRE was presented not as greed but as liberty: work for yourself so you never have to work for someone else. "Self-investing" was his term. He was also famous for speed-reading books and finishing a book a day. Apparently he listened to books at double speed all the time. Ally knew that Joe listened to podcasts and audiobooks sped up 1.7x. Everything was about efficiency and velocity. This had also struck her at the YAD pitch simulations. All "innovative" tech really amounted to (the Fourth Industrial Revolution, etc.) was velocity. Increased processing times, superior compression, and efficiency all just meant faster. Progress = speed, but no one ever questioned that equation or even the idea of progression itself. Blind pursuit of velocity in all things seemed a little effed up to her.

Mark Frosh also suggested listening to things you wanted to learn, like a new language, on subaudible levels during sleep. He had invested in an app that used biofeedback to sync deep-sleep brain waves with inserted learning pods, but it was still in beta testing because it turned out that sleep brain waves were really complex and there were unintended consequences in which the biofeedback caused the wrong waves and prevented the sleeper from getting rapid eye movement sleep.

"So we are still working on it," Frosh said, "but what a tool once we get it down."

"Totally, man, that's amazing," said Joe Rogan.

Can you imagine letting an app collect data on your sleeping brain? Ally had read that without REM sleep, people rapidly deteriorated and would go mad in like two weeks. But hey, why not use sleep for some utility other than sleep? She had also read that nobody can actually multitask and that the whole superman high-achiever dogma (Jack Dorsey, Peter Thiel, Ray Dalio, et al.) of only sleeping four hours a night just made people sick and probably gave them Alzheimer's. But sure, invade our sleep too, farm that out for ultra-achievement, for "full density productivity." Productivity was a measurement of output per unit of input; which meant you always needed to get more than you put in, which was also kind of effed when she thought about it.

Frosh and Rogan circled back to goal setting and FIRE. Okay, but financial independence and retire early for what? Maybe if you retire you won't have to speed-read (speed-listen to) books or utilize your brain waves while you sleep?

She switched off that podcast and listened to NPR. Then she turned that off and listened to the sounds of the road as she drove.

Ally loved visiting her grandma Lily's house. When she arrived, she could see Lily working in her garden, picking the last of her little perfect tomatoes for their dinner. She would cook chili or paella or pasta. Lily would have bought her favorite crusty bread from the bakery for them. After dinner they would sit on the couch and have homemade apple crisp or pie and stream a movie. It was exactly what Ally wanted and needed.

But when Ally got close to Lily, she saw how loose her clothes were. Her eyes had a puffiness under them, and her skin looked dry. Lily hugged Ally and led her into the house. She still smelled the same as she always did, like lavender soap.

They did all the things Ally counted on. Ally told Lily about her college applications, her summer activities, and her life with her dad. She told her about the fiasco of her mother's stand-up. ("You know she didn't mean to upset you," Lily said. "But she is so clueless—that was so private. She has no boundaries of any kind,"

Ally said. "When it comes to you, I'm afraid that is true.") Ally trusted Lily and almost told her about Joe, but then she felt weirdly ashamed and self-conscious. What would Lily think of Ally having a secret affair? Maybe that would be okay with her, but Ally knew that she would dislike Joe, dislike all the development stuff he did, and positively hate all the pretend benevolence that veiled the moneymaking and the power it gave him. So no, she wouldn't spill about Joe.

They didn't watch a movie, because they were both too tired. They sat in their pajamas on the sectional drinking tea.

"I have something I've been meaning to give you," Lily said. Then she pulled out a long narrow velvet box, the kind that snapped open and held nice jewelry. She handed it to Ally.

"Thank you, Grandma," Ally said. The last time she'd gotten jewelry from Lily was on her sixteenth birthday, when she gave Ally her gold cameo ring.

"Open it!" Lily said, laughing.

Ally pressed the catch and it sprang open, and there on the pale gray silk was Lily's string of real natural pearls. Ally loved these pearls (not too big, not graduated, and with the most exquisite sheen of creamy opalescence). She gasped.

"Put them on."

Ally put them around her neck and clicked in the little silver safety clasp.

Lily covered her mouth with her hand. "My god, you are so beautiful. Born to wear those pearls. I think your mother will kill me. She wanted me to wait until your graduation to give you any more of my nice jewelry. But I don't want to wait."

Ally was so glad to get them, but she sensed that it meant something bad was happening, something dreadful.

Then Lily said, "Honey, I need to tell you something serious. I have what they call leiomyosarcoma."

"What's that?" But Ally knew all about "sarcoma," had looked it up before. It was from "sarkoma," which meant fleshy substance, and "sarkoun," something that leads to a growth of flesh—i.e., a tumor. "Flesh" itself was fascinating; it was from Old English, from "flaesc," meaning meat ("sarcasm" also came from the same root via "sarkazein," which meant to strip off flesh by means of a sneer or taunt).

Her grandmother had a tumor.

"Isn't that some kind of cancer?" Ally said, staring at her tea.

"It is. Cancer of the soft tissues."

"What stage is it?"

"You know so much about cancer, huh? It's stage four."

Ally nodded but felt oddly calm. "That's terrible news."

"I know it's a shock, but I have a great doctor. I am doing some treatments to make the time I have left the best it can be. That's all I want."

The time I have left. Ally sipped her tea, felt the mug in her hands. "Does Mom know?"

"She knows some of it. Not all the specifics yet. I have to tell her in stages, because she gets very upset."

"Yeah, I know how she gets."

"She has enough to worry about right now. But I knew you could handle it."

Ally nodded. Ally was calm partly because she was stunned, but partly because it was just how she reacted to things. That was one reason she did so well in competitions. Unflappable. The higher the stress, the calmer she became.

"We'll talk more in the morning, okay?" They hugged and then went to bed. Ally lay on the couch under the comforter and looked up "leiomyosarcoma." She read all the pages on the Mayo Clinic website and then stopped looking. She closed her eyes, exhausted, and thought about Lily dying. It was something she had feared her whole life. But it was also something she'd expected. Many of her friends had lost grandparents. She knew it would happen, and yet she knew this would change everything in a way she couldn't quite imagine. She tapped her phone back on and the blue light hurt her tired eyes in the dark. She really, really wanted to call her mom. But what would she say, whispering in the dark? Plus she was still mad at her mother, wasn't she? What about Dad? No calls—she might wake her grandmother, who needed her sleep. It never occurred to her to call or text Joe about it. She fell asleep, clutching her phone.

In the morning, Lily was cheerful. She made them bacon and eggs. Ally would stay a little longer and help Lily in the garden. They didn't talk about the leiomyosarcoma, although Ally had continued to read all about it on her phone when she'd woken up at six.

They weeded and picked. Lily seemed fine, like nothing had changed. But for being a bit thinner, she didn't seem sick. When they were done, she made Ally coffee for the road.

"Thanks, kiddo," she said, her hand brushing Ally's face. Big, long hug. They pulled apart and looked at each other.

"I love you, Grandma," Ally said.

"And I love you. You and your mom need to come out here soon, because I'm not as keen on driving to Syracuse."

"Of course," Ally said.

"Your mother is having a hard time."

"I know."

"Ally, I need you to forgive her."

Ally sighed.

"I'm serious. You need to take care of her for me."

Lily took Ally's hands in hers and made Ally look at her.

"Okay," Ally said.

"You promise?" Lily said.

"Of course."

"She's my darling baby girl, you know. Just like you are to her. She needs you."

Ally nodded.

She had two missed calls from Joe. Then he texted her that they should FaceTime when she got home. When she arrived, her dad wasn't there, so she took the opportunity of privacy to call Joe back.

Before she could tell him about her trip and her grandmother, he said, "We need to talk."

"Okay," she said.

She guessed what was coming. She watched him as he spoke. It was a glitchy connection, but she got the gist. He wanted to "take a break." He loved her but felt she wanted more than he could give. After Labor Day, after she'd kissed him in public, he'd realized how dangerous things were getting. So some time off to think about things, yadda yadda. He was breaking up with her.

"I agree," she said. She was calm. She was ice.

"We'll still be friends, of course. I hope that for us."

After she got off the phone, she didn't cry, but she took a long bath and delineated, out loud to the tub surround, as if she were on a podcast, all the things about Joe she didn't like. "Let me walk you through it," she said to the tub.

He listened to audiobooks at 1.7x speed. Not 2x or 1.5x. The precision of that and what he thought it implied really bugged her.

He tried to "zero" his inbox every day.

He rode—no, "crushed"—randonneur 400K endurance bike rides.

He followed Elon Musk's productivity hacks.

He told her to "level up," to "do purpose" and assess "SWOT" (strengths, weaknesses, opportunities, threats).

He spoke of "bringing things to scale"/"scaling up"/"scalability."

He dated a girl who was still in high school.

She got out of the tub. Before she dried off, she picked up her phone and texted him:

Delete my photos.

After her bath, she got back in her car. Ally thought she would drive to Loomis House and surprise her mother. She texted her dad (where was he?) and then took off, listening to Patti Smith instead of fucking podcasts. She figured Patti Smith = the opposite of Joe. Patti Smith did not optimize her productivity. Ally's mood lifted a little.

She hadn't been to Loomis House in years. Her mother had started working there after she'd chaperoned Ally's school field trip to the house back in sixth grade. Her mother had lamented at how run-down and unloved it was. So she'd ended up volunteering and then getting hired by the jankiest historical house in New York State.

It was even lamer than Ally remembered; all the informational plaques had a flimsy, low-budget look. All the rooms were threadbare, musty, and dull. Why was seeing someone's house interesting? Ally didn't have a feeling for these things, not like her mother, who seemed to channel entire lives just by looking at someone's writing desk.

Mrs. Delven was working. Her mother was off this afternoon.

"But she's added some new things in the history and information room. You should take a look."

Ally nodded and went into the room. There was a giant glass case. "A Cabinet of Curiosities," it said, curated by Samantha Raymond. And a pamphlet about Syracuse history, written by her mother.

She picked one up and ran her finger over the type. What was that called, the print that you can feel on the heavy paper? Her mother had put a lot of effort into these items that no one else cared about. Ally looked at the curios cabinet, which contained objects her mother had collected and then identified with little explainer cards. Ally read them all and looked at the objects. My weirdo mom. The care and detail her mother applied to the things she loved. Her freaky enthusiasms all on display. All this work for something hardly anyone would see. As Ally read her mom's pamphlet, she felt an unexpected rush of affection for her dear, silly mom. And at long last, Ally missed her.

She texted her.

Hi! Where r u?
I'm at freakin' Loomis House, lol

Ally walked outside to her car and waited for her mom to text her back. Which, shockingly, did not happen instantly.

I like the exhibits u made

Maybe her phone was turned off.

SEVEN

Syracuse

I

SYRACUSE: A PAMPHLET

compiled by Samantha Raymond of Loomis House
(please take one)

Why was Syracuse built?
Salt. From natural salt springs and marshes. In 1656, Jesuit missionaries first came to the area where the people of the Onondaga Nation had been living for centuries. A (brief, failed) misson was built near Onondaga Lake, which was the place where the Great Peacemaker brought the five original Nations of the Haudensaunee ("Iroquois") Confederacy together. Although missionaries noted the brine water, they soon left. During the Revolutionary War, American colonists burned down Onondaga villages from the lake to what is now Nedrow. The 1784 Treaty of Fort Stanwix gave salt processers access rights to the land, and in 1797, the state legislature took control of the southern part of the lakeshore and named it the Onondaga Salt Springs Reservation.

What else was manufactured in Syracuse?
Typewriters (Smith Corona). Lanterns (Dietz). Automobiles (Franklin). Air conditioners (Carrier). Soda ash (Solvay process). Furniture (Stickley).

What is, and has been, the crossroads of New York, the Empire State?
Syracuse. Salina Street—named for the salt flats that powered early development—crossed East Genesee Street, at the center of the new

city. These streets were laid over two trails that crossed at the center of New York State, the east-west and north-south passages used by Native peoples and then the settlers who took over the Native lands. The center of the city = the center of the state.

What came after salt demand slowed and salt mining died off?
Soda ash manufactured from local (now much less valuable) salt and limestone.

What is soda ash? How was it made and what was it for?
Soda ash is sodium carbonate, Na_2CO_3, accomplished by means of the Solvay process, patented and licensed from France. Soda ash is used for glass, for soap, for papermaking.

What waste does it make?
Sodium chloride, which leaches from waste beds into the ground. So began the process of turning the pristine Onondaga Lake into what would become the nation's first Superfund site. Two decades of cleanup and it is considered "recovered," yet you should not eat the fish from it if you are pregnant or if you are a child. Nevertheless, one can see people fishing the lake. Signs warn. An image of a black bar crosses out the fish. But the fish, it seems, will be eaten, polluted or not.

Why is Onondaga Lake still so polluted, so many years after the Superfund designation and cleanup?
"Metropolitan Syracuse Wastewater Treatment Plant (Metro) contributes 20% of the annual flow. No other lake in the United States receives as much of its inflow as treated wastewater." (Yeah, Wikipedia.)

What did the city boosters call Syracuse over the years?
The Salt City, which was scotched in the 1980s for the Emerald City, which didn't seem to convince anyone, no matter how green it became in the summer.

What else was the city known for?

Many people escaped slavery via Syracuse, where reformist and anti-slavery sentiment ran so deep Daniel Webster called the city "a laboratory of abolitionism, libel, and treason."

What are some of the notable empty structures downtown?

—The abandoned train platform: only fully visible as you zoom by on 690 East. Statues now stand where humans used to. The train tracks have been relocated. If you look at this spot on Google Maps, it actually says "Abandoned Train Platform." It even has Google reviews (4 out of 5 stars).

—The Carnegie Library on Montgomery Street: built in 1905 of yellow brick and white limestone, all Beaux Arts grandeur with columns and a parapet. In the 1980s a developer built another structure of cheap utility and minimal solidity and, in order to get tax breaks, included in it space for the downtown library. The books moved. The old library building remains.

—The People's African Methodist Episcopal Church of Zion, built in 1911. Designed by Charles Colton in collaboration (perhaps) with one of the first Black architects practicing in the United States, Wallace Rayfield. In the early 1960s, the interstate overpass was built nearby, and the church building, with its poignant Gothic revival arch and three-story bell tower, has been empty since 1975.

—The old entrance gate to Oakwood Cemetery (built as a "Beautiful City of the Dead" in 1859, where the living and the dead could peacefully commune in the fresh air with views of the city). The marble gate was abandoned (but not torn down or moved). I discovered it one day when I got on 1-81 North at Colvin Street and saw the stone remnants, only visible once you were on the highway. I almost crashed my car when I saw it. It had been there my whole life, but I had never noticed it before. I once tried to walk to it from the new entrance on the other side of the cemetery, but it is difficult to reach.

—The First English Lutheran Church on James Street. Every time I drive by the silhouette of its stucco tower with its iron Arts and Crafts mission-style cutouts, I think that it looks so beautiful but also ridiculous, like it should be in Santa Fe. It used to hold services that were frequented by African refugees, Congolese Christians mostly. But it also gave space to a food bank, AA meetings, Syracuse Streets, and other community organizations. Old buildings are expensive to maintain. It can't be torn down because of historical protections, but it can be empty.

—The Syracuse Central High School on Harrison Street. A whole city block, empty for a decade. Boarded-up windows outside, but an intact wood-paneled two-story auditorium and sweeping staircase inside. Rumors have it that it will become a Tech Garden, or a Tech Hub, or a Tech Incubator in the coming future (and I tell you, the future is coming) by dint of 5G, by becoming a Smart City, by what is called the Syracuse Surge.

What is 5G? The Syracuse Surge? What is a Smart City?
Your guess is as good as mine.

What about the Erie Canal?
Sometimes, when I leave the Home Depot parking lot and pass Dunn Tire and approach the intersection of Erie Boulevard and Bridge Street (Sunoco on the southwest corner, Wendy's on the northeast corner, a closed gas station on the southeast corner), I imagine the Erie Canal flowing by, before it was paved over. All that remains is the name, Erie, and what one tries to envision before every single thing I see was built. One thing I know is that it must have been better. No matter how much garbage was thrown into the canal, no matter the smell of a canal, with no natural sloughing or tide. No matter coal burning. Erie was made into a multilane, pedestrian-hostile boulevard, and it progressively became uglier, ruined by corporate archi-

tecture and branded plastic facades so familiar to Americans as to be almost invisible (but not, alas, invisible). I am not a snob, not precious, but the orange face of the Home Depot sign, its inoffensive letters and colors, fatigued me, made me sad and dull. What happened to us? When did progress become so ugly?

A CABINET OF CURIOSITIES

a glass box containing local and historical artifacts
curated by Samantha Raymond of Loomis House

1) Syroco Wood wall hanging made from wood pulp constituted with a polymer and then injected into a mold. 1950s. Relief of two Scottish terriers frolicking among peonies.

2) Syracuse China glazed porcelain charger plate, "Millbrook" pattern, 1940s. Airbrushed shadow tone image of an aeroplane, white outlined in deep blue against light blue, with the city skyline below.

3) Heart pin cushion, 1901. Haudenosaunee. Red wool challis, velvet, green and silver glass beads, cotton backing. Stuffed with sawdust.

4) A felted orange college pep-rally flag, slightly tattered, that reads "Syracuse Orangemen." 1900s. (Name later changed to the Orange, for obvious reasons.)

5) Silver-plate flatware, one spoon and one fork, "Tudor" style, 1890s, manufactured thirty miles outside the city of Syracuse by the Oneida Community, a financially successful Perfectionist commune that abolished private property and, notoriously, advocated complex marriage, communal child-rearing, and stirpiculture, the horticulture of children for maximum spiritual

qualities. Clara Loomis lived there for two years. It was where she met her eventual husband, Henry Loomis.

6) *The Wonderful Wizard of Oz,* by L. Frank Baum, illustrated, cloth-bound, with green and red lettering and an image of a bespecta-cled lion with a ribbon in his mane. First edition, 1900. Children's novel written in Chittenango, New York, ten miles east of Syra-cuse, which was the model for the Emerald City.

7) Small porcelain fragment with a translucent turquoise glaze and delicate incisions. Made by Adelaide Alsop Robineau in 1920.

8) *The Craftsman* magazine, vol. 1, no. 1, 1901. Sand-colored paper with a black ink decorative border and red letters. Gustav Stick-ley's magazine to promote his utopian ideas about Arts and Crafts houses and furniture (his iconic designs were then built at his fac-tory in East Syracuse). This first issue was dedicated to William Morris and was largely written by Irene Sargent, an art historian and eventual Syracuse University professor.

9) A political or advertising flyer (both), embossed letterpress on card stock. Printed and distributed around the city in 2017. Leg-end reads: "Embrace NTE."

10) A pamphlet written by Clara Loomis, "On the Avoidance of Pregnancy and Male Continence," for the League of Deliberate Population, 1895. Offset black type on cream-white paper, hand-bound. Although it was a medical instruction pamphlet, it was flagged as pornographic by Anthony Comstock's New York Soci-ety for the Suppression of Vice.

EIGHT

Clara Loomis

18 October 1868

Dearest Mother,

I know that you will one day understand why I left home. I hope
that you can forgive me. By the time you read this, I will be far
away. I can't tell you where I am going, but I want you to know that
I will be sound and healthy. God has led me to this place, and I
think I will have greater purpose than if I had stayed at home.

I draw upon this verse from Romans as my guide, which is very
well known to you: "And be not conformed to this world: but be ye
transformed by the renewing of your mind, that ye may prove what
is that good, and acceptable, and perfect, will of God." I try to be
humble and yet have the will to not be conformed. I must discover
what it means to renew my mind so that I can be good.

As joyful as I am for my new life, I already miss you terribly. I
miss the garden. I miss sitting with you by the fire. On the Sabbath,
I can see everyone gathering after supper to hear Papa read from
the Bible. Please tell him not to worry after me.

When I am settled, I will write with my address and all my news.
Until then, please be patient and try to understand God's plan for
me. You and Papa have always said that I was different, that I had a
too curious mind for a girl. You were right, Mother.

Yours humbly,
Clara

15 January 1869

Dearest Mother,

Today, on the eve of my seventeenth birthday, the time has come for me update you and reveal where I live now; for the past three months I have been living in the Oneida Community near Sherrill, not far from Oneida Lake. I know there are many rumors about this place, but it is simply like no place else, a community built on love instead of greed. We believe that through confession in Christ, we attain Perfection, which means we can have Heaven on Earth; we renounce the pride and evil of ownership and private property. It is a matter of upmost importance that we share everything. We try to radiate the goodliness of true Christian life unmarred by competition or striving for material things. Instead we strive for spiritual exaltation, for the sublime in ordinary life, and regard everything that distracts us from that as petty vanity. We live in the midst of daily ecstatic expression; we discover the glory of God in ourselves and one another. Moreover, Mama, I am part of something bigger than myself; living here has untangled me from worldliness, from servitude, and from the degradation of a woman's lot in life.

Do you remember my friend Nellie Wallingford? She lives here, and I consider her one of my sisters now. She wrote me about this place and invited me. What a life girls can live here. We can study what we want. We get to wear pantaloons instead of long skirts; we cut our hair short. We don't waste time longing over styles, jewelry, and fancy dress. We get to do any occupation God draws us to: teaching, working in the wonderful, extensive library, cultivating the garden, child tending, cabinet making, cooking, but also type-setting and operating our printing press, editing and writing stories for our circular, and even designing products for our metal manufacture business. We rotate the work. The drudgery doesn't take up your every day when all the labor is shared.

O Mama, the mansion house is so beautiful! It has a Mansard roof like a grand house in Paris. We are building another wing as we grow. I have my own pretty little room, but none of us stays too long alone. We rejoice in our community with one another. No one is hungry or poor. No one is excluded. It is as if a family could grow to be a whole village, with everyone caring for everyone. It is so clear to me that is what God wants for all of us. I see that Heaven can be ours if we want it. Suffering is not required for life; it is the wages of greed and pride. We don't have to fight other people or jealously guard what poor things we grab in the material world. There is enough on God's great Earth for all to prosper if we share equally. Possessiveness and ownership make one mean and small. What have the recent years taught us? No one should be possessed by another or ruled over by anyone but God.

I wish I could send you a photograph. This year I will sit for an Ambrotype; one of the older women here, Elsie More, makes such portraits. Until then, I enclose a drawing that Nellie made of me. I think the likeness is accurate. I have become as healthy a girl as you will ever see. We are all very active and go out of doors every day, even in the winter. Women don't faint in the parlor here. Women don't wear corsets or other binding attire. I can dance. I can breathe. I can sit cross-legged on the grass if I want. I have never slept better. We eat the food we grow right here on our farm. We don't eat animals. We make a delicious, healthful basket cheese, though, and I am never wanting for anything. The Community is famous locally for its straw-berry shortcake, and anyone who doubts the divine in the everyday here need only taste it to believe! Remember the special Gold Cake with pink boiled icing you made for me on my last birthday? As wonderful as the baking is here, I will miss your cake tomorrow. As I write this, I indulge in a lunch of sweet-cucumber pickles and Graham Flour biscuits. Truly, I have a wonderful appetite from all the activity, but I don't overindulge. None of us, not man or woman, smoke tobacco or drink ardent spirits. At night we listen to music in the grand piano room. Sometimes we perform plays and always we read Scripture. My life is filled with beauty and love.

We live in miraculous times. We are not cloistered here. I eagerly follow the news of the day. I read the New York papers, which are mailed to the library every week. At last wretched President Johnson has been overruled, and this year I know we will see real emancipation and true civil rights for the former slaves. Soon we will address other forms of bondage and inequality. All of us deserve to be free, to be safe, to be fed, and to express love. How could God not want us to work for that every day? In this small Eden, I hope we will show others it is possible to live communally.

Please write to me here. I have enclosed the address. I am anxious for news of you, Papa, and all my brothers and sisters. I miss Ella every day and pray for her. I think she looks down from Heaven and rejoices over the life I chose.

Yours faithfully,
Clara

January 15, 1869

Father Noyes has suggested that I keep a journal of my spiritual practice and my Perfection with God. I have done that with earnest and regular obedience. He has looked on it and been satisfied with my progress, although he is careful to say only God knows what is in anyone's heart. "He knows us better than we can ever know ourselves." In my daily contemplation, I discovered that I have need of a more private accounting. How does one understand anything in this life unless one uses language, either spoken or written? And how can one tell the deepest truth if she knows it will be examined by others? I need to work toward my own clarity.

Yesterday, Henry had to sit for Mutual Criticism; it was a hard thing to witness. Father Noyes accused him of excessive self-esteem, and Henry nodded in agreement. I sat in the very back of the Great Room and felt tears of shame come to my eyes. Father Noyes has told us we would be free of shame. I am confused.

I have not yet had to sit for Mutual Criticism, but in truth I wonder if I ought to suggest it myself. I am guilty of a terrible vanity; I feel especial love for Henry. I know that Father Noyes says we must resist exclusive, possessive longing. I know that we all belong equally to one another. Yet when he comes with me to my room, he is Henry and everyone else slides away from my eyes.

It was only six weeks ago that Father Noyes—John—invited me to his bed for my very first time with anyone. He knew I was ready for deeper Fellowship because of my spiritual joy. "Joy is you, Clara, and you are joy. God's Perfection radiates from you." He was careful with me. We lay naked together under the blanket, and he gentle touched all the slopes and valleys of my body. He let me do the same for him; how odd male bodies are. His beard so full and wiry. I liked the tickle of it on my breasts. "Surrender everything to the spirit, for we are truly beyond sin." He stayed with me until I was released of all my suffering and sadness. He practiced the discipline of male continence and held his own pleasure back. This allowed amative, spiritual coitus instead of procreative coitus. We were liberated from the fear of pregnancy and childbirth.

After, when I told him how nice it felt, John said what you have experienced is a celebration of God, a manifestation of Heaven on Earth. "As we are told in Peter, 'ye rejoice with joy unspeakable and full of glory,'" he said to me. Truly, I was happy and at peace. He laughed at my expression.

"Why do you laugh?" I asked, drowsy with the warmth of our bodies' heat.

"Dear Clara, why do people settle for worldly tribulations? They pray over the after-life, over the future, yet they chase trivial things. Here we are, with the bodies God gave us, in Heavenly ecstasy, already in Paradise."

This recalled to me what he preached the first night I stayed here. He is a magnetic and, in truth, mesmerizing speaker. He spoke to all the younger members, but I felt as if he were speaking directly to me. To my spirit. He smiled as he preached, and his eyes twinkled in the candle-light of the high-ceilinged Great Room.

"What if what you are waiting for has already happened? What if happiness is yours if you want it? Do you think God wants us miserable? Our happiness celebrates God, honors the gifts He hath given us."

In my first interview with him, he spoke with such feeling about the slavery of pregnancy and childbirth. How cruel it was to make women suffer over and over when it did not have to be this way.

I told him about watching my sister Ella die; he told me about his four premature babies when he first married; God was showing him the need for "male restraint and continence."

I admire Father Noyes's mind and his generosity, I do. How grateful I am that he spied me reading the newspapers in the library; he recruited me to edit his articles for "The Circular," from which I have learned so much. His complex ideas on well-ordered procreation are our future. He gave me Darwin and Galton to read. I have so many ideas about stirpiculture and human cultivation, on how to make our species deliberate and not mistaken, furtive, and indentured to chance.

We grew so close, but now I think he has changed toward me because he senses my attachment to Henry. But also because of a change in our own sexual congress. We are told we can say no, but can we really, and to John, God's own emissary on Earth? What an ingrate I am to write this, but we are also told that God wants us to pursue the light of truth wherever it leads us.

Fellowship with John was and is precious and loving. He is a great and good man. But it was with Henry that I understood the true Godliness in our human bodies. It was with Henry that I felt the "joy unspeakable." Henry is not as ascended in Fellowship as Father Noyes. He is practically as young as I am, but despite his youth, he is master of his ardor. Usually the young men must be paired with the older women because they need to master male continence. But Henry has ascended fast. John himself had identified him as being of a special spiritual category. Even the Committee on Stirpiculture had chosen him as someone who should be allowed to procreate. How can he be so harshly criticized when he did everything right? Henry asked Father Noyes if he could have Fellowship with me, and Father Noyes took it to the Committee, which allowed it despite Henry's youth.

My confession: how often I revisit in my mind the very first time Henry and I lay together. It bewitches me; it intoxicates me as if it were happening to my body as I remember. Henry came to my room, and we were soon naked like the children angels we knew ourselves to be. Henry is sturdy and much taller than I am, yet he is soft to touch. All of his skin is as smooth as my inner wrist, or the nape of my neck, where he first kissed me. We simply stroked each other and whispered for hours with no coitus. We kissed, and our bodies grew less and less foreign to each other. Then he told me to lie back, for he wanted to kiss me everywhere. I said, "Yes! But I will have my turn too, to kiss all of your body." When we finally had intercourse, it was as natural and gentle as those easy kisses. Then I felt it, a mystical quickening—as if the spirit came to a pinpoint inside of me and then flowed and stuttered out to every part of my body. I knew it was God, it was Heaven, my body had a divine gift. After that first night, all I have to do is look at Henry; think of Henry; and I feel the same light of God in my body. They call some people Old Lights and other people New Lights. I don't think that is right. My light is new and old at once. Inside me but beaming out to the world too.

My confession: I long to realize my own Perfection. I pray, but it is very hard for me to want anyone but Henry. When others ask for Fellowship with me, I want to say no, but I feel that I should not. I should love them all, especially Father Noyes. I should be open to them. Yet it must be some weakness in me, for I cannot stop the feelings I have. I confess that when I see Henry with the other girls, my very sisters here, I grow faint and get a terrible pain in my stomach. Father John has noticed; he gave me a look of disapproval when I left the dinner table last week, looking faint and unable to swallow anything.

I fear for what will happen. I have to hide my heart from everyone but Henry. He too wants only me. If we confessed it to anyone, they would make us stop laying with each other. I cannot bear that, wanting only him. But even those words, "wanting only," is a form of enslavement. Why would God make us so confused? Can God make us need to deceive? But what if it is possible that love between two can also be Perfect and a part of Heaven on Earth? Can it be possible that Father Noyes is wrong? Writing these words, thinking these words, will lead to expulsion. I must stop if I can. Tear this up. I do not want to leave here and go back to the worldly ungodly cruel life that lay ahead for me in Syracuse.

.   .   .

I wrote Mother tonight. Father Noyes insisted. I explained that she may try to get me if I tell her where I am. He told me that many mothers suffer from the pride of motherhood. That I can resist her, but not to shut her out. He told me to guard against my own "philo-progenitiveness." My phrenology was similar to hers, and we should know our own weaknesses. Many women get too attached to their own children, when all your fellows deserve your attachment and love. We are all God's children. No one is your child, your possession.

I listen to what he says and obey him; but he does not know my mother. If she knew the full story of this life, she would see it as wanton. She would not see it as a sacrament; she would not see that conventional marriage is akin to slavery. She would not see that. I remember when we talked about the Free Love Society and what they espoused. She viewed it as Jacobin Godlessness. But other times she conceded that women were no better off than slaves if they married the wrong man, or if they had pregnancies they couldn't bear, like Ella did. Is there a chance that she would reconsider if it wasn't Godless? I long to talk to her. I miss her. But I can't go back. Twice I watched my mother almost die in childbirth. I had seen her pale and writhing in pain. I had wiped her brow and prayed. Both times she recovered. She lost one of the babies she had in those terrible cruel births. Samuel, born breech and still as a doll. Mother let me hold his little body. We wept together. All of it is part of life, especially the life of a woman.

None of it prepared me for my sister Ella dying. She was too young, too slight, but she was healthy. She could have lived a long life. The two miscarriages before this pregnancy were a sign that everyone ignored. This pregnancy was painful and mistaken from the start all the way to the end. She vomited every day of it. Maybe some women's bodies are not meant to give birth; with birth as a constant possibility, how can women tolerate sexual congress at all? No one asks those questions. Perhaps some women may not want to give birth, regardless of health. Our options are so narrow. That or be a wayward, shameless woman or a loveless spinster. Susan B. Anthony is a Quaker schoolteacher who never married and never had children. She lives the life of the mind. Women must renounce physical love, giving up the life of the body, or we can give birth over and over and be a slave to the body, be haunted by death, our own and our children's. I don't want to leave Oneida, this God-struck paradise, no matter how I love Henry, no matter how confused I am.

Thank God for Nellie writing me of this place, where women have equality with men. The women don't get pregnant unless they want to, and they are able to have sex with whomever they want whenever they want and not only dwell in God's light but become God's light. I must remind myself of why I came and not squander this haven.

The morning after my sister's funeral, I packed a small satchel and hid it under my bed. I took the little money I had from the sewing and embroidery I took in. In the very middle of the night, I woke up. I was not tired, and I was not scared. I dressed quietly in the dark, and I crept out of my room on stocking feet. Only my dear Jack heard me, but he is a sleepy old dog. He watched me but never made a sound.

I crept out into the city night. The gas lamps made James Street beautiful and lonely. I sat on a bench in front of our house to tie my boots. I brushed leaves off my stockings. Thank Heaven it wasn't very cold or wet. I pulled my satchel onto my back; I was ready. I walked to the train platform and climbed the steps. I could see my house and my street in the distance below me. I bought a ticket for the 5 a.m. train. As the train pulled away from my city, it still felt like an ordinary trip, not quite real. I reached Oneida an hour and a half later, just as the dawn was starting to break.

I had the directions from Nellie in my bag. It was a half hour walk to the Oneida Mansion.

I walked and the sky grew pink and bright. After I passed through a little village, I saw in the distance a grass-covered hill and the beautiful new building that surely must be the Oneida

Mansion. I didn't yet have bloomer pants or comfortable boots. My hair was still long. But I untied and removed my little bonnet and started to run.

I ran fast and my legs felt strong. My hair came loose and I could feel it flying behind me. Faster and faster I went toward that hill, my lungs burning and my breaths coming hard. When I finally got there, Nellie would greet me at the door. She would exclaim at my rosy cheeks. I would laugh and embrace her. She would take me to the kitchen, where I would be given a slice of bread, soft butter, a small dish of prunes and raisins, and a big glass of sweet milk.

But before then, I ran toward the hill and the house, my new life unfolding ahead of me, and my old life left behind. I ran faster than I ever have, my body warming to the task. I lifted my head, my legs pumped in great strides. Up the hill they propelled me. I felt as if I had wings and I could run forever. What a thing this body is; what discoveries I will make with it.

NINE

Blood

Sam opened her eyes. Her face pressed against something. Stuck to something. She tried to turn her head, her cheek pulled, heavy, not all hers. Ow. She realized—slowly, because the world felt slow—something was terribly wrong. She touched the back of her head where the pain was coming from. Sticky. She looked at her finger the way she had seen in movies. Blood. She put her head back down to rest. Her face was wet; she realized, before she again lost consciousness, that she was lying in a puddle of blood, her blood, a deep crimson she had seen so many times. She recalled that she had been hit, knocked to the red oak floor, where she watched the pool of blood get bigger. She didn't worry. She was too weary to worry. Instead she wondered.

In her dream, the blood flowed from her body and filled the whole world.

In her dream, she was not scared of the blood. She laughed. What was blood to a woman? There was menstruation, the monthly bleed: "A flow of blood and other material from the lining of the uterus, lasting for several days and occurring in sexually mature women who are not pregnant at intervals of about one lunar month until the onset of menopause."

There was menopause: "The cessation of menstruation for at least twelve months."

There was the in-between, the perimenopause, where Sam lived, in which you bled still, randomly and erratically, so that it would surprise you the way it did when you were a fourteen-year-old; it would stain things, unnerve you with its heaviness or clots or darkness.

Sam lay on the ground in her blood and hallucinated that all the blood was yet another period. She dreamed of her recent period, her painful, leaving, weird period, maybe her last ever period.

It began with the gurgle in the lower gut, the bloated, full feeling, but with movement. It was familiar to her, but it had been months, so it came with an odd distance to it: again? This again? There was a strange cathartic quality in the process. The doubled-over, lie-in-bed cramps. She visualized her uterus as she felt the intense period pain. She imagined it squeezing out the shedding lining. This made the pain feel better: productive, almost cleansing. This was probably the last one, certainly one of the last ones. And it was voluminous, intense, relentless. On and on it went. As always, after the pain, the bleeding was profuse. Copious. Overflowed. She had wadded up toilet paper to get her through the night. When she stood up, she had to hold the wadded tissue to keep it all from whooshing out of her. She waddled awkwardly to the toilet. Messy, her body was a mess. Disgusting yet fascinating. (Classic misogynist joke: Can you trust a creature that bleeds for three days but doesn't die?) She had to go out and buy tampons and pads again. What a thing, this out-of-control body. It made her aware of how her body was alien to her, progressing toward its decline, its next phase, regardless of her desire or collusion. Her participation was not required.

Just like her pregnancy. At a certain point it had occurred to her that being forty weeks pregnant was like being on a terrifying ride at an amusement park. Once you are on it, you can't get off. You will see the thing through no matter what, no matter how scared you are. Her body would do what it would do, her willing participation an illusion. Yes she could breathe and push. She could help it happen. But she could not stop it, she could not get off the ride. These wacky menopause periods reminded her of that feeling. She was a body, a highly complex organism in which there were many autonomic activities that she didn't command. Her "cycle." This was the last time, probably. After the first day, the pains lessened and she enjoyed the relief of the flow. Get it all out. What if her hormones, the things that kick that last period into action, what if they crap out before she got rid of the last lining, the mess of blood, the unneeded stuff of the uterus? Would it stay there for the rest of her life? Get it all out. She wanted it all out of her, and then it could shut down. Would she be at all sad that it was gone, this monthly process? Odd to have something so intimate and regular and pretty unpleasant stop. Would she forget what it feels like, actually feels like, the way you forget the body pain of childbirth?

Childbirth, another blood-ridden affair. A gush of effluvia, cleaned up by nurses, but then Sam bled for two weeks. Not a period, but it felt cleansing and draining, both, that postpartum bleed. And also sort of powerful. How could you not be in awe of your body and all its workings after it gave birth?

Blood had always been an elemental part of who she was. She

had never been one of those women with an IUD or birth control pills who didn't get her period. She had the monthly clock. Her amazing body had been so precise for years. She knew when she ovulated, knew when she would become ravenous, knew when she would bleed. But now, it had been haywire for over a year. Destabilizing. Transitioning. Her maybe last one. You of course can't know your last period when you get it. Only later, looking back, could you realize it was your last. So maybe this one was it. Should she enjoy it more, feel sad in some way? She was no longer fertile (which had been mostly a burden, a horrible lifelong threat). No, she was glad to see it go. To see what her body would be like next, when it was no longer occupied with reproduction. When it was no longer blessed with this "special secretion." Apparently, sleep mattered less. Would it change her relation to time passing? Was her cycle a measure of her life, and now days would turn to months to years without her noticing?

What did that come from, "special secretion"?

A nineteenth-century book of female sexual function by Alice Bunker Stockham. "Eve, having through her transgressions entailed upon her daughters a curse, they needed more renovation and regeneration than men; and that aside from ordinary depurition this special secretion was given to them."

Right. The monthlies, the menses, the blood, was also called the Curse. Curse or blessing, her own blood did not alarm her.

What you didn't want to see was someone else's blood. What Sam didn't want to see. She had walked past the street where she saw the shooting, but she was too scared to walk down the block where it happened. She was worried that there would be stains from where his blood had seeped into the concrete. She was worried there wouldn't be stains from where his blood had seeped into the concrete.

Rust-colored, faded.

Her blood, Sam's, was a sticky bright pool on the floor under her face. Where was it leaking out from? The back of her head but also her nose and her mouth. If enough blood sat on the waxed wood floor for enough time, it would stain the oak floorboards. Even if cleaned, some tiny amount would have seeped into the cracks between the planks. When it was cold, tiny gaps opened at some of the floorboard seams. This pleased her—if she died today, on the floor right here, she would be secretly absorbed by the house. Her body would become part of her house forever.

She heard the distant sirens coming her way, but before the EMTs pounded on the door and then came inside, she passed out again.

Sam

Sam woke in the hospital bed and her entire body ached, especially her head. She was told that she had a concussion, and the less she thought, the better. She laughed. Her head hurt. She winced but still laughed.

"What's so funny?" the nurse said.

"Just thinking about not thinking is impossible," she said. "I'm thinking about that."

"Try to relax."

"Trying to relax is like not thinking," she said. She drank some juice through a bent straw.

At last the doctor came to talk to her. Sam told him she remembered being hit, but not who hit her. Would her memory come back?

"You weren't hit by anyone."

"What?" she said. "That's impossible."

"You had a transient ischemic attack. A TIA. You passed out. And you hit your head when you hit the floor, so you also have a concussion."

"But I felt something hit the back of my head before I fell."

"TIAs can cause a sharp pain in the back of your head, like a blow."

This couldn't be true.

He explained that a TIA was a stroke event, but the good news was that it didn't seem to have done any damage. She wasn't confused or having difficulty speaking.

But she was confused.

"A fucking stroke? I'm only fifty-three!"

"It happens," he said.

"I'm so healthy, my god, my blood pressure, triglycerides, HDL, body fat, my liver enzymes, my kidneys, my A1C, my CRP—"

The doctor nodded. And he smiled.

"You need to rest. Stress is the problem here. Have you been under a lot of stress lately?"

Sam didn't speak.

"Have you been getting enough sleep?"

Sam shook her head.

"You need to rest. You're healthy. You'll be fine," he said. "Very little damage. Many, many years to come, I promise."

Thank god! Thank god that I sustained very little damage after my mini-stroke. Eye-roll emoji, Sam thought, and laughed at her own pathetic joke. She was tired, and thankfully, her body let her sleep.

She didn't dream about what had happened because she didn't remember much about the entire night, really. When she woke, she tried—but trying to remember actually hurt. Memory was not a thing that responded to willful straining. It was delicate and temperamental. She had hit her head on the edge of the tile was what the EMTs had surmised, and this was what the doctor explained to her. You are lucky, he said, that you were able to call for help. The concussion and the cut were bigger concerns than the TIA.

No one had hit Sam. No one had persecuted or targeted her. No one to blame or be angry with.

Matt had been in the night before with Ally, but Sam was sleeping. He called her, and after she told him she had had a small stroke event, he sighed. "Yeah, the doctor told me," he said.

"It isn't that serious," she said. "At least it wasn't a cardiac event. Or an arrhythmia or an aneurysm or a seizure."

"Stay off the internet, Sam."

"Okay, okay."

"No screens, concussion, you know the drill."

Later he brought her some takeout food from Vince's deli, her favorite: sliced porchetta with rosemary and garlic on a ciabatta roll, which she couldn't eat, not yet. She picked it up. Put it down. She had become a person overwhelmed by substantial food, like a frail little old lady.

She should call her mother, but Matt said he had spoken to her. Everything could wait.

"What do I do? I can't read or look at any screens."

"I'll stay until you fall asleep."

"Really?"

He nodded. "But close your eyes. Do that thing where you don't think, you relax your body part by part."

"Meditation?"

"Yeah, do a breathing meditation," he said and held her hand.

After a few minutes of this, she rested, but she wasn't sleepy. Not a cacophony of thoughts, but thoughts just the same. Ally. Also Aadil and his mother's photo in the paper and the street that night. The street so close to her house. She opened her eyes. Matt was staring at her. She tried to smile at him, then winced.

"You aren't sleepy?" he said.

"No," she said, "but this is nice, thank you."

He nodded. Squeezed her hand.

"What do you want now, Sam?" he asked, adjusting her pillow.

"I think—" Sam said. "I think—"

"Don't think, remember? Your concussion, your cognitive rest?"

"Right," she said, and smiled. "That." She touched her bandages, which made an odd, muffled sound in her head, as if she were underwater. She looked up at him.

What did she want? She wanted an honest life. More than that. She wanted a good life. You can do nothing or you can do better.

After she was released from the hospital and went back to where she lived (the old beautiful wrecked house), Sam sat and took stock (her old beautiful wrecked body). She was recovered, but not completely. She would never entirely be the same as she was before. She knew this was true, but it didn't upset her. Wasn't that always true? After all, what is a body for? Her body, *this* body, and its glorious, sad flesh? Shouldn't your body be inscribed with every thing that ever happened to you, every thing you did or saw or felt?

Her phone pinged. Ally texted to see if she could stop by.

yes please!

Sam hesitated and then added an emoji face with a head bandage.

She watched out the window for her daughter to pull up. When she did, Sam opened the door and watched Ally walk toward her (so tall and lovely), smiling and holding a giant white bakery box. "I'm so happy to see you, Ally-oop," Sam said. They awkwardly touched each other's arms, not quite hugging, and when they pulled back, Ally looked her mother over and frowned.

"Are you okay, Mama?" Ally said, and hearing Ally say "Mama" made Sam start to tear up.

"I am," she said. "My head hurts because I hit it, but no permanent damage to the brain. I am concussed."

"You do cuss," Ally said.

"I must concuss that I cuss a lot," Sam said. They laughed. Ally put the giant white box tied with pink string on the table. Sam pointed at it.

"Is that?"

"Cannoli cake from Nino's. You need to eat. You're too skinny." Cannoli cake from Nino's was Sam's favorite. Sam wanted to jump up and get the elegant silver-plated Oneida cake cutter she had found at a yard sale, but she was tired, so she just waited and let Ally figure it out. Sam sat on her bed and watched. Ally opened the box, and with a dull butter knife she lopped off two giant, awkward pieces. She plopped them onto two small bread plates. Then Ally grabbed two tablespoons from the dish rack and placed them on the plates alongside the cake. She handed a plate to Sam. The smell of the cake woke Sam's brain up. The most perfect dopamine delivery system ever. They ate their cake together with the big spoons and it was intoxicating.

"This house is so pretty. And cozy. Exactly as I pictured it," Ally said.

"You pictured it?"

"Yeah, when you texted me, I imagined you here."

"Can I show you?" Sam started to get up.

"Later, Mom."

Sam nodded, sitting back on the edge of her bed, watching Ally eat her cake at Sam's table. Ally scooped a large frosty chunk with her spoon, slowly chewed, and then swallowed.

"You saw us at the fair, didn't you?" Ally said.

Sam nodded. "I did." (So Ally knew that Sam had seen her!)

"But you said nothing. You walked away."

"I thought I should leave you alone. Not that I liked it."

"You didn't like leaving me be or you didn't like me being with Joe?" Ally said.

"Both. I'm worried he'll hurt you."

Ally stared down at her plate. She was now prodding the cake with her spoon. She pushed it away, to the center of the table.

"It's already happened. Or is happening. He dumped me, which is strange because I had started to question things with him, but I wasn't expecting him to do that. It upset me a lot more than I would have guessed."

"Oh, honey—" Sam said.

"But I'm fine," Ally said, shaking her head at her mother. "Look at me. Here I am, still standing somehow. I will never love again, of course. But otherwise, fine."

"Oh, Ally—"

"I'm joking!"

Sam smiled weakly. "Oh."

"Sam, sometimes I think you lack faith in me."

(Now it was "Sam," not "Mama.")

"You panic. I'm resilient. I'm okay," Ally said.

"I know you are. I really do know."

Ally looked intently at her, the serious girl again. "Do you think you will come back home now?"

"I'm staying here," Sam said. "I can't live there."

Ally didn't look surprised or mad. "I kind of feel the same way—I can't wait to leave for college."

"Good," Sam said, and nodded. Her head hurt with the nodding, and she touched the bandage.

"Does it hurt a lot?" Ally asked and moved from the table over to her mother. They sat side by side on the little bed. Sam shrugged.

"Can I see?"

Sam turned the back of her head to Ally. Lifted the edge of the giant bandage.

Ally sucked in her breath. "Oh, Mama!"

"Looks worse than it is, I guess." Sam pushed the bandage back into place.

"Grandma's sick," Ally said.

"Yes. What did she tell you?" Sam said.

Ally looked down. "She didn't go into much detail about it." Then Ally's mouth started to quiver. She put her hand over her mouth and then she reached for Sam, who pulled Ally to her. Sam heard Ally cry against her chest.

"I was so scared when you got hurt, Mama," Ally said into Sam's shoulder. "I didn't think anything could happen to you—" She pulled back and looked up at Sam. She laughed and shook her head, her eyes red from crying. "Because you're—"

"I know. I know," Sam said. She rubbed her daughter's back, and Ally let her. Ally leaned back on the bed.

"What a comfy little bed," she said. "I like it."

"Why don't you rest," Sam said. Ally stretched out. Sam tucked the blanket around her. She closed her eyes. Sam continued to gently rub her back through the blanket. To Sam's surprise, Ally's breathing slowed and she fell asleep.

Sam sat on the edge of her single bed and watched her daughter sleep. This moment, she thought. This moment. If only her mother, Lily, were here with her too. But Lily was here with her.

Sam knew that after her mother died, the last worries and pains would fall away. Sam would see her mother as not merely her mother, but as a full, perfect human. Sam would apprehend the whole of her mother's life, her girlhood through her old age, the whole of her body, her mind, her heart. Her existence on earth would be clear and perfect. Sam was from her, a part of her, and Sam would feel, in a profound way, that she remained a version of her, a derivative. This soothed Sam, to feel her mother's traces in every molecule, her light in every aspect. Her mother would die, but Sam would still be here. She didn't quite believe it yet, but she knew it just the same.

When Ally stirred from her nap, Sam made her coffee. Then Ally drove back to Matt's. Tomorrow Matt would pick up Lily and bring her here, and that night they would all have dinner together: Ally, Matt, Lily, and Sam.

Sam's head ached, and she was very tired. She turned off the lights in the living room and looked out through the leaded windows at the city. It was cold and wet and beautiful. She made a fire, and then sat watching the firelight making the glaze on the tiles glow. She touched the bandages on the back of her head and winced. She lay down to rest.

Sam slept for nine hours without waking. In the morning, as her consciousness streamed in with the sun, a vision came to her, unbidden but not unwelcome: of the ends of things, the time between now and then, the world without her.

Acknowledgments

While writing this book, I relied on a number of people to guide my research. Thank you to Christine Healy for her time, intelligence, and hilarious insights; and to Peter McCarthy for his knowledge and thoughtful conversations, as well as for being an early reader. Thanks also to Lynne Della Pella Pascale, Samuel Gruber (and his beautiful *My Central New York* blog), Clifford Ryan, Carol Faulkner, Scott Manning Stevens, Beth Crawford, Tro Kalayjian, Mike Goode, David Haas (and his @syracusehistory Instagram), and Eric Bianchi. And gratitude to Joan Farrenkopf for space in her Hawley-Green house for my writing retreat weekends.

Thank you to the writers who read early versions of this book: Chanelle Benz, Anna Moschovakis, Jonathan Lethem, Elizabeth Horvath, Don DeLillo, Sarah Harwell, and Jonathan Dee.

Much gratitude to Melanie Jackson (as always but in particular with this book) for her insightful advice, her friendship, and her faith in my work. Thank you to Jordan Pavlin: her wisdom, encouragement, and fine attention made this novel much stronger.

My husband, Jon, and my daughter, Agnes: thanks for putting up with my eccentric (and endless) writing demands and for letting me steal words right out of your mouths.

Many answers, questions, and ideas came from the Onondaga Historical Association, The Arts and Crafts Society of Central New York, the Onondaga Nation website, and the Erie Canal Museum. The Oneida Community Mansion House was an inspiration, both staying in the building and the lectures (Anthony Wonderley's especially). *The Stammering Century* by Gilbert Seldes and *Desire and Duty at Oneida* by Tirzah Miller and Robert Fogarty (among other books) helped me imagine life in the Oneida Community.

The dictionary definitions of "period" and "menopause" quoted by

MH and Sam come from Google Dictionary. The song lyrics "Once upon a Dream" are by Jack Lawrence and Sammy Fain. The many etymologies that Ally looks up come from Etymonline (app) and *Webster's Third*. The line Sam quotes about wastewater in Onondaga Lake comes, as she admits, from Wikipedia, as does the perhaps apocryphal story that Wallace Rayfield was one of the architects on the People's AME Zion Church. The quote from Alice Bunker Stockham is from *Tokology: A Book for Every Woman*. The bible quotes in Clara's letters and journal are from the King James Bible. All the T-shirts described at the 2017 Great New York State Fair are actual T-shirts I saw for sale at the Great New York State Fair. I owe a debt to the city of Syracuse, a place I find endlessly fascinating. Inspiration for this novel came from the many beautiful old structures in Syracuse, especially the houses Ward Wellington Ward designed (including the Garrett house).

Thank you to the American Academy of Arts and Letters for support at a crucial period. Thank you to the Syracuse University College of Arts and Sciences for giving me the time and resources to write. And thank you to the Syracuse University Creative Writing Program's faculty and students.

Dana Spiotta is the author of four previous novels: *Innocents and Others*, which won the St. Francis College Literary Prize and was a finalist for the *Los Angeles Times* Book Prize; *Stone Arabia*, which was a National Book Critics Circle Award finalist; *Eat the Document*, which was a National Book Award finalist and was awarded the Rosenthal Family Foundation Award for Literature; and *Lightning Field*, a *New York Times* Notable Book of the Year. Spiotta was a recipient of the Rome Prize in Literature, a Guggenheim Fellowship, a New York Foundation for the Arts Fellowship, and the John Updike Award from the American Academy of Arts and Letters. Spiotta teaches in the Syracuse University Creative Writing Program. She lives in Syracuse with her family.